Grassroots Grants

To aid you in developing
your grant proposals,
all exercises and worksheets in this book
are available FREE on-line.

If you would like to download electronic versions
of the exercises and worksheets,
please visit

www.josseybass.com/go/grassrootsgrants

Thank you,
Andy Robinson

Second Edition

Grassroots Grants

An Activist's Guide to Grantseeking

Andy Robinson

With contributions from

Jean Lewis

John Pomeranz

Wendy Wilson

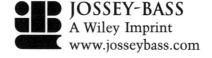

JOSSEY-BASS
A Wiley Imprint
www.josseybass.com

Published by Jossey-Bass
A Wiley Imprint
989 Market Street, San Francisco, CA 94103–1741   www.josseybass.com

Library of Congress Cataloging-in-Publication Data
Robinson, Andy.
  Grassroots grants : an activist's guide to grantseeking / Andy Robinson—2nd ed.
    p. cm.—(The Chardon Press series)
  Includes bibliographical references and index.
  ISBN 0-7879-6578-2 (pbk.)
  1. Proposal writing for grants—United States—Handbooks, manuals, etc. I. Title. II. Series.
  HG177.R65 2004
  658.15′224—dc22   2004002749

Printed in the United States of America
SECOND EDITION
PB Printing   10 9 8 7 6 5 4 3 2

THE CHARDON PRESS SERIES

Fundamental social change happens when people come together to organize, advocate, and create solutions to injustice. Chardon Press recognizes that communities working for social justice need tools to create and sustain healthy organizations. In an effort to support these organizations, Chardon Press produces materials on fundraising, community organizing, and organizational development. These resources are specifically designed to meet the needs of grassroots nonprofits—organizations that face the unique challenge of promoting change with limited staff, funding, and other resources. We at Chardon Press have adapted traditional techniques to the circumstances of grassroots nonprofits. Chardon Press and Jossey-Bass hope these works help people committed to social justice to build mission-driven organizations that are strong, financially secure, and effective.

Kim Klein, Series Editor

For Jan

Contents

List of Exhibits, Exercises, and Worksheets

xiv   List of Exhibits, Exercises, and Worksheets

Preface

Several years ago, I was hired by a well-known national nonprofit to visit their regional offices and teach their staff to be better grantseekers. The organization was decentralizing its fundraising and wanted to make sure that everyone had the opportunity to develop appropriate skills.

At the first office, the staff gave me a proposal to review. It was miserable—overly long, technical, boring, and almost unreadable. When I say "unreadable," I mean literally. The font was tiny, the margins minimal, and too many words were crammed onto the page. I spent an hour with this mess of a document, wrote all over it, made suggestions, and handed it back.

"Did you submit this?" I asked, a bit dubious.

"Yes," they replied. "We got $75,000."

Well, I led the workshop, got on a plane, and went to the next town. I was given another application to critique. This one was worse: longer, denser, filled with jargon and lots of extraneous details. I was tempted to carve it up with a razor, but I took out my pen, edited the proposal, and returned it.

"What happened with this one?"

"They gave us $150,000."

By the time I got to the third city, one thing was abundantly clear: these folks sure knew how to build good relationships with their funders. In talking with them, I learned that they made their phone calls, met with foundation officers, and in many cases worked collaboratively with them to develop their proposals. By the time the paper was formally submitted, *the deal had already been done.*

The first edition of *Grassroots Grants* was subtitled *An Activist's Guide to Proposal Writing.* With this edition, I've taken the words "proposal writing" out of the title because, in the end, grantseeking encompasses a broad range of strategies and techniques, and writing is perhaps the least important of these.

Using a series of examples, worksheets, and role plays, this book will teach you four basic skills you need to be effective:

- *Grant thinking:* how to think as funders do, so you can conceive and structure your work to attract grant money. As an additional benefit, learning to see your work more objectively, as grantmakers do, will make your programs and campaigns more effective.

- *Research:* how to identify the most likely prospects to support your work.

- *Relationship building:* how to reach out and educate and involve grantmakers. (There's a technical term for this—*schmoozing*—which I'll define later.)

- *Proposal writing:* how to create compelling, easy-to-read, good-looking documents.

Along the way, I will touch on a number of other topics, including the pros and cons of grantseeking, leverage (how to use money to create more money), grant reporting, and keeping yourself fresh for the long haul. I'll also examine several successful proposals, page by page, to see what makes them work. Please note that all the worksheets and exercises included in this book are also available on the Jossey-Bass Web site, www.josseybass.com.

Fifty funding officers and trustees contributed their wisdom to this project. You'll find their quotes and suggestions throughout the book. They fund groups working for social justice, human rights, and environmental conservation. Like you, they're passionate about social change. Many started out as activists and community organizers and still think of themselves that way. Like you, they sometimes feel overwhelmed. Like you, they're learning as they go. By the time you finish reading, I hope you'll think of grantmakers as potential allies and peers.

Many people who are new to grantseeking—indeed, any sort of fundraising—feel intimidated. Be not afraid. If you can think clearly, if you like people, if you don't mind doing your homework, you can find all the money you need to change the world. This book will help you.

Plainfield, Vermont   Andy Robinson
February 2004

Acknowledgments

By its very nature, a book like this one involves a lot of collaboration. It's a privilege to thank the following people for their help and support:

- Contributing writers John Pomeranz of the Alliance for Justice, Wendy Wilson of River Network, and Jean Lewis of the Tucson Pima Public Library, who share their wisdom on nonprofit lobbying regulations, collaborative fundraising, and grant research, respectively. Jean has helped with many projects over the years, and I am grateful for her continuing friendship and generosity.

- The many foundation officers and trustees who took the time to fill out my survey and talk with me in person and on the phone. You'll find their names and comments throughout. By sharing their inside knowledge of grantmaking, they've added veracity and substance to this book.

- The nonprofits and businesses that offer electronic grant research tools and allowed Jean Lewis free or low-cost access to their products so she could evaluate and review them.

- The staff and supporters of the Mesa Refuge, who provided a serene place to work during the very early stages of this project.

- For their professionalism and patience, Johanna Vondeling, Allison Brunner, and their coworkers at Jossey-Bass. Considering the detours and difficulties that come with researching and writing a book, one can scarcely imagine the complications of editing, designing, publishing, and bringing it to market. For a job well done, thank you.

- Editor Nancy Adess and production editor Carolyn Uno continue to inspire me with their hard work, thoughtfulness, skill, and grace under pressure. Fun working with you both again!

- I am indebted to Kim Klein and Stephanie Roth of Chardon Press and the *Grassroots Fundraising Journal* for their encouragement, loyalty, and good humor. It's been ten years since we first became colleagues, and our relationship is one of the great pleasures of my professional life.

Several organizations allowed me to publish and critique their proposals and letters of inquiry. For their graciousness and exemplary work, both in the field and in their grantseeking, my thanks to

- Anthony Thigpenn and Lalee Vicedo, AGENDA, Los Angeles
- Kimble Forrister and Jamie Keith, Alabama Arise/Arise Citizens' Policy Project, Montgomery, Alabama
- Virginia Rasch, Association of Vermont Conservation Commissions, Adamant, Vermont
- Franki Patton Rutherford, Big Creek People in Action, Caretta, West Virginia
- Juri Peepre, Canadian Parks and Wilderness Society, Yukon Chapter, Whitehorse, Yukon Territory, Canada
- Alisa Bierria, Communities Against Rape and Abuse (CARA), Seattle
- Nancy Johnson and Pramila Jayapal, Hate Free Zone Campaign of Washington, Seattle
- Geoff Ramsey-Ray and Eric Mann, Labor/Community Strategy Center and Bus Riders Union, Los Angeles
- Susana Geliga, Little White Buffalo Project, Rapid City, South Dakota
- James Plourde, Manchester Area Residents Concerned about Health (MARCH), Manchester, Connecticut
- Johanna Miller and Hans Voss, Michigan Land Use Institute, Beulah, Michigan
- Patrick Flaherty, Milwaukee LGBT Center, Milwaukee, Wisconsin
- Tim Baker and Bob Decker, Montana Wilderness Association, Helena, Montana
- Evelyn Rens and Kevin Dahl, Native Seeds/SEARCH, Tucson, Arizona
- Cheryl King Fischer, Linn Syz, and Ginny Callan, New England Grassroots Environment Fund, Montpelier, Vermont
- Mike Graham-Squire, Seattle Young People's Project, Seattle
- Taylor Barnhill, SouthWings, Asheville, North Carolina
- Gilda Haas and Denise Duffield, Strategic Actions for a Just Economy (SAJE), Los Angeles
- Joni Halpern, Supportive Parents Information Network (SPIN), San Diego

- Jonah Vitale-Wolff and Peggy Middaugh, Urban Garden Resources of Worcester (UGROW), Worcester, Massachusetts

- Brigette Sarabi, Western Prison Project, Portland, Oregon

- Mike Ballard, Lina Miller, and Leanne Klyza Linck, Wildlands Project, Richmond, Vermont

- Rona Fernandez, Youth Empowerment Center, Oakland, California

Finally, a big kiss for my beloved, Jan Waterman, a fine companion who also happens to be a terrific research assistant, editor, and proofreader. How about I make dinner tonight?

A.R.

The Author

Andy Robinson has been raising money for social change since 1980. As a trainer and consultant, Andy has assisted nonprofits in forty states and Canada, leading workshops on donor fundraising, grantseeking, board development, strategic planning, marketing, and earned income strategies.

Andy specializes in the needs of organizations promoting human rights, social justice, and environmental conservation. In addition to hundreds of local groups throughout North America, his clients include the American Friends Service Committee, National Wildlife Federation, Neighborhood Reinvestment, National Trust for Historic Preservation, the Evangelical Lutheran Church in America, and the New England Grassroots Environment Fund, where he served as training and outreach director. You can reach him at andyfund@earthlink.net.

Andy is a columnist for *Contributions* and a regular contributor to the *Grassroots Fundraising Journal.* Writing in *Whole Earth,* author and trainer Tracy Gary praised his latest book, *Selling Social Change (Without Selling Out),* for its "good news, innovation, and sterling examples of ethical entrepreneurship . . . full of imagination and creative commercial charisma." *Selling Social Change* is available from Jossey-Bass.

The Contributors

Jean Lewis is an information services librarian at the Tucson Pima Public Library in Tucson, Arizona, with twenty years of on-line database experience. As manager of the Grants and Nonprofit Information Center there since 1989, she teaches grant research. She assists local nonprofit and community organizations in gathering information to increase their effectiveness. The Web site of the Grants and Nonprofit Information Center is www.lib.ci.tucson.az.us/grants/.

John Pomeranz is nonprofit advocacy director at the Alliance for Justice, a national association of public interest advocacy organizations in Washington, D.C. An attorney with law degrees from Georgetown University and the University of Southern California, John works with nonprofits around the country to enhance their capacity to participate in the policy process. The assistance he provides includes workshops on the rules governing nonprofit lobbying and political activity, plain-language legal guides for nonprofit organizations, and information on federal legislative developments that affect organizations with 501(c)(3) tax status. Before joining the Alliance, John taught at the Harrison Institute for Public Law at the Georgetown University Law Center. He has also worked as a lobbyist for a group representing the interests of consumers of legal services.

Wendy Wilson works with River Network, a national nonprofit that helps grassroots river and watershed protection organizations become more sustainable. She has worked for more than twenty years as an environmental activist, lobbyist, and political organizer. Wendy founded Idaho Rivers United and was a founding board member of the Save Our Wild Salmon Coalition. She lives in Boise, Idaho, where many of the rivers run free.

Grassroots Grants

Up from the Grassroots
The Evolution of Grants and Grantseeking

Grantees are more oriented toward results and less involved in defining themselves as victims. People speak with more verbs and fewer adjectives. There is less guilt-tripping of funders. Overall, I see more seriousness and maturity.

—MARTY TEITEL, Cedar Tree Foundation

Foundations are smarter about organizing because there are more organizers in foundation jobs.

—SI KAHN, Jewish Fund for Justice

"This book is about two things: money and power. If you didn't need money for your organization, you wouldn't be reading these words. If you weren't trying to change the world, which involves challenging and changing the relations of power, you wouldn't be so concerned about raising money."

So began the first edition of this book, which appeared in 1996. In the intervening years, our world has shifted—and the way we organize and raise money has also shifted—but what strikes me is how the fundamentals remain the same:

- There's enough inequality and oppression to keep us all busy for decades.

- There's plenty of money to do our work, if we can just get over our discomfort and shortsightedness and learn how to raise it effectively.

- We are sustained by each other. Social change work builds solid, enduring relationships.

If you find the first point depressing, well, the other two provide a strong antidote.

What follows is a summary of the trends that are changing the way we approach and practice grantseeking. Some of the news is discouraging, but much of it is cause for optimism.

The Expanding Philanthropic Sector

For grantseekers, many new funding opportunities have been created in the past decade, while thousands of new nonprofits have been established to address a wide range of community needs.

More foundations, more grantseekers. In 1996, there were roughly forty thousand grantmaking foundations in the United States. As of December 2003, the Foundation Center database (www.fdncenter.org) includes about seventy thousand foundations, along with about ten thousand corporate giving programs and public charities that make grants. Due to changes in the law that encouraged the creation of foundations—a way of shielding assets from taxation—those of us looking for grants have a lot more options.

On the other hand, we've seen an explosion in the number of nonprofits, especially groups with the 501(c)(3) tax status required to receive most grants. According to the National Center for Charitable Statistics, we now have an astounding 1.35 million nonprofit organizations in the United States, including 870,000 groups with 501(c)(3) designation. In the 1990s, the number of registered nonprofits increased by 44 percent, then increased another 15 percent during the current decade so far (National Center for Charitable Statistics, 2003). These numbers do not take into account the hundreds of thousands of informal local groups that have chosen not to incorporate but are still doing important, grant-worthy work.

I hate to use the word competition, but those of us who've been around for a while have a lot more company. As Therese Ogle at Northwest Grantmaking Resources says, "My job hasn't changed, but the piles of proposals just keep getting higher and higher."

The growth of family foundations. Most of these new funders fall under the informal category of "family foundations." Typically they are managed by a family member, or perhaps a local attorney or foundation consultant. Very few have formal guidelines, annual reports, or even an office. While their grants can be substantial, they don't give away as much money as the brand-name foundations. You might find them in the big grantmaking directories, but information about their grants and priorities is often very sketchy. (See Resource A for information on grant directories.) Most have no presence on the Internet: of the more than seventy thousand funding programs tracked by the Foundation Center, only twenty-five hundred have Web sites linked to the Foundation Center site. Family foundations tend to be invisible, and many prefer it that way.

For grantseekers, the family foundation phenomenon presents both challenges and opportunities. They're hard to find, hard to contact, and hard to figure out. Many direct their grants to "preselected organizations only," so "applications are not accepted." From the outside, it looks a bit like a gated community.

However, according to a report from the National Center for Family Philanthropy (2003), 92 percent of family foundations limit grantmaking to their local community, state, or region. They have personal relationships, business relationships, and organizational relationships. They are, literally speaking, your neighbors. With diligence, you can begin to create relationships with them.

The approach to family foundations feels more like a major gifts campaign—soliciting gifts directly from individuals—and less like a grant application. (When budgeting, some nonprofits count family foundation donations as major gifts rather than grants.) Many of these folks don't even ask for proposals. They just want to meet the people doing the work and to know that their money is being used effectively. The lack of paperwork and bureaucracy is refreshing.

A Different Set of Circumstances: Economy, Politics, Technology

In a rapidly shifting world, fundraiser-activists must be adaptable if they want to be successful.

The stock market giveth and taketh away. Since the first edition of *Grassroots Grants* was published, we've experienced one of fastest-growing stock markets in history, followed in rapid succession by one of the most persistent "bear markets" ever. (By the time you read this, who knows how the market will behave.) Most foundations are heavily invested in stocks; when the market goes up they prosper and when their portfolios decline in value they have less money to give away.

This is tough on funding officers, who already have a difficult job. "Our endowment has dropped by 40 percent," says Jon Jensen of the George Gund Foundation, "so I spend more time equitably distributing disappointment." It's even tougher for those of us who depend on grant money for our work.

Despite the stock market's swings, overall foundation funding held steady from 2000 through 2002, though many environmental and social justice funders cut way back. Because foundations prepare their budgets based on a five-year "rolling average" of their assets, we are still seeing the residual positive effects of the boom. For grantseekers, it may get worse before it gets better.

The United States has become more conservative, making our work more challenging. "It's a repressive time. Things are harder now," says Gaye Evans of the Appalachian Community Fund. "We always talk about being reactive instead of proactive, but now there's an even greater sense of insecurity. Organizations are constantly shifting gears to deal with moving targets and upcoming crises. Sustainability is a big question, both on the funding side and the political side."

This shift has hit organizers and grantmakers with equal force. "Given the national political change and the sinking economy, our strategy has changed," says Hubert Sapp of the Hartford Foundation and formerly with Oxfam America. "Before, we looked at how to build and expand programs. Now, we're looking at how to preserve and conserve gains we've already made."

Roxanne Turnage of the CS Fund agrees: "We've always been in a relatively defensive posture, but now we're in what feels like a critical time, trying to hold on to the gains of the past twenty or even fifty years. This makes it much more challenging to figure out what to fund. The stakes are higher. We can't afford to make mistakes."

The upside, says Sapp, is this: "Grantees are more realistic now about what they can actually accomplish."

Changes in technology have created both opportunities and barriers. The expanding use of e-mail has made it a lot easier to stay in touch with funders and even transmit proposals electronically. "I now read and comment on a majority of proposals, including essentially all renewals, prior to the official hard copies of these proposals being submitted," says Ed Miller of the Illinois Clean Energy Community Foundation.

On the other hand, somebody has to manage the inevitable paper. "We have an internal debate about electronic submissions," says Pat Jerido, formerly of the Ms. Foundation. "The support staff says they're a lot more work to process," because the tasks of printing and collating shift from grantseeker to grantmaker. As it becomes easier to submit applications, she says, "More proposals mean more pressure on us."

The continuing evolution of computer technology and the Internet has made it easier to research prospective funders. Thanks to the wonderful work of GuideStar (www.guidestar.org), you can now download the tax returns for 850,000 U.S. nonprofits, including virtually all charitable foundations. A variety of commercial grant research products, in both on-line and CD formats, are also available; you'll find them profiled in Resource B.

Despite the advantages of computer technology, the "digital divide" remains a significant barrier in poor communities, communities of color, and rural locales. Grassroots groups are likely to be years behind the technology curve. The benefits arrive late and, due to limited resources and lack of access to training, sometimes they never arrive at all. "GIS is the new PowerPoint," sighs Marjorie Fine of the Unitarian Universalist Veatch Program at Shelter Rock, offering one example, "and most groups are not equipped to use it well."

As media activist and foundation officer Jerry Mander has written, technology is not value-neutral: the institutions in power take advantage of nearly every technological advance to consolidate their power (Ingram, 1991). To the degree that we can use e-mail, the Web, wireless communication, and so forth to counter that trend, we should—recent antiglobalization organizing is a fine example—but without succumbing to technology worship.

Grantmaking: An Experiment in Democracy?

A common critique of foundations—from both liberals and conservatives—is that they are not accountable to anyone but themselves. Recent changes in the funding world have begun to address this problem head-on and also in more subtle ways.

The many faces of community-based, social change philanthropy. More than twenty-five years ago, the Funding Exchange pioneered a new kind of philanthropy based on two radical ideas: (1) giving should be directed toward "change, not charity," and (2) the people affected and the communities served should help make decisions about distributing the money. Gaye Evans and her colleagues at the Appalachian Community Fund call this "activist-controlled grantmaking."

The Funding Exchange network now embraces fifteen affiliate funds, including the Liberty Hill Foundation in Los Angeles. Liberty Hill staff members Margarita Ramirez and Lina Paredes describe how their version works:

> Our decision-making process lies in the hands of a Community Funding Board comprised of community and donor activists engaged in a wide range of social and economic justice issues. While staff does initial screening, the CFB interviews all potential grantees and makes final funding decisions for the foundation.
>
> Having a Community Funding Board process has its challenges. We've adjusted our grantmaking procedures to meet many of these. We now provide training for CFB members in grant review and in the foundation's

mission and goals. We also have developed a more concrete policy about conflicts of interest. We focus on funding groups that have an impact on social change, and we emphasize strategic grantmaking. We've standardized our decision-making process, and we provide CFB members with considerable background information about groups so that they can make more informed decisions. We also give groups that will receive an interview a list of questions they will be asked in advance.

At the end of a decision-making process we meet to evaluate what worked and what didn't. Finally, we have a party for our new grantees, giving them the opportunity to learn about each other's work. As a result, grantees have ended up collaborating on current or future projects.

The idea of democratic, community-based decision making has taken a variety of forms and influenced many grantmakers, both within the Funding Exchange network and beyond. According to *Social Change Philanthropy and Community-Based Philanthropy*, a report from Changemakers (2003, pp. 1-7), more than one hundred community-based social change foundations now operate in the United States.

The principles behind this movement have affected the corporate and mainstream foundation community as well. John Sterling, former grants officer for the outdoor clothing company Patagonia, reports, "We established a grants council of employees who represent and report back to their work groups. Our process is unique in that we try to involve our entire company in philanthropic decision making."

Jeff Anderson of the Oregon Community Foundation reports, "We use about fifty volunteers who do fact-finding and provide us with a sense of the overall fit [of a proposal] with our funding objectives. Volunteers review larger grant requests than ever before. We have recruited and trained additional volunteers, which may suggest a trend for my time—maybe more management of a volunteer-based program and less time spent on site visits."

While these volunteers are not the final decision makers, they have substantial influence over the results. As Barbara Meyer of the Bert and Mary Meyer Foundation notes, "In my experience, community-based reviewers are the toughest evaluators of all."

The Southern Partners Fund represents perhaps the fullest flowering of the idea of community-based philanthropy. Meyer has pledged to turn over the assets of her family foundation—currently valued at about $14 million—to a new public foundation, the Southern Partners Fund, founded and run by Meyer Foundation grantees.

She says, "As far as I know, we are making history. I am not aware of any private foundation transferring all of its assets and consequent power to a public foundation run by its grantees. We're pioneering a new model. If we believe that community members know what's best, if we believe in the wisdom and integrity of the grassroots, it makes sense to transfer the money and the authority to the community."

The founding activists, who had long and deep relationships with Meyer's family foundation, were stunned by this notion. Nevertheless, at the end of the very first meeting, they came up with a compelling idea: a dollar-for-dollar challenge. For every dollar provided by the family foundation, the Southern Partners Fund (as it was later named) would be required to raise an equal amount from other sources, until the assets were completely transferred. In this way, they could build a big enough endowment—the current goal is $15 million—to make a substantial impact throughout the region. More important, having worked to raise matching funds, community members would feel a lot more ownership over the process, the money, and the fund itself.

An endowment campaign to meet the challenge grant is now being planned, and several initial gifts have been secured. "We have the potential to step up and make this thing happen," says executive director Joan Garner, "which would be an incredible achievement."

Trading places: the community organizer as funder. Over the past decade, progressive funders have hired dozens of organizers and activists from a wide range of social movements: human rights, antiracism, economic and environmental justice, conservation, antiglobalization, reproductive rights, youth empowerment, labor organizing, media democracy, immigrant rights, civil liberties, and so on. These folks add an unprecedented level of richness and sophistication to the ongoing discussion and debate between grantmakers and the groups they support. Many come from communities of color, which has helped to diversify the foundation community—still an overwhelmingly white enclave.

"They're sensitive about how long it takes to make change," says Marjorie Fine, referring to these new program officers. "Not just policy change, but the membership change that precedes it."

Si Kahn encourages nonprofit groups to see grantmakers as peers rather than adversaries. "It's a complementary relationship," he notes. "Funder work is organizing, too—in many cases, pushing the funding community to take on new issues and new approaches." For a lot more information on building good relationships with foundation staff, see Chapter Six.

Young people rise up. We've seen an explosion of youth organizing, including donor organizing to help young people with wealth figure out how to use that wealth most effectively to create social change. Several foundations, including Active Element and Third Wave, are funded, staffed, and governed by youth. Other nonprofits, such as Resource Generation, provide training and support to this constituency. Definitions vary, but for the purpose of philanthropy, a "young person" is typically fifteen to thirty-five years old.

The philosophy of this movement is summed up on the Active Element Foundation Web site, www.activeelement.org: "We believe firmly that the active involvement of young people is critical to altering present power relationships, and we exist to help build the infrastructure that will sustain such involvement."

"Young people have always been a critical part of social movements," says Active Element's Gita Drury. "Our energy, optimism, and vision can also be applied to philanthropy. We're willing to fund less conventional work, like hip hop organizing as a tool for reaching youth."

Collaboration sells. Working together with other organizations and constituencies has always been a smart strategy for nonprofits, but in times of reduced resources, it becomes essential. "There's a new emphasis on collaboration," says Ann Krumboltz of the Brainerd Foundation. "Who do you work with? Are you engaging any non-traditional allies? We're all asking these questions more regularly." Michael Fischer, formerly of the Hewlett Foundation, concurs. "We think of grantees in 'clusters' and are most comfortable with prospective grantees who can present themselves as being part of a team seeking to further the foundation's mission."

Ron White, formerly of the Tides Foundation, is encouraged by this trend: "I'm aware of more multistate organizing and regional coalitions. They see themselves connected geographically and economically. They address regional targets: banks, utilities, extractive industries. You can't deal with a regional target without a regional strategy."

The same collaborative spirit is increasing in the funding community as well. Here's a story from Marty Teitel: "I went to the Environmental Grantmakers Association conference after five years away from the funding community, and it was a Rip Van Winkle experience. I noticed a marked increase in cooperation among funders. They're focusing more on goals and results and less on the promotion of specific groups or strategies. This opens the field to more prospective grantees."

In some grantmaking communities, such as the informal network of environmental funders based in the Pacific Northwest, foundation officers meet regularly, share notes, and identify emerging needs among their grantees. The high level of collegiality and trust has benefited grantseekers by creating more transparency and responsiveness.

The fight over payout requirements. When families establish private foundations, they make a deal with the federal government. In exchange for paying no taxes, the foundation agrees to spend at least 5 percent of its assets each year for charitable purposes. The 5 percent calculation can include the costs of doing business, including salaries, travel expenses, office costs, board member compensation, and so on.

A dogged coalition of funder activists, led by the National Network of Grantmakers and the National Committee for Responsive Philanthropy, has been working to increase payout requirements. Their goal is to make more money available for social change. Unfortunately, this argument was easier to make when the stock market was booming and foundations were earning much more than 5 percent on their investments. Despite the decline in the market—or perhaps because of the way that the tumble in stock values has made it harder for their grantees to raise money—several funders have voluntarily increased their payouts.

A 2003 Congressional proposal would have excluded board, staffing, office, and travel expenses from the minimum payout and required that at least 5 percent be spent as grants. The proposed legislation split the foundation community, with a number of mainstream funders fighting the higher payouts. This issue is likely to be with us for years to come.

Funders Don't Act the Way They Used to Act

As philanthropic models have changed, funder behavior has also begun to change.

More intermediaries are raising money and giving it away. The common term for pass-through arrangements is *regranting:* larger foundations (and, in some cases, individual donors) make gifts to public charities that provide small grants to grassroots groups. The approach is as diverse as the many movements it supports. Here are some examples:

> *The Seventh Generation Fund* assists a broad range of social justice and community development projects created by and for Native Americans. "We are both grantmaker and a grantseeker simultaneously," says Tia Oros Peters.

> *The New England Grassroots Environment Fund* supports environmental work of all types in its home region; half the grantees are ad hoc, "kitchen table" groups without formal tax status.

RESIST, Inc. funds "groups that withstand reactionary government policies, corporate arrogance, and right-wing fanaticism through organizing, education, and action."

The *Active Element Foundation*, mentioned earlier, supports youth organizing and empowerment. Says Gita Drury, "We're trying to bring a different level of humanity to the process of grantseeking. It's our job to jump through extra hoops to raise the money so our grantees don't have to."

River Network, primarily a capacity-building organization for the river and watershed protection movement, also manages a small grants program for partner groups.

These funding opportunities exist because large foundations have neither the expertise nor the infrastructure to hand out what for them are small grants of $500 to $5,000, yet gifts of this size can generate tremendous results. "The Mott Foundation is a large institution that gives away more than $100 million each year, and it's not feasible for us to do that in small grants," says Lois DeBacker of the foundation. "Our typical grants are $40,000 and larger, so we rely on intermediaries for regranting."

For individual donors, this strategy offers a way to pool their gifts for greater impact. They trust the intermediaries to identify important needs and locate effective organizations.

Funders are stepping outside their traditional roles—and it makes some activists nervous. In the not-so-distant past, foundations made grants and community organizers used the money to do the work. Grantmakers have always exercised power implicitly through their funding choices, and in some cases explicitly by creating new initiatives and forcing collaboration, but they generally limited their activities to grantmaking. Lately the roles of "funder" and "organizer" have begun to shift and overlap, raising a new set of questions about who has the power.

Gaye Evans reflects on shifting responsibilities and expectations:

We struggle with our role. Our job is raise money to give it to other groups. We have to fight the impulse to do other things, but sometimes the "other things" win. We recently organized three Dismantling Racism workshops for our grantees. No one else was offering this service in our region, and our board and staff felt that it was needed. Some grantees saw it as a command performance, but we stressed again and again that their funding was not conditional based on whether they showed up. In the end, we had to turn people away from all three events, so we'll probably do it again.

The change in roles can be traced to several factors:

- The number of former community organizers now employed by foundations. They tend to think and act like organizers, regardless of their job titles.

- The growth of intermediaries. In addition to giving grants, many of these organizations were created to provide capacity building and technical support to their grantees. Tia Oros Peters of The Seventh Generation Fund estimates that she spends 60–70 percent of her time giving technical assistance and only 30–40 percent of her time making grants.

- The rise of community-based social change foundations. If the foundation is managed and controlled by community activists, perhaps it's natural that it be involved in defining issues and organizing programs.

Funders are stepping out of their traditional roles—and behaving like investment bankers. At the height of the 1990s stock market boom, several new foundations were created by altruistic entrepreneurs who wanted to address social needs. They invented a new kind of grantmaking that combined traditional philanthropy with the principles of venture capitalism, which include creative, "out of the box" strategies; clear "metrics," or ways to measure results; and lots of hands-on tinkering (like it or not) by the investors. Many focused on commercially based solutions to problems like poverty and homelessness. They called their approach *venture philanthropy* or *social investing*.

With the gyrations of the stock market, venture philanthropy has lost a bit of its luster. Some market-based strategies worked, while many failed. A number of "investors" grew frustrated with nonprofit culture or the intractability of the problems they had set out to solve. Nonetheless, venture philanthropy has had at least two lasting impacts on how foundations and grantseekers do their work:

- Funders are pushing even harder for measurable results, which forces social change groups to attempt to measure changes in power, leadership, self-determination, and so on.

- Many more organizations are thinking entrepreneurially about how to sell their expertise—rather than giving it away—thereby diversifying their funding and relying less on grants that require them to weigh and count things that are extraordinarily difficult to measure.

Given these changes in the funding world, it's time to ask yourself a crucial question: are grants your best fundraising option? In Chapter Two, we'll consider the pros and cons of grantseeking and learn about how grants fit into a complete fundraising strategy.

What Grants
Will Get You . . .
and What They Won't

Foundation money is big money, fast money, and it seems to be
easy money—who wouldn't go for it? However, it's an illusion
that you can build a social justice organization only from grants,
especially at this time. If you want to be effective, develop a
grassroots funding base.

—SI KAHN, Jewish Fund for Justice

I'm not sure that all funders completely understand the power
dynamic—how much power they really have. Program choices are
often driven by what the grantmakers want to fund.

—GAYE EVANS, Appalachian Community Fund

Many groups consider fundraising the most unpleasant subject possible,
so they tend to avoid it. Here's a typical meeting: after fighting your way
through a discussion about the latest staffing crisis, what the recent election
means for your work, and why nobody washes the dirty dishes, you finally
get around to the hole in your bank account. Everyone is tired and cranky. You
talk of benefit events past and future, but without much enthusiasm. Finally
a voice is raised in hope: "I know! We'll get a grant!"

Watch out.

While the purpose of this book is to help you win more grants, you should
understand that grant money comes with a variety of strings attached. Some
of these strings are visible and beneficial, like the final report in which you

describe, in detail, how you spent the money. Others are less obvious and potentially dangerous.

Before evaluating the pros and cons of grant funding, let's take a quick look at the universe of charitable giving and see how grants figure in the mix.

Who's Got the Money?

Willie Sutton, the old-time gangster, was once asked why he robbed banks. "Because that's where the money is," he replied. If someone questioned you about why you submit grant applications, you might give the same answer—and you'd be wrong.

According to *Giving USA 2003*, published by the American Association of Fund Raising Counsel (AAFRC), U.S. nonprofits received an amazing $241 billion from the private sector—individuals, foundations, and corporations—in 2002. This staggering amount is more than the economic activity of most countries. You might be surprised to learn that 84 percent of that charitable money came from individuals, while only 16 percent was given by foundations and corporations (the people who read grant proposals).

AAFRC has been tracking these numbers for almost fifty years, and the percentages change very little over time. In fact, dead people, through their estates, give away more money, year after year, than all U.S. corporations combined.

Here's another surprise: the vast majority of donors aren't rich. Roughly 70 percent of U.S. households donate to nonprofits. Indiana University Center on Philanthropy data show that total giving per household averages about $2,000 a year. Among the two-thirds of Americans who take the standard deduction on their income taxes—primarily middle-class, working-class, and poor people—average annual donations are estimated to be almost $550 per family.

This book is designed to help you raise money from the 16 percent of the private-sector pie that gives grants: corporations and foundations. If you're seeking government funding, the techniques described here can also make you more effective. However, many organizations are too small, too marginal, or too radical to receive either corporate or government grants—indeed, thousands of groups are directly challenging corporate power or working to change government priorities. For these groups, the field is further reduced to the 11 percent of private-sector giving provided by private foundations. Nonetheless, we're talking about $27 billion: a significant sum and certainly worth some effort.

If you're sensible, however, you'll understand that the time you put into grantseeking should be proportional to the potential return on your effort. In other words, if you were going to build a rational private-sector fundraising program, you would put no more than 16 percent of your time and energy into preparing grant applications; 84 percent of your time and energy would be devoted to soliciting individuals. Ask yourself and your colleagues: When it comes to fundraising, are we behaving rationally?

When you rely too much on grant applications, you limit yourself to a small piece of a very large pie. Over the long run, you risk starving your organization to death.

The Downside: Ten Ways That Grants Can Drive You Crazy

Let's first consider the problems that accompany grantseeking:

1. *Long waits.* The process of proposal development, research, and relationship building will be addressed in great detail in Chapters Four through Six, but let's lay out the basics:

   - You come up with an idea for a new program. It's unique, it's practical, it solves a problem that no one else has been able to solve. What a great idea!

   - You discuss it with your coworkers, who endorse your idea and encourage you to keep working on it.

   - You take some notes—perhaps even draft a proposal outline—and share it with your coworkers, who offer feedback to help you refine your idea.

   - By talking with colleagues at other groups, conducting on-line research, visiting the library, and so forth, you begin to research potential funders.

   - If you can't get the information you need over the Internet, you contact the funders directly to ask for guidelines and application materials.

   - Having studied the guidelines carefully, you begin to interact with the grantmakers—by phone, by e-mail, maybe in person—to test out your idea. Under the best circumstances, they invite you to submit a proposal.

   - You write, you edit, you pass the proposal around, you rewrite. You get all the attachments together, being careful not to overwhelm the grant reviewer with too much stuff.

   - Perhaps you line up letters of support. You ask someone to proofread everything, then drop it in the mail (or e-mail it) with your fingers crossed.

- Perhaps you receive a follow-up call from the grant reviewer, who asks questions about your idea. Maybe the funder requests a site visit to see your work in person. This stage of the process involves a lot of waiting—the decisions are in someone else's hands, and there's not much you can do.

- Eventually you receive a letter or call informing you of the decision. In many cases, no decision has been made and your proposal is "rolled over" to the next grant round. Maybe you get a letter that says, "We love your project and have chosen to fund you"—congratulations!—"but before you receive the check, here's a bunch of paperwork to fill out."

If everything works beautifully, the transformation of an idea to a fully funded project takes six months to a year. Two years or more is not unusual. By the way, it takes two years to give birth to an elephant—and that's what this process can feel like. If you need money today, or next week—and most of us do—grants are not a good solution.

2. *Lousy odds.* No one has exact figures, but the vast majority of proposals are not funded. The Ford Foundation (www.fordfound.org) reports that about 6 percent of their applicants received grants in 2002. According to *The Grantseeker's Toolkit* (New and Quick, 1998, p. 9), a 30 percent success rate would make you a "grants superstar."

There is a lot of competition for foundation grants. Many "successful" proposals are only partially funded, which leaves the grantee scrambling to run its project on a reduced budget or find additional money from other sources. Careful research and diligent relationship work will improve your odds, but if you want the best opportunities, you have to go where the money is: individual donors.

3. *Rejection hurts.* Effective organizers pour themselves into their work and their grant applications. When the nearly inevitable rejection letter arrives, it's hard not to take it personally.

"Their proposal is their life's work and vision. We understand that," says Tia Oros Peters of the Seventh Generation Fund. "But we have dozens of proposals from other struggling communities dealing with similar issues. Unfortunately, we are limited by available funds and cannot fund every initiative, however critical or worthy."

To be fair, rejection is built into every sort of fundraising. As author and fundraising trainer Kim Klein likes to say, fundraising is a volume business. Since most prospects say no, the best way to handle rejection is to identify, research, and cultivate a lot of prospects.

4. *"Soft money."* Grants are seldom renewable. A particular foundation may provide support for three or four years, but not forever. As Si Kahn points out, "Very few funders support grassroots groups indefinitely." This problem is compounded by the fact that most foundations are interested in new, innovative projects, and are less likely to fund ongoing programs. Individual donors, on the other hand, have been known to support a particular nonprofit for decades.

5. *Restricted money.* The majority of foundation grants are directed toward specific projects, not general support, which greatly limits your flexibility. A grant is a contract, and you are legally bound to use the money as described in your proposal. Any significant changes in the program or budget must be negotiated with the funder.

6. *Grants don't empower your group.* Grantseeking does not empower people or organizations the way that community-based fundraising does. When you write a proposal, you transfer a critical decision—whether you will have a portion of the money you need to operate—to someone outside your constituency. The more money you raise from your own community, the stronger your group will be.

7. *Too few people are involved in the process.* Grantwriting concentrates organizational power in the hands of a few people. Most proposals are developed by one or two staff members (and, in some cases, approved by a board of directors). When you rely too much on grants, you miss out on the leadership development opportunities that come with campaign planning, one-on-one solicitation, house meetings, benefit events, and other fundraising strategies involving lots of people.

8. *Your work can get distorted in the pursuit of money.* If you're not careful, grants can shift power over your programs to someone outside the organization.

The process is usually subtle. Let's say your group sees a funding opportunity and develops a new project specifically to meet the guidelines, even though the project doesn't fit your mission very well. Much to your surprise, the proposal gets funded. Since this project pulls you in a new direction, it takes a lot of staff time to figure out how to manage it. Your core programs suffer from neglect. The tail—money—ends up wagging the dog, which is your mission. "You'd be surprised at how many people extrapolate from the guidelines, rather than starting with their own work," says Hubert Sapp of the Hartford Foundation.

In the worst case, you become more accountable to foundation supporters than to your own membership. You risk the charge of being under the influence of "outside interests" that don't live in the community and, according to the critics, don't have the community's benefit in mind.

9. *The "dirty money" syndrome.* Some organizations refuse to submit proposals to certain funders because they disagree with how the money was raised in the first place. For example, a number of environmental groups won't accept grants from oil companies or their corporate foundations—even when courted by those companies.

   While I understand this position, I urge a broader view. Virtually all foundation and corporate money comes from wealthy people. Great wealth is usually acquired by exploiting natural resources or other human beings. All of us are culpable to some degree, depending on where we shop, what products we buy, and where we bank, so I'm not sure we can simply blame the rich and absolve everyone else. Most environmentalists I know (including me) continue to drive cars and consume gasoline, even as we organize against "big oil."

   If you choose to claim the moral high ground on this issue (assuming you can find any), screen your prospective grantmakers carefully, as any socially responsible investor would. Foundations generally invest their assets and distribute the interest in the form of grants. Try to find out where the money came from—who or what was exploited along the way—to see if it meets your test of cleanliness. Even better, stick with grassroots fundraising and skip the grant proposals altogether.

10. *Opportunity cost.* The resources you invest in grantseeking are no longer available for other fundraising strategies. Consider the following question: Would it make more sense to prepare a proposal for a one-time grant of $10,000 or to spend the same amount of time, energy, and money to build a relationship with a donor who can provide $1,000 per year for ten years? There's no right answer to this question—sometimes you need the larger check now—but it's the kind of question you need to be asking yourself.

The Upside: Ten Ways That Grants Can Benefit Your Work

Now that you understand the frustrating aspects of grantseeking, let's talk about why grants are attractive, useful, and worth the trouble:

1. *Grant proposals are guilt-free.* Most charitable foundations exist to give away money. That's their goal. They publish guidelines on how to apply, so there's no guesswork. (Of course, you should always, always, *always*

follow the guidelines.) Since they advertise "Free Money—Line Up Here," we don't feel like we're breaking any taboos, such as those that prohibit imposing on friends.

2. *Lots of options and opportunities.* With nearly seventy-two thousand foundations, corporate donation programs, and grantmaking public charities in the United States, you can probably find one or two that will help your group. When I worked at Native Seeds/SEARCH, a regional conservation group in Arizona, I maintained files on 250 foundation and corporate prospects. Forty of them provided funding to the group at one time or another. Of course, grants research was an ongoing process, and it took five years to fill that file cabinet. You won't find 250 legitimate prospects in one trip to the library or a single pass through an on-line search program.

3. *Grants force you to get organized.* A grant proposal is an organizing plan, and by putting the details down on paper—goals, objectives, deadlines, budgets, and so forth—most of us become better organizers. The process of developing a proposal can help us do our work more effectively, even if we don't get funded.

4. *Grants provide credibility.* When I worked at the New England Grassroots Environment Fund, our grantees often said that, while the money was helpful, the endorsement that came with the grant was even more valuable—especially for small, informal groups trying to create change on a local level. A grant signals that someone outside the organization is impressed with your work and willing to invest in your success. This can improve your credibility with news media, local businesses, prospective major donors, and other foundations. Your opposition might even take you more seriously.

5. *Grants come in large amounts.* Most grassroots groups don't have major donors they can approach for gifts of $5,000 or $10,000. On the other hand, these are fairly modest grants.

6. *Seed money.* Grants have traditionally been used to create new programs or redefine and invigorate old ones. At this stage, you often need a critical mass of money to get things started. Of course, the implication is that sooner or later the project will need to become self-sustaining through community-based fundraising, earned income, or other sources.

7. *Grants enable you to further diversify your funding.* One of the best uses of grant funds is to enable you to get the training and build the infrastructure to raise more money. With the growth in capacity-building programs, more and more funders find this an attractive pitch.

8. *Good preparation for a major donor campaign.* The process of developing relationships with foundation officers and board members is a lot like courting major donors. It can help staff, board members, and volunteers develop the cultivation skills needed to approach individuals for big gifts.

9. *Grants provide leverage.* Some grants, specifically challenge grants, are designed to help you raise more money. For example, a foundation may provide a grant on the condition that you match it, dollar for dollar, with donations from your members. Challenge grants are very helpful in encouraging individual gifts. For more information on grants leverage, see Chapter Nine.

10. *It's fun.* I enjoy the detective work that goes into discovering new prospects and figuring out how best to approach them. I hope you will, too.

How Grants Fit into a Complete Fundraising Strategy

By now, you should have a clear idea of both the problems and opportunities associated with grants. Keep writing your proposals, but find other ways to fundraise, too.

If you raise most of your funds from grassroots sources, you will find it easier to get grants. This sounds like a paradox, but the idea is simple. Most foundations prefer to back solid organizations that aren't desperate for money, because these groups tend to be more effective. If your community helps to pay for your work, it shows that the community cares about your work. Furthermore, grassroots fundraising is really about mobilizing a power base in your community to help move your agenda.

A summary of your options for income sources appears in Exhibit 2.1.

Here's a quick take on some of the favorite fundraising strategies employed by community organizations:

Individual gifts include membership fees, annual donations, and any other contributions you receive from individuals. These gifts can be solicited by mail, over the phone, via e-mail, through your Web site, or in person. You can set up a monthly or quarterly pledge system and donors can advise you to charge their credit card or deduct money directly from their bank account through electronic funds transfer.

Major donors are a special group of individuals who contribute relatively large gifts. For some groups, a major donor is anyone who gives $100 a year; for other groups, the threshold is $10,000 a year. Wherever you draw the line, you need to solicit these folks differently—typically face to face—and once you receive the donation, give them special treatment.

EXHIBIT 2.1

Income Sources for Nonprofits

Nonprofit organizations can raise money in three ways: by soliciting individual donors, writing grant proposals, or earning income. Among your options are the following:

Individuals

- Membership/donor programs

- Major gifts

- Monthly giving (through electronic funds transfer or credit/debit cards)

- Benefit events

- Workplace giving (payroll plans; United Way, Earthshare, and the like)

- Planned gifts (bequests, life insurance policies, trusts, real property, and so forth)

Grants

- Foundations

- Corporations

- Public charities with funding programs

- Government

- Service clubs (Rotary, Kiwanis, Soroptimist, and so forth)

- Faith-based (from local congregations to national funding programs)

Earned Income

- Goods

- Services

- Publications

- Investment income

- Cause-related marketing, business partnerships

While not every organization can generate income from all categories, the message is clear: diversity is the key to survival. Having a broad and diverse funding base—especially money raised from your community—is the most effective way to ensure the longevity and good health of your organization.

Benefit events range from bake sales and walkathons to black-tie balls. Despite the excellent public relations value of these events, it is far less efficient to organize fundraising benefits than to simply approach potential donors and ask for gifts. Nevertheless, most successful groups still incorporate benefits into their fundraising program as a way to deepen their relationships with current donors, identify new prospects, and increase community awareness of their work.

Earned income can be a moneymaker, although relatively few grassroots groups have explored this approach. Investigate ways to earn money from your programs. If you have a skill that others want—community organizing, mural painting, fundraising, preparing environmental impact statements— why not sell your expertise through workshops and consulting? If you're working to preserve a wild and scenic area, why not charge for guided hikes or canoe tours? If you conduct public interest research, why not publish and sell your reports? Earned income, also called fee-for-service, is a great way to expand your budget while expanding your programs—assuming you can identify the right product to sell.

Resource A lists several publications to help you diversify your funding. Some of my favorites are Kim Klein's *Fundraising for Social Change*, Joan Flanagan's *Successful Fundraising*, and my own book on earned income, *Selling Social Change (Without Selling Out)*. The *Grassroots Fundraising Journal* is another excellent publication that provides information on this topic.

Now that you understand the pros and cons of grantseeking and the reasons to create a diverse funding base, it's time to consider the needs of your partners—the funders. Who are these folks and what do they really want? For an inside look, turn to Chapter Three.

chapter

3

Why People (and Funders) Give Away Their Money

What grabs my attention in a proposal? A community base plus optimism. Our people are up against such tremendous odds. When you see the strength that's carrying them through to survive, you've got to respond to that hope.

—TIA OROS PETERS, Seventh Generation Fund

There's nothing more beautiful than a strategic pitch that fits with the current reality.

—MARTHA KONGSGAARD, Kongsgaard-Goldman Foundation

A great deal of unnecessary mystery surrounds the process of philanthropy, which is a fancy word for "giving away money." Dozens of books, articles, and sociological studies have analyzed the typical donor, trying to understand the philanthropic impulse. Professional fundraisers study these documents like sacred texts. Because the task of raising money makes so many people so uncomfortable, much foolishness has been written—and sold—to help people deal with their discomfort.

I'm going to boil down the research and save you a bunch of reading. The number-one reason people give away their money is simple: somebody asked. If it's someone they know and trust—their sister-in-law, parish priest, or car mechanic—so much the better. All fundraising, including grantseeking, begins with the simple act of one person asking another for money. This chapter explores the motivations and criteria of grantmakers.

Who Gets the Money? Criteria for Giving

To be a savvy grantseeker, you must learn to see your organization from two perspectives simultaneously—as both solicitor and donor. This chapter challenges you to consider both points of view at once. This isn't as difficult as it sounds. You may not think of yourself as a philanthropist, but you probably are.

People ask you for money every day. They send you mail, call you on the phone, ring your doorbell. Your neighbor collects for her daughter's softball team. Your son wants an increase in his allowance. Even the panhandler at your bus stop is a fundraiser. Unless you're very wealthy or incapable of saying no, you have to be selective in your giving—which summarizes the job of a foundation officer.

Before you research potential grantmakers and write proposals, it's useful to consider the criteria foundations and other funding programs use when giving away their money. What follows is a list of factors likely to influence giving decisions at both the personal and institutional level. Don't be intimidated by the length of this list. Your organization is not required to address every item for every donor—what's important to one individual or institution may be inconsequential to another—but you will have to address several of them.

As you read through the list, think about how it relates to your own personal "giving behavior." How do you evaluate requests for donations? The staff and board members of foundations are human beings, and their criteria are similar to yours and mine.

Issue. Do you care about what the organization does? Are the group's concerns also your concerns? Is the issue timely? If you don't really care about whales, then a "Save the Whales" appeal from Greenpeace will end up in your trash can. On the other hand, you might respond to a Greenpeace appeal focusing on reduction of toxic pollution. In that case, the issue (and not necessarily the organization) is your primary motivation to give.

Nearly all foundations clearly articulate the issues that interest them. If you're seeking grants for other things, you need not apply.

Constituency. Who will benefit if the organization succeeds? Most foundations are trying to reach specific groups of people; grantseekers must define their constituency.

Uniqueness. Are other nonprofits already doing what this group has set out to do? Are they organizing a different constituency? Or are they trying to solve a new problem? As a grantseeker, you must distinguish yourself from other groups.

"What gets my attention," says Janice Fong Wolf of the San Luis Obispo County Community Foundation, "is an indication that the program is unique, either in the community or the field of work."

Credibility. Have you heard of the organization? Do they strike you as being well organized, competent, legitimate? Do they get things done, or do they just talk? Have you seen them on television or in the newspaper? News media coverage is helpful for most groups because it lends instant legitimacy. (Of course, there are many legitimate organizations that haven't made the news—yet.)

Track record. What have they done in the past? How do their accomplishments reflect on their ability to get things done in the future? The best predictor of future success is past performance. However, sometimes a history of courage is more important than tangible success. Si Kahn of the Jewish Fund for Justice says he's moved by both "concrete victories and concrete defeats; battles worth taking on, even if they lose."

Big ideas. "Ambitious and aggressive is more saleable than defensive and modest," says Bill Dempsey, formerly of the Unitarian Universalist Veatch Program at Shelter Rock. "Humility and caution don't help. If you're doing good work, don't be shy."

A thoughtful, realistic plan. Big ideas are attractive, but how will the organization make things happen? Is there a step-by-step plan to move the issue and implement the work?

As a grantseeker, if you can be both ambitious and practical at the same time, you've got a terrific strategy—and a very fundable proposal.

Personal relationships. What happens when you're solicited by a friend? When you get a fundraising letter, do you check the letterhead to see if you know the board members? The oldest cliché in fundraising—"People give money to people"—certainly holds true with many foundations and institutional donors.

Like most grantmakers, Irene Vlach of the Lazar Foundation is unapologetic about the value of relationships. "We fund people whom we know and whose work we are familiar with and like," she says, "so make it as personal as you can—pick up the phone, come visit. Whenever a proposal gets on the docket, we've already worked with those folks extensively."

Personal experience. Many of us donate because we have direct experience with a particular issue or need. Perhaps a family member gets ill and we give to a group working to prevent that type of illness, or we enjoy hiking in a particular forest, so we support the forest protection organization. Foundation guidelines are sometimes created in response to the personal experiences of the decision makers.

To make amends or give something back to the community. Perhaps you give because you've directly or indirectly benefited from the group's work, or maybe you're hoping to rectify past mistakes.

Reflecting on her family's history in the resource extraction business, one conservation funder calls herself "an environmental train wreck," adding with a laugh, "I should sue myself." Her foundation is not afraid of aggressive advocacy. "We fund the unfundable," she says proudly.

Referrals. Do you know about this group because a friend or family member has been involved? When we lack direct experience, most of us will take the recommendation of somebody we know and trust.

The most effective referrals may come from your peers. "When grantees recommend other groups, I take that really seriously," says Lois DeBacker of the Charles Stewart Mott Foundation. "Sometimes I solicit these references. A recommendation from another group indicates that these organizations are part of a broader community." She adds, "I appreciate the non-competitive groups; they're generous in spirit. It shows that they want to win."

Leadership. Who's running this thing? Decisions are made by the organization's leadership, and grantmakers want to know who the decision makers are: their experience, relevant training, community base, and so on.

Virginia Kemendo Martinez of the El Paso Community Foundation emphasizes the importance of personal leadership. "I'm not sure that prospective grantees realize the importance of their personal reputations, in addition to the reputation of the organizations they represent. If you know that the person is creative, thoughtful, and so on, he or she will probably do good things with the money."

"We like to see evidence of community empowerment in the project," say Margarita Ramirez and Lina Paredes of the Liberty Hill Foundation. "It goes beyond simple involvement and includes investing in the leadership development of community members and actively involving them in decision making."

Joni Craig of the San Diego Foundation for Change offers a similar assessment with a different twist:

Unlike many funders, our grantmaking committee is very much a part of the community it serves. Nearly all of the committee members are or have been activists. Funding decisions are often based, in part, on an activist's reputation among his or her peers. If one or more members of a group are known for being fiscally irresponsible, for never finishing what they start, or for doing more harm than good in their work, rest assured that these issues will be discussed at a committee meeting. Likewise, applicants who have a strong track record and are respected among their peers will be acknowledged and given credit for their efforts. The lesson here is to be aware that your words and actions may have long-term consequences, and that you never know who might be a potential funder.

Enthusiasm. Do the grantseekers really care about their work? Can you sense their excitement? As Jeffrey Hedgepeth of the Pride Foundation says, "I like proposals that sound energetic and demonstrate the writer's passion for the project."

Innovation. Does the proposal demonstrate a new way to address an old problem? Tia Oros Peters of the Seventh Generation Fund, which supports Native American communities, puts it this way: "We look for the innovative ways that culture can inform the response to local problems; in other words, culturally based innovation. This energy fuels the cultural renaissance in Indian country."

Collaboration and combining issues. Will there be any new collaborations, new combinations of constituencies or interest groups? On the principle of strength in numbers, a group that broadens its base and gets more people involved is more likely to succeed. Many foundations are particularly intrigued by joint projects involving new and existing organizations.

When asked what gets her attention in a proposal, Robin Carton of RESIST says, "Thinking outside the box, particularly showing the ability to cross issues and agendas with other organizations."

Program and organizational development. What will be the long-term effect of the project, if successful? Will it build the organization? Will it significantly affect the lives of the constituents? Does it have the potential to develop into an ongoing program? Can it be replicated somewhere else? An organization is less likely to be funded if donors perceive it is heading for a dead end.

Sources of funding. Grantmakers want to know who provided funding in the past and which funders will be approached for new projects. Information about previous grants helps establish the group's credibility; a list of current prospects allows foundation staff members to check with each other, discuss competing proposals, and avoid duplication of funding.

Financial self-sufficiency. Organizations that can support themselves, rather than rely on outside sources such as foundations, are more likely to survive, grow, prosper, and get things done. "We look for individual donations from the community," says Pat Jerido, formerly of the Ms. Foundation. "We want to see that grantees are rooted in the community. We don't want to be the sole funder, so we ask for a plan that shows other sources of support. This could include fundraising events or using a strong volunteer base to promote the mission."

We all like to back a winner. Most applicants will be more successful with foundations if they can show a diversified funding base.

Financial management. Can the grantee organization handle money in a professional way? Will they produce timely, accurate reports?

Intuition. Not all funding decisions are rational or predictable. While grantmakers must fulfill their "due diligence" requirements, the process often starts with a feeling, as Roxanne Turnage of the CS Fund describes: "Sometimes you have a hunch about a proposal and you go digging—phoning, meeting, going to the next level—and you find what you're looking for. As a grantmaker, you hope your intuition is good enough to know when to put in that extra effort."

John Powers of the Educational Foundation of America describes his approach to grantmaking:

> This is the way I review proposals:
>
> - Is the *project* important to me?
>
> - Can the *organization* deliver? Of the organizations working on this topic, is this the one to fund? Is the organization businesslike, efficient, and frugal? Will this be a one-shot effort or will the organization endure? What is this organization's record?
>
> - Is the project or issue *timely*? Is there an urgency or a window of opportunity on which to capitalize?
>
> - Does the organization *need the limited funds* our foundation has, or could it raise what it needs from other sources? Is the budget realistic, lean, or padded?

Foundation Culture

First, let's get our terms straight. According to the Foundation Center Web site, www.fdncenter.org, there are four types of foundations:

Independent foundations established by wealthy families or individuals, sometimes in the form of a bequest, otherwise know as "a gift from the grave."

Company-sponsored foundations, also called corporate foundations, created and funded by businesses.

Operating foundations established to operate research, social welfare, or other charitable programs. Operating foundations seldom give grants to other nonprofits.

Community foundations supported by and operated for the benefit of a specific community or region.

The first three are private foundations. Community foundations are classified as public charities—a different status for tax purposes—and sometimes called public foundations. (Note: Canadian law is different; check the Canada Customs and Revenue Web site, www.ccra-adrc.gc.ca, for specifics.)

A number of other granting sources, including other types of public charities, service clubs, religious organizations, and corporate giving programs, also make grants. They may look and act like foundations, but technically they are not. From the grantseeker's perspective, these technicalities matter little, since these organizations accept applications and give away money. (For more on approaching faith-based funders, see Resource C.) In this book I use the terms *funder, grantmaker,* and *foundation* interchangeably, with the understanding that not every grantmaker is formally organized as a foundation.

Most independent foundations—the biggest category—are started with a large chunk of money. Foundation officers and advisors invest this money in stocks, bonds, business loans, or real estate, with the intention of earning more money. The income is typically held aside and reinvested.

In exchange for their tax exemption, foundations are currently required to spend only 5 percent of their assets annually as grants and to cover their own operating expenses, including staff salaries, office costs, travel, and so forth. Under most economic conditions, with assets growing at 8–12 percent each year, the majority of independent foundations earn more money than they grant. During the boom years of the late 1990s they earned a lot more than 5 percent. On the other hand, when the economy sours and the stock market declines, their assets shrink. Under these circumstances, funders perceive that they have less money to give away. (For a discussion of fluctuations in the stock market and attempts to increase foundation payouts, see Chapter One.)

Foundations traditionally support religious charities, education, medicine, the arts, and mainstream social service agencies, such as the YMCA or the American Red Cross. Relatively few give grants for advocacy or social change organizing, despite their common rhetoric about funding risk and innovation. The more controversial your efforts, or the greater your challenge to the status quo—in social relations, politics, art, or whatever—the harder it will be to fund your work with grants. This makes perfect sense because the rich, who underwrite most foundations, *are* the status quo.

Happily, there are exceptions, as I found among the fifty staff and trustees I interviewed for this book. Be aware that the folks I surveyed are among the most progressive in the foundation world (which is not a terribly progressive community), so their views are not meant to represent "philanthropy in America."

Since there are so many more applicants than grants to fund them, the people who make funding decisions have a lot of control over the health and success of applicant organizations. "You can't remove the power imbalance between grantmaker and grantee. It's always there," says Jon Jensen of the

George Gund Foundation. "The best you can do is make it transparent and humane." This power imbalance is one of the most important reasons why you need to develop an active grassroots fundraising program.

Most foundations are structured like other nonprofits, with paid staff and volunteer boards. Some also use community review boards or consultants. "Each foundation has its own culture," says Irene Vlach of the Lazar Foundation. The differences—and similarities—are often unexpected. Mark Ritchie notes, "I have shifted from a small foundation (Foundation for Deep Ecology) to a large one (Kellogg Foundation), and I am surprised at how similar they are in terms of my experience working there. I had assumed that the smaller organization would be more informal, but Kellogg is surprisingly informal and family-like."

The following section describes the roles of various people at foundations.

The staff. "The Archaeology of Philanthropy," an exhibit by David Bergholz of the George Gund Foundation, was featured in the July 24, 2003 issue of *The Chronicle of Philanthropy*. Nearing retirement after fourteen years as foundation president, Bergholz had filled a Cleveland art gallery with 13 annual reports, 27 desk calendars, and 1,002 name badges from meetings. The walls were covered with 2,451 hand-written cards detailing his daily schedule and 21 steno pads with memos dictated to his secretary.

One photo shows the amused Bergholz with a dozen name tags strung around his neck. "I had cryptic notations on my calendar, such as 'lunch,'" he writes for the exhibit, "but no clue as to where or with whom. Because I could not read my own illegible writing, we had mystery guests appear in the office. I was forced to perfect the question, 'So why are we meeting today?'"

In 1996, Bergholz's colleague, Jon Jensen, compared his own job to being under "an avalanche of information." Now, Jensen says, "The avalanche is worse than ever. As grantmakers, we are balancing keeping groups alive with the desire and capacity to do new things. We do much more juggling than ever." Even the smaller funding programs review hundreds of proposals each year, so the feeling of being crushed by words is very real.

In addition to digging out from beneath the paper, foundation staff (the typical job title is *program officer* or *funding officer*) manage other day-to-day chores, including answering the phone, handling correspondence, and preparing materials for board review. Staff members also research new issue areas and seek out new organizations to fund, sometimes in the face of their own budget problems and staff reductions. "We cut our staff in half to spend less on salaries and move more money out the door," says Soya Jung Harris of A Territory Resource Foundation. "We lost a full-time grants person and a finance person. As a result, we're all working harder." Sounds familiar, doesn't it?

Traditionally, foundation staff members tended to come from academia, government, and other foundations. As mentioned in Chapter One, more and more staff of progressive foundations now come directly from the social change community. Many of these funders make a point of hiring people with community organizing backgrounds, which has significantly changed grant-making assumptions and methods.

While these employees seldom make final decisions about who gets the money, they advocate for applicants whose work they admire. As Roxanne Turnage of the CS Fund says, "Our board consists of four family members. After seventeen years, I know these people so incredibly well, I can look at something and say, 'this isn't going anywhere' or 'they're going to love this.' My primary skill is sifting through the mounds of information in a proposal and figuring out what the board will want to know in order to fund it. I'm always thinking, who is my champion on the board for this proposal? I'm an intermediary—I'm looking for a match between the work and my board."

An entire chapter of this book, Chapter Six, is devoted to how to build relationships with funding officers. Bottom-line advice: if you want to improve your odds, make friends with these folks.

The board. The board of directors (sometimes called the board of trustees) defines the philanthropic goals of the foundation, reviews proposals screened by the staff, and selects which groups to fund. Both staff and board members sometimes conduct site visits with applicant organizations to get a better feel for their work. Thousands of smaller family foundations have no paid staff, so volunteer trustees handle all the chores—which explains why many won't accept unsolicited proposals.

In many cases, trustees are themselves donors to the foundation or heirs of the original donors. They are giving away their own money. You'll find a lot of relatives serving together on foundation boards. As in any organization, decision-making power can be concentrated in the hands of a few particularly active or persuasive board members.

Trustees are sometimes experts in the issue areas supported by the foundation. Others are chosen for their knowledge of investment strategy or tax law. Still others serve because of their corporate affiliations. Some are simply friends and neighbors of other board members.

With most foundations, it is considered bad form to contact trustees directly, and that strategy may actually backfire. "Going directly to the trustees won't work," says Terry Odendahl, formerly of the Wyss Foundation. "Talk with me first and we'll work with the trustees together."

Si Kahn, who serves on the board of two grantmakers, Changemakers and the Jewish Fund for Justice, offers the following caution: "If you're asking me to lobby on your behalf, tell me up front. Be honest about it. I will follow up with the program officers and tell them I know the group. But then, we're always asked, 'Do you know the group?' So lobbying won't make a big difference. Like a jury, we have to put friendship aside. I don't believe there's a formal protocol about contacting board members, but please understand: at a fundamental level, I am not lobbyable."

At other foundations, contact with the board is acceptable or even encouraged. "At Northwest Fund for the Environment," says Zoë Rothchild, "Our process is unusual in that our trustees are very active in the review of the proposals. They each act as program officers on their assigned grants. Our board is stocked with professionals or activists in the field and they make the phone calls to follow up on proposals."

The moral of this story is clear: know your prospect. If you're uncertain about the rules of a particular grantmaker, ask.

Community review boards. Several community-based social change foundations add an additional layer of review: a community board, grants committee, or allocations committee. Proposals are reviewed by a group of peers—organizers and activists—to ensure that the community's wisdom and priorities are reflected in the grants. In some cases, these peer panels make final grant decisions; in other cases, they forward their recommendations to the board of directors for a vote. As mentioned in Chapter One, this model has become so popular that some traditional community foundations are beginning to restructure their decision-making processes.

Jeffrey Hedgepeth of the Pride Foundation describes a typical use of this model: "A committee of community volunteers and board members reviews applications and makes the decisions. We try to get a diverse group of people—ethnically; bisexual, gay, lesbian, and transgender; geographically; and professionally. Since we get a wide range of applications, there is almost always someone on the committee who knows a little about a topic. Staff members organize the process but don't vote on the grants. This enables us to be more of an information resource to applicants."

Consultants. Some foundations hire consultants to manage their grants programs. The consultant might be a local tax attorney specializing in the needs of small family foundations, or a former foundation officer providing grantmaking advice. Small foundations sometimes join together to create an umbrella organization and hire common staff to handle proposal review, bookkeeping, tax forms, and other tasks.

A consultant is, by definition, a walking catalog of ideas, names, and organizations. You should make it a point to find out which grants consultants cover your region or your issue, and introduce them to your work. If suitably impressed, they can open a lot of doors to potential funders.

One of the best ways to attract funding is to be successful at your work. In Chapter Four, we'll discuss the planning that precedes grant research and building relationships with grantmakers. Planning always comes before asking: if you know where you're going and you've got the route worked out, it's a lot easier to raise money for the fare.

chapter

4

The Grant Proposal as Organizing Plan

> While background information is good, with so many proposals, it's not clear how the work will happen. We need plain, specific information about what you're going to do and how you're going to do it.
>
> —GAYE EVANS, Appalachian Community Fund

> If the promise looks extravagant, it probably is.
>
> —HUBERT SAPP, Hartford Foundation

Grassroots groups tend to operate minute by minute and hand to mouth: dealing with crises, putting out "brush fires," worrying about the payroll. When the world is falling apart and your group is close behind, long-range planning is considered a luxury. For many of us, it's hard to justify taking time—our most precious resource—to create a comprehensive plan to guide our strategy.

Under these conditions, improvisation becomes a way of life and, for many people, a badge of honor. After years of improvising their way from project to project, some organizers resist planning, fearing it might limit their flexibility or autonomy. As activist and financial consultant Terry Miller writes in *Managing for Change* (1992, p. 6), "Some will argue that they cannot plan because something unexpected may happen. There is no better way to ensure something unexpected happening than not to plan. If you have a plan and the situation changes, you will be working with a revised plan; otherwise, you will be working with revised instinct."

This is where the process of developing grant proposals can really help your work. For many groups, writing a proposal is the closest thing to creating a community organizing plan. If you take the time to design your project thoroughly and outline the plan in your proposal, you will benefit in at least three ways:

- *Focus.* The discipline of putting details on paper—goals, objectives, deadlines, expenses—will focus your efforts in the field. Your project will be more successful and you'll have a bigger impact.

- *Involvement.* The planning process provides an opportunity to involve both your coworkers and your constituency in choosing the future of your organization. As Bill Dempsey, formerly of the Unitarian Universalist Veatch Program at Shelter Rock, points out, "Good ideas don't always lead to grants. We see sharp proposals from groups presenting themselves as something they are not. They often have no base in the community, no accountability to the community."

- *Funding.* You are more likely to win the grant, since you'll be so organized and professional.

The process discussed in this chapter will help you clarify the case for support, solicit input from your peers, test the feasibility of your ideas, and turn those ideas into effective programs.

Building the Case for Support

At an early stage in the planning process, you need to develop a set of background materials outlining why your organization exists—defining the problem you're trying to solve, describing your plan for solving it, and confirming your ability to do the work. The contents of this document, which is called a case statement, are nicely summarized in Kim Klein's book, *Fundraising for Social Change* (2001, pp. 27-28):

> The case statement includes the following elements:
> 1. *A statement of mission* that tells the world why the group exists.
> 2. *A description of goals* that tells what the organization hopes to accomplish over the long term—in other words, what the organization intends to do about why it exists.
> 3. *A list of objectives*—specific, measurable, and time-limited—that tell how the goals will be met.
> 4. *A summary of the organization's history* that shows that the organization is competent and can accomplish its goals.

5. *A description of the structure of the organization,* including board and staff roles and what kinds of people are involved in the group (such as clients, organizers, teachers, clergy).
6. *A fundraising plan.*
7. *A financial statement* for the previous fiscal year and a *budget* for the current fiscal year.

Notice the sequence of the first three items. The mission statement tells *why* (the need); the goals statement tells *what* (your ambition); the objectives—along with a list of methods for reaching these objectives—tell *how* (your plan). Each step flows logically from the previous one. For this reason, you should not try to develop a work plan (or a grant proposal) without reaching some sort of consensus within your group about how you define the need and your long-range goals for addressing the need.

A case statement is an internal document—it's too long and detailed for public consumption—but you can easily condense it for the public. You can also borrow entire paragraphs or pages from the case and insert them into your brochures, newsletters, membership recruitment letters, news releases, and even your grant proposals. In fact, the contents of a case statement look a lot like the sections of a proposal. If you take the time to develop your case boilerplate (the standard language about who you are and what you do) with care, your grantwriting chores will be much easier.

It's heresy to mention this in a fundraising book, but your nonprofit can survive and even prosper without a formal case statement. The key word is "formal." I've held development jobs with six organizations during twenty years, yet only one group had a formal case statement (and I can't recall ever seeing it). But—this is important—every one of those groups had the elements of the case written down and available. When needed, I would assemble the necessary pieces from the mission statement, articles of incorporation, previous grant proposals, newsletters, bylaws, and other fundraising and publicity materials. Gathering them in one easily accessible folder would have saved a lot of time. You don't need a shiny embossed binder with the words "Case Statement," but you'll be more effective if you have all the components at your fingertips.

Programs, Projects, and Campaigns

Your success in raising grant money will be based, in part, on your ability to plan your work strategically to make the most of available funds. What this usually means is breaking down your work into programs and projects, each with their own specific goals and deadlines, budgets and headaches.

Before going any further, let's get our terms straight. In describing their work, organizers and activists use words like *programs, projects,* and *campaigns.* Throughout this book, I use *program* and *project* interchangeably (and limit the use of the word *campaign,* for reasons I will soon explain). Some grantmakers, however, encourage a more formal definition of these terms, as follows.

Programs are broad, ongoing areas of your work that are defined by the issues you address: health care reform, environmental justice, reproductive rights, and so on.

Projects are more narrowly defined activities, typically focusing on constituencies, geographic areas, or portions of the larger issue. A project can be a piece of your regular program, or it can be something new that moves your work in a different direction. Projects have specific, measurable outcomes; they begin and end on certain dates. Over time, some successful temporary projects become permanent programs, or spin off other projects.

The word *campaign* has several meanings. In fundraising, the term is often used to describe a series of connected activities that move the organization toward a monetary goal—for example, a major gifts campaign or a capital campaign to raise funds for buildings or land.

Campaign is also used to define a broad coalition effort to achieve a specific goal having little or nothing to do with fundraising or elections. The South Africa divestment campaign of the 1980s is a good example. Thousands of individuals and community groups from around the world pressured foundations, corporations, universities, and municipal governments to denounce apartheid by selling off their investments in companies doing business in racially segregated South Africa. The economic pressure from this "investment boycott" helped to end apartheid. Issue campaigns are an important and useful strategy for bringing groups together to create social change.

Among the general public, the word *campaign* is usually associated with elections, which is why I don't use it much in this book. The IRS prohibits 501(c)(3) organizations from spending money to elect or defeat candidates for public office and sets limits on how much money public charities can spend on lobbying (including ballot initiatives). If your group focuses on traditional electoral campaigns or does substantial lobbying, you're probably registered as a 501(c)(4) or a political action committee and won't be eligible for many grants. (For a comprehensive look at different IRS designations and their effects on lobbying and electoral activities, see Resource D.)

If you're confused about the terms *program, project,* and *campaign,* here's an illustration to help you sort things out. Let's say you work for a hypothetical citizen's group, People Before Profits, which organizes working-class communities around economic issues. Your organization might be involved in three ongoing programs or program areas: public transit, fair lending, and tax equity. Each of these programs could incorporate multiple projects. For example, your work on public transit might include two projects: working for discount passes for students and encouraging increased service to low-income neighborhoods. People Before Profits could also be involved in a coalition campaign, under your tax equity program, to repeal the state sales tax on food and medicine. Exhibit 4.1 gives a visual representation of this work.

EXHIBIT 4.1
Programs and Projects of People Before Profits

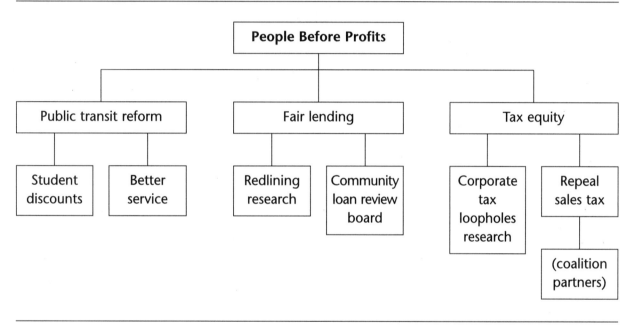

General Support Grants

It is much more difficult to win grants for general operational support than it is for specific projects. As Terry Miller (1992) writes in *Managing for Change,* "There is constant pressure from funders to get you to apply for funding only for 'special projects,' and yet your biggest need is general support money" (p. 11).

Some grants officers are aware of this dilemma and are working to correct it within their own foundations and among their peers. Despite foundations' increased attention to the general support gap, you'll have a hard time raising unrestricted funds through grants. This is one of the most important reasons to diversify your funding base with membership development and general donations, since these funds can be used for general expenses.

If you choose to seek general support grants, you'll have the best chance with a current or past funder who already knows and respects your work. Except for very small grants, it's rare to receive general support on your first approach to a grantmaker. To improve your odds, you might try to package your general proposal as program or project support. Outline the full range of your work, program by program, and ask the funder to underwrite a portion of each. Remember, the more clearly you show how the grant money will be used, the better your chances of getting funded.

Designing Fundable Projects: The Grantwriter as Feasibility Tester

As you gain more experience with fundraising and grantseeking, you'll get a better feel for what is "grantable" and what isn't. The best way to learn is to bounce your ideas off other grantwriters, community organizers, nonprofit managers, and foundation staff. As you evaluate the feasibility and fundability of your work, consider the following questions:

Does your project fill a real need, and how much of that need will this project address? In other words, are you creating a problem and trying to solve it because you think there's money available, or did the problem exist before you discovered the money? If the need is real, will this project meet the need or a significant portion of it?

Is anyone else working on a similar project? Is the niche already filled? For example, here's a story from Janice Fong Wolf of the San Luis Obispo County Community Foundation: "An applicant claimed they were 'the only ones' working on the issue—in this case, outreach to Latinos for citizenship education—yet it is well known in the community that another group does similar work. Either they hope that we don't know what's going on, or they haven't bothered to get connected. Reviewers wonder how successful they can be if they haven't gotten involved with existing groups."

If your work overlaps with that of other organizations, can you build productive alliances? Nonprofits are often competing for the same funding, so it benefits you to create partnerships with other groups to share the wealth. If you do this effectively, funders will notice. "We look at the strategy embodied in a cluster of proposals," says Shelley Davis of the Joyce Foundation. "In their proposals, applicants speak to each other and about each other."

A unique combination of issues or constituencies will capture the grantmaker's attention. Soya Jung Harris of A Territory Resource Foundation recounts two interesting examples they helped to fund:

- Faced with the prospect of an anti-immigrant ballot initiative, Oregon farmworkers aligned themselves with the gay-lesbian-bisexual-transgender community, which had organized in previous years to defeat a series of discriminatory ballot measures. This alliance forced a lot of folks in both communities to rethink stereotypes around homophobia and racism. "When they see the word 'homosexual' in a discriminatory law," says Larry Kleinman of the farmworkers union, "we encourage our members to substitute the word 'Mexican.' Then we ask, 'How does that make you feel?'"

- When it was founded, Communities Against Rape and Abuse (CARA) focused on the needs of survivors; they didn't really think about the implications of locking up abusers. With education and support from women of color active in the national antiviolence movement, they came to understand that the prison-industrial complex, by its very nature, makes the problem of violence even worse. Says Alisa Bierria of CARA, "We believe that activists have to take a stance against mass incarceration, because putting people in prison will not solve the problem of domestic violence and sexual assault. The U.S. prison system facilitates the cycle of violence; it does not help to end it."

For more on strategies for collaborative fundraising, see Resource E.

Have foundations funded similar projects? If so, which foundations? Go on the Internet, go to the library, talk with other nonprofits, call foundation offices. In judging the feasibility and fundability of your program, try to see your work through the eyes of prospective grantmakers by studying their guidelines, reviewing their annual reports, and talking with foundation staff. Do your homework before you apply. You will only develop your sense of what's fundable and what isn't through ongoing research.

As you create a long-range plan, it's appropriate to take into account the fundability of your various programs, but be cautious about shifting your mission or direction just for the sake of bringing in additional funds.

For more information on grants research, see Chapter Five.

How controversial is it? As the controversy factor increases, fundability decreases. When describing the characteristics of projects they prefer to support, foundations often use the words *risk* and *innovation*, and some actually put money behind these words. If you're trying something revolutionary, however, you'll be working from a smaller pool of prospects.

Some funders, however, are attracted to projects that demonstrate a high degree of difficulty because of their controversial nature. As Bill Dempsey says, "Do you know what gets my attention? People doing aggressive work on hostile turf—for example, promoting gay rights in Utah rather than Massachusetts. I feel bad for the groups in [progressive communities like] Madison and Berkeley—it must be harder to make the case."

Will your program make people sit up and take notice? We return to rule number one: distinguish yourself. You don't have to use gimmicks, but if your project contains a unique "hook," use it. It will make a difference.

A hook can be something visual and compelling. The late artist Alan Gussow created an event called the Shadow Project in 1982 after viewing photos of atomic bomb victims at Hiroshima, whose "shadows" had been burned into sidewalks and buildings by the intense heat of the blast. As participants in the Shadow Project, artists and activists painted their own silhouettes—thousands of them—in public places to commemorate the dead of Hiroshima. After Gussow's project took place in New York and a similar one occurred in Portland, Oregon, coordinated by Donna Slepack, leaders in these two communities came together to organize the International Shadow Project on Hiroshima Day in 1985. Nearly ten thousand people in four hundred cities participated. In this case, the hook was the shadow image itself and the unusual collaboration between visual artists and peace activists. Even today, the Shadow Project continues to be organized as a memorial and a warning against nuclear holocaust.

Sometimes the threat or problem—rather than the solution—is the hook. I once designed a fundraising mailing for a conservation group working in such a hostile community that they received death threats. A photo of the group's staff had even been tacked up in the local post office, with the crosshairs of a rifle drawn over their faces. We used these death threats as the fundraising hook—the newest endangered species, we wrote, is your local environmental activist. This mailing, which more than doubled the group's membership, was their most successful up to that time. The same story could have been adapted for use in a grant proposal.

Do you have the skills to run the program effectively? Think big, but don't ask for more work or money than you can handle. To judge your capacity, consider how the proposed project will affect your staffing, budgeting, bookkeeping, management procedures, and other programs.

Many nonprofits fail for lack of funding, but a surprising number die from accelerated growth. To live a long life, your group needs to grow in a rational, sustainable way. A giant infusion of cash can damage your organization in a number of ways:

- Changing the culture of the organization—how it feels to participate in the work—which can lead to staff turnover

- Rapidly shifting power and accountability within the organization

- Reducing the need for community financial support, which reduces your accountability to the community you serve

- Exposing the flaws in your management systems, for example, book-keeping and time management

For an inside look at how one grantmaker might evaluate your project, consider the following evaluation form developed by the El Paso Community Foundation to screen proposals. My favorite questions include "Does the project use a creative approach to get something done?" and "Does the request raise more questions than it answers?"

How would your project measure up?

EL PASO COMMUNITY FOUNDATION: CRITERIA FOR REVIEWING PROPOSALS

- Is the request outside the giving parameters of the foundation?
- Does the project fill an unmet need?
- Is there a depth of awareness of the subject area in which the project will operate?
- How does the project fit into the organization's overall mission?
- Does the project use a creative approach to get something done?
- Does the request raise more questions than it answers?
- Does the request promise too much?
- Does the project show collaboration with other organizations?
- Does the request show promise in developing local capacity?
- What is the reputation of the organization?
- What is the record of past work by the people involved?
- Is the budget reasonable?
- Is the proposal well thought-out?
- Will the project produce a long-term benefit for the community?
- Is the project area a priority concern?
- Has the foundation recently funded in the area of the request?
- Is there a compelling reason to make this grant?

Prepared by Virginia Kemendo Martinez, El Paso Community Foundation. Adapted from materials prepared by Bill Somerville, Philanthropic Ventures Foundation.

Involving Your Coworkers, Your Allies, Your Neighbors

While I would never argue for grantwriting by committee, try to find ways to involve and empower your colleagues and your community. The proposal development process tends to concentrate power in the hands of the people who write the grant applications. In preparing proposals, they make choices—some subtle, others more visible—about how the organization will behave and how the project will be run. To spread responsibility for the work, you need to develop strategy for involving several people.

To start the process at Native Seeds/SEARCH, we held a "grants brainstorm" at the beginning of each year. Our program managers would fantasize out loud about what they could accomplish with more money, and then we would begin to shape these fantasies into projects with specific goals and outcomes.

As the resident grantwriter, I tried to evaluate the fundability and feasibility of each idea. The process of brainstorming, by its very nature, generated more ideas than we could ever manage. Once all these project ideas were on the table, we tried to ask tough questions about our management skills, staffing, and other financial needs related to each of them. If the proposed project survived these concerns (and many did not), we roughed out a timeline and a budget.

Following the brainstorming meeting, I would often prepare a brief outline of those ideas that had passed muster, then circulate it to the appropriate staff members for review. Members of the board or the relevant program committee were sometimes asked for their comments as well. I urge you to develop a similar summary for your next project, especially if you're new to proposal writing. Outlines can assist you in several ways:

- *You must reduce the project to its main points.* This provides another way of testing its feasibility.

- *The strengths and weaknesses of the program are easier to see.* You can't mask potential problems with fancy words.

- *Almost anyone can find the time to read and respond to a two-page document.* Hand your colleagues a ten-page proposal, however, and you might wait a long time for a reaction.

- *Outlines can save you a lot of work.* Nothing is more discouraging than writing a long, detailed proposal, passing it to your supervisor, and hearing her say, "I thought we agreed to drop this project." It works better to get everyone's input and approval at the outline stage.

Once the outline has been passed around, edited, and approved, make sure to involve the project managers in designing a specific work plan. They will be responsible for carrying out the plan and are probably the best people to figure out the tasks and timing. This is also a good stage to involve your constituency, through your program committee or board members with relevant expertise.

At some point in your brainstorming process—preferably early—you may want to include allies from other organizations to help evaluate your ideas. For brainstorming and evaluation instructions and a worksheet to help you record the results, see Exercise 4.1 and Worksheet 4.1. Worksheet 4.1 also provides a way to analyze the elements of your proposed project.

Project Brainstorming and Evaluation

1. Gather between five and eight people in a semicircle around an easel, chalkboard, or something large you can write on. Include at least a few people not actively involved with your group; they will bring a different set of assumptions and experiences.

2. Identify one person (the presenter) willing to have his or her project idea discussed and critiqued.

3. Ask another person to facilitate the process and take notes; you can split this into two jobs if you wish. The facilitator or note taker marks three columns on the paper or chalkboard as follows: +, –, ? (See Worksheet 4.1.)

4. The presenter takes two or three minutes to explain the proposed project: the need it addresses, who will be involved, how much it will cost, anticipated results, and so forth. The participants can ask clarifying questions to sort out the details.

5. After answering a few basic questions, the presenter stops speaking (this is very difficult to do) and all attention is directed to the board. The facilitator asks for feedback from the group and the note taker marks responses under the appropriate columns. The facilitator structures the responses by asking the following questions:

   Strengths (+): What's interesting about this project? What's the "hook"? How is it unique? Does it offer a new take on an old problem, or perhaps a new combination of players? Does it suggest an emotionally compelling story or good handles for public education? Is the solution realistic? How about the budget? Do we know any "role model" groups that have tried something similar? If so, what was the result?

   Weaknesses (–): Do they face opposition? Is the idea controversial? Has it been tried before? How does public opinion line up on this subject? Is the project feasible? Are they asking for enough money? Who are these people, anyway?

   Questions (?): What information are we lacking to make a good assessment?

   Participants are encouraged to respond in any order; it isn't necessary to itemize all the strengths before moving on to weaknesses. The presenter will have a strong urge to defend every weakness and answer every question verbally, but must resist this urge, or the exercise bogs down. Simply note any concerns and questions in the appropriate columns.

6. When all responses have been teased out of the group—this typically takes ten to twenty minutes—the presenter gets the last word.

The goal of the exercise is to teach you how to think like a funder. Most of us are too close to our own work to see it with any objectivity. A group of engaged outsiders will see strengths you didn't know you had, identify weaknesses you've been avoiding, and ask a whole lot of questions you didn't think to ask.

In short, this is what a funding officer does when reviewing your proposal. To the degree that you can build on your strengths, address your weaknesses, and anticipate and answer any questions, you will create a much stronger project and a more fundable proposal.

Project Evaluation Form

Organization _____ Project _____

+	−	?
Write down all the strengths and selling points of the project.	Write down all the factors working against the project's success.	Write down all unanswered questions about the project.

The following outline of a proposal for Native Seeds/SEARCH is a bit dated (check out the budget!), but as an example it holds up well. This project was funded; the work proceeded pretty much as described; and New Mexico staff member Brett Bakker served Native Seeds/SEARCH with distinction for almost a decade. To see the arc from idea to outline to fully implemented project, take a look at the final report from the first full year of this program in Chapter Ten.

NATIVE SEEDS/SEARCH
NEW MEXICO FIELD OFFICE PROPOSAL OUTLINE

INTRODUCTION AND PROBLEM STATEMENT (WHY)

1. Loss of crop diversity in Northern New Mexico; important area for native crops.

2. Assimilation pressure on traditional Native American and Hispanic communities has greatly reduced the number of farmers, leading to loss of crop varieties and changes in local culture and agriculture. Non-farm jobs, changes in economics of family farming.

3. Other groups attempting to preserve genetic diversity in the region failed due to mismanagement, poorly defined goals, too broad a mission, and commercial pressure (the need to make money). Brief review of problems or limitations of Talavaya, Ghost Ranch (High Desert Research Farm), SNAC, San Juan Pueblo Project. NS/S has not previously worked in area to avoid duplicating work of other groups.

4. Role of NS/S in addressing these problems; track record. NS/S started due to requests from Native Americans for seeds and information. List of tribal groups we've helped in Arizona. Opportunity to expand our program to Hispanic farmers. Appropriate expansion of our range, given the Native American population of the area and the threat to native farming practices.

5. Proposed field rep, Brett, has exceptional qualifications, farming skills, and contacts among NAs in New Mexico.

PROGRAM GOALS (WHO, WHAT, WHERE)

1. Seed collection from New Mexico for NS/S seed bank and catalog. Create small back-up seed bank in office for NM collections.

2. Provide support and expertise for creation of tribal and local seed banks.

3. Distribution of seeds to Native Americans, and provide follow-up information on gardening techniques, as needed. Seed sales to general public during regular hours.

4. Distribution of educational materials (literature, slide show, videos, diabetes info) to NAs in NM.

5. Coordination of seed grow-outs for NS/S from NAs.

6. Educational outreach to schools, churches, gardening clubs, seniors, and the like. Could include gardening workshops stressing traditional techniques.

7. Local fundraising to support local programs.

8. Provide call-in or walk-in support for local gardeners and those interested in native crops. Staff office one day per week; have phone machine for message pick-up.

9. Provide articles on NM crops and farmers for NS/S newsletter and public media.

10. Coordination and networking of seed-saving groups and farmers in the area; for example, work on organizing next seed summit.

METHODS (HOW, WHEN)

1. Set up office, phone, bank account. Establish regular hours.

2. Send mailing to New Mexico members and those on mail list announcing opening of NM office (hours, menu of services, and so forth) and seeking donations.

3. Send announcement to local and regional press, including office hours, available services, and so on. Call media to arrange for feature stories on NS/S.

4. Schedule and hold grand opening event (Gary Nabhan as speaker?)

5. Recruit volunteers to help staff office and provide support.

6. Make periodic seed collection and technical support trips to regional NA and Hispanic farmers; offer support services as necessary.

7. Bring collections to Tucson for storage (fall); pick up seeds for distribution in Tucson (spring). Restock supplies.

SPECIFIC OBJECTIVES AND EVALUATION (MEASURING SUCCESS)

1. Add fifty new accessions to NS/S seed bank.

2. Arrange for grow-out of fifty varieties for NS/S catalog distribution, preservation, or research.

3. Increase NS/S seed distribution by 25 percent in New Mexico while improving the quality of follow-up support for our growers.

4. Provide six educational presentations to local groups.

5. Arrange for five articles and stories on NS/S, seed saving, genetic diversity, diabetes, and so on in local and regional media.

6. Attend or support three regional gardening or seed-saving events to distribute NS/S information and seeds.

7. Raise $2,500 in local and regional support for program through increased membership, outreach, and seed sales in first year; $5,000 in second year.

1992 BUDGET (HOW MUCH $ FOR ONE YEAR)

Salary and fringe (half time = $935/mo)	$11,220
Rent and utilities (Peace Center)	1,200
Phone service:	
Hook-up	85
Basic local	500
Long distance	500
Typing and word processing support	500
Furniture (desk, table, chairs, shelves, lamp, file cabinet; all used)	300
Equipment:	
Phone	45
Answering machine	100
Slide projector	150
Office supplies	250
Postage and shipping	1,000
Printing and photocopying	500
Travel	1,650
TOTAL:	**$18,000**

Letters of support requested from:
- San Juan Pueblo
- Ghost Ranch
- Flowering Tree Permaculture

See Worksheet 4.2 for an outline of the elements of a complete proposal.

Once the proposal is funded, it's important to keep your colleagues actively involved in documenting the program for the purpose of grant reporting. The project manager is generally in charge of spending the money, but it will probably fall to you, the grantwriter, to produce the interim and final reports for the grantmaker. Let the staff know in advance what information you will require to prepare thorough and accurate reports. For more detail on grants administration, see Chapter Ten.

Proposal Outline

Mission and organizational history

1. Mission: Why do you exist?

_____

_____

_____

_____

_____

_____

2. Constituency: Who do you work with?

_____

_____

_____

_____

_____

_____

3. Accomplishments: What have you done to meet your mission? (If appropriate, discuss the relevant skills and expertise of individuals involved with the group.)

_____

_____

_____

_____

_____

_____

_____

_____

_____

Problem statement. Define the problem you're trying to solve. Be as specific as possible—talk about how this problem affects real people in your community. Tell stories. Avoid clichés. If you have statistics, this is a good place to include them.

_____

_____

_____

_____

_____

_____

_____

_____

_____

_____

Goal. In tackling this problem, what's your goal? (Hint: What will your community look and feel like once the problem is completely solved?) If this ends up sounding like your mission statement, fine.

_____

_____

_____

_____

_____

_____

Specific objectives. (These can also double as your evaluation points.) How will you count, weigh or measure your work? How will you know if you succeed? (Hint: Most of these items should have numbers attached—for example, number of students enrolled, number of meals served, number of community meetings organized, number of people present at these meetings. Add more if needed.)

1. _____

2. _____

3. _____

4. _____

5. _____

6. _____

Methods. What *specific tasks* will you undertake to reach your goal? When will they begin and end? (Add more if needed.)

Task 1: _____

Start date: _____ Completion date: _____

Task 2: _____

Start date: _____ Completion date: _____

Task 3: _____

Start date: _____ Completion date: _____

Task 4: _____

Start date: _____ Completion date: _____

Task 5: _____

Start date: _____ Completion date: _____

Task 6: _____

Start date: _____ Completion date: _____

Task 7: _____

Start date: _____ Completion date: _____

Task 8: _____

Start date: _____ Completion date: _____

Task 9: _____

Start date: _____ Completion date: _____

Task 10: _____

Start date: _____ Completion date: _____

Budget. On a separate page, outline how much money you will need to complete the project (expenses) and how you plan to raise the money (revenues). List all prospective sources—individuals, foundations, government agencies, program fees, benefit events, and so on—and the status of funding from each.

_____

How Much Money? Developing Budgets for Grant-Funded Projects

Whenever I teach a grants workshop, someone always wants to know, "How much money should we ask for?" The simple and intuitively correct answer is, "Ask for as much as you need." Of course, this answer seldom makes anyone happy, so I'll try to provide a more thorough explanation by asking a few additional questions. This discussion covers general budgeting issues. You'll find the nuts and bolts of preparing and formatting a project budget in Chapter Seven.

How much money will you need to do the job right? Calculate all relevant expenses. Novice grantwriters remember the "hard costs," such as printing expenses for the new outreach brochure, but tend to forget the staff time needed to write, edit, design, and distribute the brochure. A standard checklist for most project budgets should contain the following items:

- Salary (organizers, supervisor, support staff)
- Benefits (social security and payroll taxes and, if relevant, worker's compensation, health insurance, retirement plan)
- Printing and photocopying
- Postage and shipping
- Communications (phone, fax, Internet access)
- Materials and supplies
- Mileage and travel (air fare, rental car, hotel, meals)
- Outside services, consulting, non-staff support

Not every project requires all these items, and many project budgets will include expenses not covered here, but this list is a good place to start. For examples of how this checklist has been adapted for the real world, look at the proposals featured in Chapter Eight.

As a first step, estimate staff time. Most staff are involved in a variety of activities; apportion their time accordingly. How many hours a week is each person expected to work on the project? If a staff member is assigned to the project quarter-time, then one-quarter of her salary should be covered under the grant budget.

For most other items, consult your past expense records and use these numbers to calculate future costs. For some items you'll need outside assistance. To estimate the cost of your new outreach brochure, for example, don't guess—call your printer, give the specifications, and ask for a bid. To figure the price of a plane ticket, contact the airlines or a travel agent.

The following tips, adapted from Terry Miller's book *Managing for Change* (1992, p. 9), are designed to help with your annual organizational budget, but can be applied to grant-funded projects as well.

- Use last year's records for developing your estimates.

- Save your calculations on work papers in the budget file.

- Involve other people—ask them to check your thinking.

- Break larger estimates into smaller subestimates.

How much of your overhead can you include in the budget? All organizations have certain fixed expenses: rent, utilities, basic phone service, and perhaps office staff. It also takes money to manage grants, since you pay for bookkeeping, bank fees, supervisory staff, and so on. Your group can't survive without paying these bills, but relatively few foundations provide general support to underwrite the basic costs of doing business.

The traditional way to solve this problem is to divide up your overhead and include a fraction in each of your project proposals. This line item is usually called "administration and overhead" or "indirect costs." Some funders refuse to pay indirect costs, but others will consider overhead that is calculated as a small percentage of the entire project budget. While big institutions such as universities have been known to double their grant requests just to cover overhead, I suggest that you limit indirect costs in your project budgets to 15 percent or less.

As a preferred alternative, develop specific budget lines for all items listed above—rent, office staff, and so on—and include them in the project budget. If you anticipate that 10 percent of the bookkeeper's time will be spent administering the grant, then bill 10 percent of her hours to the project. You can do the same with supervisory time, local phone charges, rent, and so forth. Funders are wary about paying indirect costs, in part, because they want a specific record of where the money goes. If you can show them—in advance, in detail, on paper—it will increase their comfort level.

Who is likely to fund your project, and how much are they likely to give? As you conduct your grants research, pay attention to both the interests of prospective foundations and the typical range of their grants. If your project will cost $50,000 and your best prospects give grants in the $10,000–$25,000 range, you should try to raise the total budget from several smaller grants. This is a common and effective strategy.

When approaching a grantmaker who has not previously funded your organization, it's wise to ask for a relatively small grant—less than their median amount. In other words, if the foundation gives grants of $5,000–$25,000, don't ask for more than $15,000 on your first approach. If you receive the grant and demonstrate credibility by doing a good job with the project, you will then be in a position to ask the same funder for more money, since the largest grants generally go to grantees with a proven track record.

The amount of your request should also be measured against your overall budget. Start small. If you try to double your organizational budget with one grant, you are likely to be turned down.

Your project budget should include not just anticipated expenses but also an accounting of revenue in hand, pledged, and sought. In other words, don't just describe how you're going to spend the money—demonstrate how you plan to raise it, including how much you've already raised. The first grant is always the hardest, so once you've secured partial funding, trumpet your success. When foundation officers see a commitment from one of their peers, they are more likely to provide additional grants. For an example of how to format the revenue section of your budget, see Chapter Seven.

How will you manage the difference between the amount you need and the amount you think you can raise? At some point in this process—preferably before you start writing the proposal—your fantasy must be measured against reality. If you need $50,000 for your program and think you can raise only $25,000 in grant money, reevaluate and plan accordingly. Here are your choices:

- Scale back the work and reduce the budget. Organize in fewer neighborhoods, print fewer brochures, be less ambitious.

- Use a "special appeal" to try to raise the balance from your members or donors. To help motivate these donors, you might encourage foundation supporters to make challenge grants. (For more information on leveraging money, see Chapter Nine.)

- If you can afford it, cover some of the costs with funds from your general budget. These contributions should be itemized and included in the revenue portion of your project budget. Be very cautious with this strategy— you can easily overextend your staff and budget by trying to pay for line items you can't afford.

- Intensify your research. Identify additional foundation prospects and submit more proposals. Be prepared to do less work, and spend less money, if the grants don't come through. To protect yourself, develop a contingency budget based on a lower level of funding.

Partial funding, in my experience, is the rule rather than the exception. "Grassroots" means learning to make do with less. This doesn't mean that you should set your sights low, but be prepared to scale back if you don't receive all the money you want.

How much uncertainty can you handle? This is a critical question, because budgets are prospective documents. When you write a budget, you're trying to predict the future, so you estimate. You guess. You make up the numbers. When you invent these numbers and put them on paper, you begin to shape an uncertain future, because these figures determine your goals for both fundraising and spending.

Don't be afraid. Make your most realistic guess, then plunge forward into the mist. As time goes by, you'll keep raising the money and paying it out, and the fog will lift. If the proposed budget turns out to be significantly different from your actual income and expenses, you can always contact the funders and negotiate changes.

Now that you've convened your colleagues, evaluated your ideas, and begun to shape them into fundable projects, it's time to identify grantmakers who might pay for the work. For tips on grants research strategy, turn to Chapter Five.

chapter

5

Finding Funders

Did you go to the Web site? Did you read the guidelines? We are in a less fundable disposition when groups haven't done their homework.

—IRENE VLACH, Lazar Foundation

As the saying goes, when you know one foundation, you know one foundation.

—ANN KRUMBOLTZ, Brainerd Foundation

I once had a student who wanted to paper the world with grant proposals. When I described the odds of raising funds through grants—on average, less than 20 percent of all proposals get funded, and many "successful" ones receive only partial funding—she responded, "It's a numbers game, right? If we submit enough applications, eventually we'll get all the money we need."

Her response touched a raw nerve and I reacted. In the course of my foundation research, I had discovered dozens of promising entries marked with the words "preselected organizations only—unsolicited applications not accepted."

"Don't do it," I told her. "You'll bury the funders under piles of useless paper. Eventually they will stop accepting applications. If you choose to be lazy or greedy by sending out your proposals at random, you risk poisoning the well for everyone."

You don't have to paper the world to raise money. In this chapter, you'll learn how to sift through thousands of grantmakers to identify the best prospects for your work.

Do Your Homework!

According to the numerous funders quoted in this book, between 40 percent and 75 percent of the proposals they receive don't fit their guidelines. Terry Odendahl, formerly of the Wyss Foundation, speaks for many when she sighs, "Two out of three applicants haven't done their research." Jeannie Appleman of Interfaith Funders says, "We don't have a Web site, we don't advertise, we accept proposals by invitation only—and we still get a zillion calls from organizations that don't fit." When asked what annoys her, Pat Jerido, formerly of the Ms. Foundation, says, "Proposals that clearly do not fit the criteria—it happens a lot."

Why are we doing so poorly with our homework? Let me venture a few answers:

- Grassroots groups are too overwhelmed to invest the time or energy, which in the long run reduces their fundraising success, making them feel even more overwhelmed.

- People who prefer print (they call us "ink readers") are less comfortable doing research on the computer, while computer geeks don't want to study the print sources. Thorough research requires both.

- Like the student described earlier, some activists prefer the "shotgun" approach, assuming that sooner or later they will find a good match through volume and luck. Since fundraising is primarily about relationships—strangers seldom give money to strangers—this strategy seldom works.

- Research requires diligence and organization, and a lot of us don't follow through as well as we should.

- Soya Jung Harris of A Territory Resource Foundation identifies a more subtle and distressing reason: "It's disheartening that groups will apply for anything, whether or not it's appropriate. It's a measure of people's desperation."

That's the bad news. Here's the good news: the more thoroughly you conduct your research, ask smart questions, and cultivate foundation contacts, the more your organization will stand out from the crowd. When sloppy work is the norm, competent, well-organized groups have a big advantage. By doing your homework and building good relationships, you can raise a lot of money.

Follow the Guidelines

Before we dive into the research process, I must emphasize the most obvious point, which is also the most important point: follow directions. Most grant-makers—especially those who are bold enough to accept unsolicited applications—publish guidelines to help you, the grantseeker, decide if you meet their criteria. Not only that, they even tell you how to format your proposal, when to submit it, how many copies to send, and what to attach. Unfortunately, many grantseekers are too desperate or lazy or blindly optimistic to follow (or even request) the guidelines.

Gita Drury of the Active Element Foundation echoes the concerns of many funders when she says, "It breaks my heart, the ridiculous number of really irrelevant proposals that don't fit our guidelines."

Joni Craig of the San Diego Foundation for Change adds, "Follow directions! Some funders will actually trash applications which do not conform to their guidelines, and all of your hard work will go to waste (literally!)"

At the risk of redundancy, I repeat: Before submitting your proposal, study the guidelines to determine if your project is appropriate for that funder. If you're uncertain, pick up the telephone and ask. By doing your homework, you will use your time more efficiently, submit fewer proposals, get more grants, simplify the lives of dozens of grateful grantmakers, and reduce the volume of frivolous paper in the world.

The remainder of this chapter outlines four phases of grant research: sleuthing, using computer resources, visiting the library, and studying foundation guidelines. Follow these steps diligently and you'll greatly improve your odds.

Phase One: Sleuthing

Fundraising, like any other task, becomes second nature if you do it long enough. After twenty-five years of doing this work, I never stop tracking the scent of money. When I pick up a nonprofit newsletter I automatically flip to the donor acknowledgment page. When I go to the theater, the usher hands me a program; everyone else reads about the actors, I read about the benefactors. When the word "foundation" appears in a newspaper, I review the article with a little more care.

You can, and should, reserve time for grants research. In the next few pages I'll tell you how to proceed. But before we begin, remember this: your research never ends.

- If you stop thinking about prospecting when you go offline or leave the library . . .

- If you collect data on a dozen foundations and forget about grant research for the rest of the year . . .
- If you have ten conversations with ten colleagues and the word *fundraising* is never mentioned . . .

. . . then you're not doing your job properly. A good detective is always sniffing around for clues, asking questions, drawing conclusions, and testing those conclusions against the evidence. For fundraisers, clues are everywhere. The following steps will help you hone your detective skills.

Get information from nonprofit newsletters. Contact all the groups you can think of—national, regional, and local—that work on issues similar to yours or work with similar constituencies, and request their newsletters and annual reports. Even better, make a donation and have your name added to their mailing lists. If you can't afford to contribute, suggest a free publication exchange between your groups. More and more organizations have Web sites and post their publications on-line. By looking over the shoulders of your brother and sister groups, you can learn who is funding them.

Keep an eye on local nonprofits, regardless of their issues or programs, as well as groups in other geographic areas with programs that resemble yours. The local connection is important, since most foundations restrict their giving to certain communities or states. The program connection is just as important, because regional and national grantmakers tend to focus their funding on certain issues and populations.

Check with your peers in other groups. Call up your colleagues and say, "I've been reading your newsletter and I saw that you got a grant from the XYZ Foundation. How did that happen?" Shelley Davis of the Joyce Foundation says, "Talk with your peers and ask, 'What's the process? What were you funded for? Who did you work with at the foundation?'" Soya Jung Harris agrees: "Activists don't talk with their colleagues enough about sharing funder contacts and experiences."

In my experience, colleagues are willing to share this information on the assumption that, sooner or later, you will provide similar information in return. Understand that when you receive funding from an institution—a foundation, public charity, corporation, labor union, faith organization, or government agency—that information is part of the public record. Anyone can get it from the Internal Revenue Service or other sources, such as GuideStar.org. (Conversely, contributions from individuals are generally considered confidential, unless the donor tells you otherwise.)

You can choose to be secretive about where your grant money comes from, but secrecy won't benefit you. It's wiser to share funding information so you can receive new information in return. Perhaps you can strategize with your colleagues about a joint grant proposal. For more information about collaborative proposals, see Resource E.

Talk with funders. People who give away money for a living know a lot of other people who give away money for a living. They talk on the phone, share notes, and go to conferences together. To varying degrees, they try to influence each other's funding priorities. "Foundations tend to run in packs," says Ron White, formerly of the Tides Foundation, "so use that pack behavior. Encourage your funders to work their relationships as hard as they can on your behalf."

Begin by asking your current foundation supporters for suggestions. Because they work in the funding world, they often have the most up-to-date information and the strongest relationships with their peers. They might be willing to recommend your organization to other grantmakers or write letters of support.

Who else do you know in the philanthropic world? What other relationships can you call upon to help raise money? Everyone in your organization should be involved in identifying and cultivating prospective donors, including foundation officers.

As a next step, compile lists of board members of foundations that fund in your geographic area and are interested in your issues, then circulate these lists to your board, staff, and key volunteers. Anyone with a "live" relationship should be involved in sounding out the funder. Be careful here—some foundations don't want you talking with their trustees about a pending proposal. If you're not sure about the protocol, ask.

Make appointments to meet the staff of your local and state community foundations. These people serve as professional matchmakers and, if impressed with your programs, can recommend you to prospective donors. For more information on how to work with community foundations, see the section in Chapter Six on donor-directed grants.

As you do your research, you will start to gather leads, names, and ideas. I encourage you to create a file marked "Grant leads—to be checked." When you find a list of foundation supporters in an annual report, tear it out (or photocopy it) and put it in the file. If you see a story about a local foundation in the newspaper, clip it. When a colleague says, "You should investigate the Justice for All Foundation," ask additional questions, write down what you learn, and file it.

As you're reading through donor lists and talking with colleagues, practice "grant-thinking": How can you present or package your work to interest the widest range of potential funders? As mentioned in the previous chapter, your success at getting grants will be based, in part, on your ability to divide your work into separate programs and projects. If you haven't done so by now, start to think about your work in terms of categories and constituencies. What's your issue or subject? Who are you trying to reach, to serve, to empower? Do you work with a variety of population groups? Do you have a variety of projects? Do you operate in more than one city or state?

In other words, how many fundraising "handles" can you create?

Phase Two: Using Computer Resources and Web Searches

The Internet is overflowing with information for grantseekers. Many Web sites and services are credible and helpful, and while others are less useful and some are downright bogus. Despite the sheer volume of data, keep in mind that the Internet is *not* a comprehensive source of free grant information.

For example, the Foundation Center reports that we now have about seventy thousand private and community foundations in the United States, but the Foundation Center search engine—one of the best in the field—provides links to fewer than three thousand funder Web sites. It appears that the vast majority of grantmakers do not have their own Web site. To access some of the most useful data, you may need to pay for search products, purchase printed directories, or visit your closest Foundation Center cooperating library collection to look at this stuff for free.

To get you started in your Internet research, here's a list of relevant Web addresses:

Foundation Center, fdncenter.org. The Foundation Center is a national nonprofit that provides services to grantseekers. Their Web site includes several useful tools, including a search engine, a list of cooperating library collections (fdncenter.org/collections/) and a listing of state and local grant directories (fdncenter.org/learn/topical/sl_dir.html) that profile many smaller, locally based funders.

Canadian Centre for Philanthropy, www.ccp.ca. This organization researches Canada's charitable sector and publishes the *CCP Canadian Directory to Foundations and Grants,* the most comprehensive national listing of grantmakers.

GuideStar, www.guidestar.org. Thanks to GuideStar, we now have free access to the tax returns of more than 850,000 U.S. nonprofits, including charitable foundations. While funder tax returns (Form 990-PF) are often less comprehensive than we would like, they offer the best available information on small family foundations. (Warning: these are PDF files; if you have a slow dial-up connection, they take a long time to download.)

National Network of Grantmakers, www.nng.org. The National Network of Grantmakers represents the most progressive wing of the funding community. Their members are interested in social change, human rights, economic and environmental justice, and so forth. They advocate for more democracy and accountability among foundations, and also publish the *NNG Grantmakers Directory*, which lists more than two hundred progressive funders.

Council on Foundations, www.cof.org. The Council on Foundations is the mainstream professional association of grantmaking foundations and corporate giving programs. Through the Council's Affinity Group Network (click on "Networking"), funders interested in similar issues or constituencies work together to share information and develop common strategies. Examples include the Neighborhood Funders Group, Native Americans in Philanthropy, Grantmakers Concerned with Immigrants and Refugees, and the Disability Funders Network. Thirty-eight affinity groups are currently affiliated with the Council.

Environmental Grantmakers Association, www.ega.org. The Environmental Grantmakers Association is an extensive network of funders that support conservation and environmental activism. Their Web site includes a brief but useful directory of environmental funders.

Once again, the process is pretty straightforward. These sites will provide you with relevant background information and steer you to specific funders and funding opportunities. Keep your eyes open for links between grantmaker interests and your work, and take good notes.

The extensive material in Resource B, prepared by librarian Jean Lewis of the Tucson Pima Public Library, provides an evaluation of eight commercial search products for grantseekers. If you're ambitious and diligent, you can do quite well with the free research tools available on-line and at the library. On the other hand, the fee-based products and services reviewed in Resource B can save you time and help identify funders you might not find on your own.

Phase Three: Doing Library Research

Depending on the scope of your on-line research and your access to the electronic products presented in Resource B, you may be able to skip the library phase, which sounds a bit archaic in our database age. Unfortunately, since grassroots organizations seldom have the money to afford electronic research products or buy print directories, an occasional trip to the library remains an important part of the research process.

The Foundation Center operates reference collections in New York, Washington, D.C., Atlanta, Cleveland, and San Francisco. It also helps libraries, community foundations, and other nonprofit agencies create cooperating collections with grant research and proposal writing materials. More than two hundred cooperating collections are spread throughout all fifty U.S. states and Puerto Rico.

Each cooperating collection includes a core set of reference books published by the Foundation Center as well as a copy of their searchable CD-ROM database, *FC Search*. Some grant collections serve a broader function as local nonprofit resource centers, with books and magazines on general fundraising techniques, major donor solicitation, benefit events, earned income strategies, board development, publicity, strategic planning, incorporation and tax issues, philanthropic trends, and nonprofit management.

The following research strategy can and should be adapted to meet your own needs. If you'd like assistance or other ideas, talk with your local librarian. Some libraries offer a hands-on orientation session to get you started.

1. When you go to the library, bring a pen or pencil, paper to write on, scrap paper (to tear into strips for bookmarks) and money for the photocopy machine. Don't forget your "Grant leads to be checked" file, with leads gleaned from reading newsletters, calling up your colleagues, talking with foundation staff, doing preliminary on-line research, and so forth.

2. Collect several grants directories from the shelves and carry them to your work table. The most useful resources are *The Foundation Directory, The Foundation Directory Part 2, The Foundation 1000, The Foundation Grants Index* (all published by the Foundation Center) and the *Foundation Reporter* (published by Taft). There are also many subject-specific directories. If you're seeking grants from major corporations or corporate foundations, start with Taft's *Corporate Giving Directory* and the Foundation Center's *National Directory of Corporate Giving*. (For a list of additional resources, see Resource A.)

Many grantseekers find that state or regional funding directories are more relevant to their local funding needs than the national directories and databases. State or regional directories may also capture local funding opportunities that the national databases miss, providing the best prospects for community-based groups. As of this writing, sixty-five state or regional directories now cover forty-seven U.S. states. They are compiled and produced by a variety of nonprofits, universities, and private businesses. Most are published in print or CD-ROM formats, but twelve are available on-line; subscription prices range up to $500 per year, with most costing about $200.

Check with your local library for free public access to these print directories and databases. For a list of state and regional directories, check the Foundation Center's Web site at fdncenter.org/learn/topical.sl_dir.html.

3. Work through the names in your file. *The Foundation 1000* and the *Foundation Reporter* have the most in-depth information, so look up your prospects in these directories first. If you can't locate a particular prospect, try *The Foundation Directory, Part 1* and *Part 2.* These books cover a lot more grantmakers, but in much less detail.

    As you read through the entries, be aware of the following types of information:

    -   *Geographic restrictions.* Most funders limit their donations to groups working in certain cities, states, or regions. Does your group fit within their geographic boundaries?

    -   *Fields of interest.* These define the issues, subjects, and types of organizations grantors prefer to support. Broadly speaking, are they interested in the kind of work you do?

    -   *Grant size.* Do they offer an appropriate amount of money for your project? Too small is fine, since you can piece together multiple grants—unless you're trying to raise $50,000 from funders who give $1,000 grants. On the other hand, you're unlikely to raise $2,000 from a foundation whose normal grants range from $25,000 to $200,000.

    -   *A recent list of grants.* Review the list, if one is available. Are any current grantees doing work that relates to, or overlaps with, the work of your organization?

    If the answer to these questions is yes, you've identified a prospect. Write the appropriate information on a piece of paper or use a bookmark to hold the page so you can photocopy it later. (Make sure to follow all applicable copyright laws.) Sooner or later you should check the foundation's Web site for current guidelines and annual report information, although this task can wait until you return to the office. If the foundation doesn't have a Web site, request this information via letter, e-mail, fax, or phone; more on this in the next section.

4. Learn how to use *FC Search.* Each Foundation Center cooperating collection has a copy of *FC Search,* which compiles all their directory information onto one CD-ROM. The librarian can teach you how to use the database. Expect to pay a small fee for every page you print, or buy a diskette from the librarian so you can save your results and take the information with you.

Since the data in the Foundation Center print directories is also on their CD, in principle one would not need to look at both. My experience has proved otherwise. Perhaps as one develops greater database skills the printed books become redundant, but I'd encourage you to try both. You're likely to find information and leads in one format that you would overlook in the other.

Even if you go to the library without a list of leads, you can still identify lots of prospects, though the process will take a little longer. Grant directories and databases are generally indexed by the name of the foundation, the names of their officers and trustees, the geographic areas in which they contribute, and the subjects, issues, and constituencies they fund. Review the subject index and find your program area(s). If, for example, your group helps Hispanic women to develop their own businesses, look for headings such as "women's issues," "minorities—Hispanic" and "entrepreneurship." Beyond that, it's simply a matter of reading the entries of each foundation listed in your subject and geographic areas and matching your programs with the interests of potential grantmakers.

If you choose to solicit help from your board and staff in developing relationships with foundation officers, the best resource is the *Guide to U.S. Foundations*, which is published by the Foundation Center. This massive directory lists the board members of more than sixty-five thousand foundations and includes an alphabetical index of trustees by name.

Another good resource is *The Chronicle of Philanthropy*, which is published twenty-four times a year. Each issue contains a feature called "New Grants," which you can use to identify new prospects and update your older foundation files. The publication also includes a regular "Deadlines" feature that describes current requests for proposals (RFPs) from a variety of foundation, corporate, and government grants programs. Check your local library for the *Chronicle*; subscription information is included in Resource A.

I urge you to spend some time at your nearest funding information library. Even without a research plan, you'll learn something useful just looking through the stacks. Try to spend three or four days throughout the year in your local grants collection. If you need to travel from out of town to get there, budget the time and money for at least one trip each year, and plan to stay at least one full day (two is better).

Phase Four: Studying the Current Guidelines

Foundation directories and computer search tools are incredibly helpful, but they have two significant drawbacks.

First, the information is incomplete. There's a lot to learn about each prospective funder and the necessary data can't be adequately covered in a few paragraphs or even a few pages.

Second, the information is dated. Most data are drawn from federal tax returns that are typically two to three years old. Foundation programs and guidelines change, and you need to know what the grantmakers are funding now—not three years ago.

To complete your research, go straight to the source—the grantmakers themselves—and ask for three things:

- *Guidelines*—information about funding criteria and the application process

- *Annual report*—the foundation's goals, programs, and accomplishments

- *List of grantees*—which groups receive funding (this is often included in the annual report)

If the funder has a Web site, you're likely to find the information on-line. If not, you'll need to ask directly with a query letter. This is a request for information, not money, and can be sent via e-mail or the postal service. As an alternative, you can request this information by phone (though I've always had better luck through the mail).

The query letter is your first contact with the funder and might spark the interest of foundation staff, so be sure to include a bit of background information on your work. In a paragraph or two, briefly outline your mission, programs, budget, and sources of revenue, including other foundation supporters. Then request the grantmaker's guidelines and annual report, including a list of recent grantees.

In my experience, about 80 percent of grantmakers will respond, although some require a reminder letter. Their responses range from polite, one-paragraph notes ("Sorry, we do not publish our guidelines") to glossy, full-color annual reports. Occasionally you will be turned down on the basis of your query letter, even though you have not explicitly asked for money. This is one of the benefits of including information about your organization in the query: if you're going to face rejection anyway, be grateful you didn't go to the trouble of preparing a full proposal.

Read these materials carefully. Get out your highlighter or red pen and mark them up. Compare the foundation-produced materials (including information drawn from the Web site) with whatever data you gathered from library directories, and note any important discrepancies, such as changes in deadlines, program focus, or grant amounts. Once you've read and digested the guidelines and reviewed the list of grantees, write down any questions you have that aren't answered in the written materials. This is a good time to create prospect files for all promising grantmakers. Include their guidelines, annual reports, and any relevant research data gathered from the library and on-line searches.

Now try to match your programs and projects with the funders' interests. Compare their language with yours: Do they describe the problem in a similar way? If not, can you use their language and feel comfortable with it? How about their approach to social change: Do they emphasize the same strategies as your group? Do they focus on the same constituencies? "Be sure that your project falls within the grant guidelines," says Jeff Anderson of the Oregon Community Foundation, "and then see whether you can read between the lines and search out the nuances."

Based on a very careful review of the information, you're likely to eliminate half the prospective funders because you don't fit the guidelines. Don't feel bad. The ones that remain are good candidates and worth investigating further.

We've reached a crucial moment: reaching out to the people on the other side of the process. For many novices, this is the most intimidating aspect of grantseeking. Never fear—everything you need to know about relationship building is covered in Chapter Six.

Building Peer-to-Peer Relationships with Grantmakers

Most proposals say, in some form, "Give us money to do the work." Few say, "We are doing this work regardless—join us." What gets my attention is a proposal that invites partnership rather than saying, "If you don't fund us, the world will end." If you act powerless, you are.

—MARTY TEITEL, Cedar Tree Foundation

Build the relationship. Don't forget that funders are in social justice work, too. We got into this to make the biggest contribution we could, so try to learn more about the funder as a person.

—MARJORIE FINE, Unitarian Universalist Veatch Program at Shelter Rock

In his classic book *The New Joys of Yiddish,* the late Leo Rosten (2001, p. 355) defines *schmooze* (spelled various ways) as "a friendly, gossipy, prolonged heart-to-heart talk—or to have such a talk." He cites as an example, "They had a little schmooze and settled everything." Rosten adds, with a note of sadness, "In our cynical age, *schmooze* has also come to mean a more manipulative sort of banter: 'Don't try schmoozing me—no deal!'"

When I ask workshop participants to define the word, most of them use phrases like "butt-kissing" and "sucking up." Clearly, the more cynical view is winning out, so it's become my policy—nay, my passion—to restore *schmoozing* to its former glory.

Schmoozing is a frank and friendly discussion between peers. It's the place where honesty and camaraderie sit down together to share the news (and maybe a good meal). Schmoozing is the ethical, transparent way we build relationships.

In this chapter, you'll learn how to schmooze—in other words, how to reach out to funders to educate and involve them in your work.

Leveling the Playing Field

The relationship between grantmaker and grantseeker is, at first look, a power relationship: one has money, the other needs it. Even the most self-effacing funders exercise a certain amount of clout simply by creating guidelines, setting up an application process, and making choices about who and what they support. Others behave more assertively by promoting pet theories of social progress, limiting their funding to particular strategies, or imposing collaboration on unwilling nonprofits. In this age of "venture philanthropy," some funders want a hand in running your organization, too. "We need weekly injections of humility," says Marty Teitel, addressing his colleagues in the funding community.

Under these circumstances, says Marjorie Fine, "The partnership between funder and grantee may feel false, because it is, due to the power inequity. What we should strive for is an honest, transparent relationship."

In preparing the current edition of this book, I've been struck by how many grantmakers yearn for a more level playing field. What's driving this, I suspect, is the expansion of activist-controlled grantmaking and the increasing number of community organizers and activists who now earn their livelihoods reading proposals and interacting with grantseekers.

Bill Dempsey, a former coworker of Marjorie Fine, says, "Funders don't have that much power. We just react to what you send us." Ron White, formerly of the Tides Foundation, says, "Understand the value of your work. Grantseeking isn't begging." Ann Krumboltz of the Brainerd Foundation adds, "Don't be shy—remember that we are required by law to give out grants. Your work helps us accomplish our goals, too."

You might be surprised to learn that some of the biggest bullies are on your side of the table. Marty Teitel recounts, "I was once confronted by an applicant who said, 'The world will suffer thermonuclear war because you didn't fund this proposal.' Frequently, we get proposals from environmental groups that say, 'The only way to stop this problem is for you to give us money.' The relationship is built in terms of guilt."

John Sterling, former grants officer for Patagonia, points out a variation on this theme. Some proposals, he says, take the attitude that the organization will go belly-up if it's not funded.

On the other end of the spectrum, applicants try to curry favor with foundations. Although guilt-tripping and rudeness are bad, false friendship and submissiveness are possibly worse. When asked what annoys him the most, Jason Halbert of the Oak Hill Fund replies, "Obsequious behavior."

Ethical grantmakers are sensitive to the power dynamic and do what they can to tread lightly and professionally. Shelley Davis of the Joyce Foundation puts it this way: "After three years, I'm just learning how to bring along new grantees. The question is always 'Who can we bring in [to fund] and how do we have this conversation without raising expectations?' We might say, 'If you can frame your work this way I can help you, but I don't want to tell you how to do your business.' It's a tricky dance."

Over the long run, as the roles of "activist" and "funder" continue to shift and overlap, perhaps the perceived power imbalance will equalize. "Being a grantmaker has helped me to become a better fundraiser," says Si Kahn, a board member with both Changemakers and the Jewish Fund for Justice and executive director of the nonprofit group Grassroots Leadership. "I'm more empathetic; I see grantmakers as peers rather than adversaries. Many come out of the organizing world. Ask their advice on fundraising, communications, strategy, public relations. Funders are happy to be treated like activists."

Grantmaking: It's a Job

Compared to the exhilarating, stressful, random, caffeine-fueled, overcommitted and underpaid life of a community organizer, the foundation world is a bit more structured and redundant, filled with recurring deadlines, phone calls, meetings, and staggering amounts of paper. "Before we switched to a letter of inquiry process," says Roxanne Turnage of the CS Fund, "we received eight hundred or nine hundred proposals each year. Half didn't fit the guidelines." But when things work well, it's also a very satisfying job, as nearly every funding officer will attest.

Grantseekers should also understand that foundation staff must serve multiple masters. "I'm trying to meet the needs of three constituencies," says Marty Teitel. "In order of priority, they are my board, the grantees, and the IRS and other rule makers." With that in mind, here's an abbreviated, informal job description for your friendly neighborhood program officer.

Talent scout. Funders are always searching for effective, strategically positioned organizations. "We're proactive—we go out and look for groups," says Terry Odendahl, formerly of the Wyss Foundation. How do they find them? "I'm out in the world and run into somebody who's interesting, or I'll get leads from colleagues, friends, even other grantees," says

Roxanne Turnage. For many grantmakers, this is the most fulfilling part of the job. "It's rewarding to identify a new group that the trustees really like," says Odendahl.

Trend spotter. Grantmakers interact with hundreds of organizations: by phone, in person, via e-mail, or through the printed word. They also talk with their colleagues at other foundations. By its very nature, the job provides a certain critical distance that allows funders to see emerging issues, approaches, and connections. "We weigh broad strategies for change, not just specific proposals," says Si Kahn. "It's a complicated business."

Proposal reviewer. The staff members quoted in this book see anywhere from a few hundred to nearly one thousand funding requests each year. Some of the requests are well organized and well written; most are not. Some of the work described is unique, exciting, and provocative; much of it is not. Diligent proposal review requires the stamina of a marathoner, the concentration of a gem cutter, and the patience of a preschool teacher. This is not easy work.

An ongoing challenge for grant reviewers is that many applicants don't follow the guidelines or respect the format. As Zoë Rothchild of the Northwest Fund for the Environment says, "We want applications to come in a uniform manner. Please don't assume that your proposal or idea is more valuable than someone else's and therefore worthy of breaking the rules. We want to view each proposal on a level playing field."

Pat Jerido, formerly of the Ms. Foundation, has the same concern. "When we're reviewing many proposals," she says, "we need consistency to be able to review them fairly. That's why we ask for a specific format."

Risk manager. Lois DeBacker of the Charles Stewart Mott Foundation stresses the need for groups to prepare a good proposal but says, "It's also about trust and confidence in individuals. We're placing bets on individuals' integrity, clarity, commitment, vision, leadership, and skill." Some of these bets pay off; others do not.

Field reconnaissance specialist. As time and money allow, funders conduct site visits, go on field trips, attend conferences, and do what they can to get out of the office and into the world to identify prospective grantees and educate themselves about the issues. When they're not in the field, they're working the phones.

"We call everybody," says Cheryl King Fischer of the New England Grassroots Environment Fund. "Then we call everybody who knows everybody. We do more homework on the marginal or poor proposals than on the obvious yeses."

Mediator and go-between. Most program officers serve as intermediaries between the applicants and the decision makers, who double as the program officers' supervisors. "I'm the translator between the nonprofit and our board," says Terry Odendahl. After reading proposals, talking with applicants, and gathering necessary background information, staff members make recommendations to the trustees—who may or may not agree with staff guidance.

Customer service representative. Foundation staff answer your questions, meet with you, slog through your letters and proposals, suggest edits, deal with your peculiarities, try to position your work to its best advantage so they can sell it to the decision makers—and then they get judged on how well they do it. "Our program officers are evaluated annually on program goals relating to the speed of response to applicants," says Lois DeBacker, "along with adherence to grantmaking strategies and meeting multiyear program goals."

Processing the large number of inquiries "is becoming a capacity issue," says Gita Drury of the Active Element Foundation—especially from people who don't fit the guidelines. "We can't return everyone's phone calls, and we feel bad about that."

Mentor and counselor. If you need a guide to the funding world, who better than a grantmaker to provide that service? "Mentoring in how to relate to funders is a really important role for program officers to play," says Denise Joines of the Wilburforce Foundation.

"When our grantees get rejected by other funders, they take it personally," says Tia Oros Peters of the Seventh Generation Fund. "We help them work through it."

Bearer of bad news. Someone has to write those rejection letters, make the phone calls, and deal with devastated or irate applicants. "We make 'rejection calls,' rather than sending letters," says Irene Vlach. "It's the toughest part of my job. We often love the work, but don't have enough money. Some of these people are so gracious when we turn them down; I really admire that." Others get nasty.

Evaluator. After the grants are made, the money is spent, and the project is completed (or not), the foundation must review the results and make judgments about the effectiveness of the grant and the value of the work. At most foundations, this job also falls to the program officers—as if they didn't have enough to do—which may explain why evaluation tends to get less attention than it probably deserves.

Fundraiser. Engaged grantmakers spend time with their peers, and some of that time is devoted to pitching their pet projects and organizations. According to Joel Solomon of the Endswell Foundation, based in Canada, "Money is tighter and the grantee relationships are well established, so I spend much less time on orientation and due diligence. My time is ever more focused on helping to raise money—getting other foundations to invest and expand in our issue and our region."

Since you're a fundraiser, too, don't be shy about using this behavior to your advantage. "Ask for help," says Si Kahn. "Funders can go to bat with other funders."

Community organizer. Many social change grantmakers work hard to encourage their peers to be inclusive, democratic, and self-aware. "We try to expose mainstream funders to progressive organizations and ideas," says Soya Jung Harris of A Territory Resource Foundation. "With more people of color in the funding community, it creates opportunities to promote racial justice."

Are We Partners or What? The Value of Honesty

"If you're asking a foundation to be your partner," says Jeff Anderson of the Oregon Community Foundation, "then behave as you would toward a partner. Maybe this is too idealistic, but I believe that most foundation staff members would prefer to recommend grants for projects that they understand pretty well, warts and all, so don't be evasive." David Karoff of the Rhode Island Foundation puts it simply: "If you're transparent and honest, you'll get further in the process."

Reciprocal relationships are built on trust, and without honesty there can be no trust. Grantseekers often wrestle with the question of how many "warts" to reveal. The problem with limited disclosure is that, sooner or later, everything is revealed whether you like it or not. "We hear about groups that are effective," says Loretta Horton, a grantmaker with the Domestic Hunger Program of the Evangelical Lutheran Church in America, "and we hear about the ones that aren't working so well, too." Would you rather have somebody else tell your troubles to the funder, or initiate that conversation yourself?

"With my favorite grantees, the common thread is honesty," says Ann Krumboltz. "They're willing to be vulnerable. They call me up and say, 'We're struggling with this issue. What are you hearing from other groups?' In that way, we create a feedback loop between partners."

Because program officers play a mediating role between you and their trustees, be aware that your candor both helps them and makes their jobs more difficult. As Terry Odendahl says, "Don't sugarcoat your work. Be really honest with me, but realize that I have to find a way to bring it to the board. When I was honest with the board [about the challenges faced by a particular group], they turned me down, so I have to avoid talking about shortcomings. They have an unrealistic notion about what nonprofits should be like. If I don't play it right with the board, that's my responsibility."

Of course, by being thoroughly truthful, you set the tone for the relationship. You can and should expect the same level of candor in return.

Pick Up the Telephone

Let's review your research strategy so far. You have collected leads from other nonprofits and solicited suggestions from your best contacts in the funding world; researched your prospects on-line and possibly at the closest Foundation Center grant collection; gathered and studied the most current materials—guidelines, annual report, list of grantees—from your best prospects; and sorted the list based on how well your programs match their interests.

If you think you see a viable match, or if you have questions about the guidelines, it's time to pick up the phone. David Karoff speaks for hundreds of funders when he says, "Talk to us before you start writing. It's in everyone's best interest to build the relationship first." Jon Jensen of the George Gund Foundation agrees: "Call before you mail. I hate the proposal that comes out of nowhere with no prior contact. Perhaps 20 to 30 percent of our applicants send 'cold proposals.' We favor people who pick up the phone first and provide a two- or three-minute description of the work. When things work well, this leads to a meeting and ultimately a proposal."

If you're like me, sometimes you're afflicted with phone phobia. "I don't want to pester them," I'll say to myself, feeling timid. "I'll just ask a lot of stupid questions. Besides, my project is really marginal." To be honest, I often gave in to this urge—perhaps one-quarter of the successful proposals I've written were submitted without any prior phone calls or personal contact. But I can also testify that the personal touch makes a big difference. Conquer your phone phobia and make that call.

Listen to Denise Joines at Wilburforce: "Don't be so nervous about picking up the phone. I can't do my job without talking to you, so it's always helpful to have a phone call first. Do research before calling. It's very impressive when someone has obviously done their homework."

Foundation staff are terrific sources of information. They can help you interpret their guidelines, tell you how best to pitch your project and, if it's a poor fit, they might recommend other sources of funding. Best of all, they can guide you through the peculiarities of the grants process. Jim Abernathy of the Environmental Support Center says, "We have as many conversations with the applicants as needed to clarify their intentions and give them the opportunity to submit new information or even apply for a different program, if their initial application would stand a better chance there."

If you've been referred to the foundation by a colleague at another nonprofit or, even better, by someone in the funding community, don't be shy about mentioning that. As Shelley Davis says, "Name-dropping isn't a bad thing. It happens every day. It makes sense to call and use the names of people you have in common."

Now that you're eager to pick up the telephone, be aware that some funders discourage phone calls. If you're not sure whether to call, read their written materials, visit their Web site, and recheck the information you've gleaned from the grant directories. If you don't see the words, "No phone calls, please," pick up the phone. To help you prepare, try the role-playing activity in Exercise 6.1.

Honor the Gatekeepers

A word about receptionists, secretaries, assistants and all others known as "gatekeepers": treat them with respect. Like all people, they are worthy of your respect, and they also have a lot of power. "When people walk by my desk without acknowledging that I exist, I won't go to bat for them," says Irene Vlach of the Lazar Foundation. "When they're friendly, I go out of my way to help. Be nice to gatekeepers; we don't make the decisions, but we have influence."

Here's a story to illustrate the point. Several years ago, I contacted a foundation by phone, looking for the president, whom I will call Joe. He wasn't available, but his assistant asked if she could help.

"Sure," I said, and laid out the project. After a ten-minute discussion—lots of questions, back and forth—she said, "This is a terrific idea, but I have to tell you, Joe is going to be a hard sell."

"That's too bad. What can we do to bring him along?" (Notice the word "we.")

She was quiet for a moment. "Who else funds you?"

"We get regular support from Foundation A, and Major Donor B helps out, and we recently got a grant from Foundation C."

"Perfect," she said. "Joe really admires that woman at Foundation C. Can you get her to call and put in a good word for you?"

"I don't see why not."

"Then here's our plan. You ask her to work on Joe from her side, and I'll work on him from my side, and between the two of us we'll see what we can do."

This conversation eventually led to a $15,000 grant. If I had treated that woman like the gatekeeper—in other words, if I had been disrespectful or frustrated or dismissive—it never would have happened.

The moral of the story is simple: whoever picks up the phone or greets you at the door is a potential ally, so cultivate *everyone*.

How to Meet Grantmakers

Once you've mastered the telephone, the next step is the site visit. The term *site visit* generally refers to a meeting with foundation officers at your facility; in most cases, this happens after you submit a proposal. For our purposes,

Phoning the Funder

The purpose of this role play is to help you

- Learn to describe your work clearly and briefly, leaving out unnecessary details.
- Negotiate a next step with the funder.
- Increase your comfort level.

Dramatis personae ("The parts to be played"):

- The grantseeker
- The foundation officer: A staff member whose job is to read and screen proposals, meet with grantseekers as time allows, do "background checks" on applicant groups, and make recommendations to the final decision-makers—typically the foundation board.

Role play:

Find a partner to work with in person or by phone. If you're working in person, turn your chairs back to back so you can't see each other (this simulates a phone call). One person plays the grantseeker; the other, the foundation officer. Assume that you've completed your preliminary research and identified this funder as a good match. (If you need more specifics about the foundation, see Exercise 6.2.)

If you're playing the grantseeker, take a few moments of silence and ask yourself, "What's my goal with this phone call?" When you're ready to start, make the phone ring (yes, you can say "ring, ring") and your partner will respond by answering. Over the next *three minutes,* your job is to

- Introduce yourself.
- Make sure you're talking to the right person. ("I'm working on a community garden project in my neighborhood in Cleveland; who would be the best person to speak with?")
- Find out what, if anything, the foundation officer knows about your work or your issue.
- Describe your organization and your project *briefly!*
- Ask a question or two to gauge the funder's interest.
- Complete the call by getting the grantmaker to agree to a next step; options include

   Letter: review a summary or introductory letter (letter of inquiry)

   Proposal: review a full proposal

   Meeting: schedule a meeting

   Leads: suggest other sources of funding (especially if the grantmaker decides your program is not a good fit)

To debrief this exercise,

- The grantseeker goes first. She or he says two things about the phone call that went well and one thing that could have worked better, with an idea for how to improve it.
- The foundation officer goes next, following the same format.

After debriefing, switch roles and start again.

allow me to broaden the term to include any kind of face-to-face contact between funder and grantseeker.

It's hard to overstate the value of these meetings, because that's how people really get to know one another. Once again, it's about the relationship. Funders repeatedly emphasize that knowing the people behind the proposal is critical to the funding process. Jon Jensen of the George Gund Foundation says, "I remember one fellow who wrote terrible proposals, but when he came in, he was articulate and knowledgeable, so we funded him again and again." The Brainerd Foundation's Ann Krumboltz says, "We read proposals carefully, but it is the people behind them that impress me. A moderately well-written proposal submitted by an adept leader will likely be funded." Martha Kongsgaard of the Kongsgaard-Goldman Foundation adds, "It's a lot about who comes into the office. If we don't meet with them, we don't fund them. The paper is secondary."

How can you personally introduce yourself and your organization to grantmakers? Here are a number of ways:

Meet them at the foundation office. The simplest solution is to call and, after you've described your project and gauged their interest, request a meeting. "How do you become known to us?" says Terry Odendahl. "Drop by when you're in town. Call first: 'We'll be in the neighborhood. Can we talk?'"

Prior to your call, review the guidelines and assess your likelihood of getting a grant. No grants officer will choose to meet with you if your work is completely outside the foundation's area of interest, so do your homework first.

Attend "meet the grantmaker" events. A number of nonprofit resource centers host "meet the grantmakers" workshops, which include panel discussions, questions from the audience, and opportunities for grantseekers to meet foundation and corporate philanthropy staff. Check with your local community foundation, United Way, Foundation Center cooperating collection, volunteer center, or other community service centers to learn if something similar is offered in your area.

Go to conferences. Conscientious, hardworking program officers often hit the conference circuit to learn about the issues of the day and get the latest buzz on which groups are hot (and which ones are not). I often run into grantmakers at two of my favorite social change events—a biannual gathering sponsored by the National Organizers Alliance, and the Community Strategic Training Initiative organized by the Western States Center. Funders appreciate these opportunities because they can interact with many grantees and prospective grantees in a few days, which saves lots of time.

Every time you attend a conference, scan the registration list for foundation contacts. Ask the organizers if funders are expected to attend. Talk with other participants. Read name tags. Get out there and schmooze!

Be a presenter at grantmaker events. Funders also meet with each other at conferences sponsored by the National Network of Grantmakers, the Neighborhood Funders Group, the Environmental Grantmakers Association, and many other funder affinity groups. These events are generally closed to grantseekers, with one notable exception. When program officers and foundation trustees gather to educate themselves about specific issues—the health care crisis, the privatization of water resources, threats to civil liberties, and so on—they need experts to update them on the issues and describe potential solutions. Who are these experts? Community organizers, activists, and nonprofit program staff. In other words, *you.*

Make friends with a few grantmakers and ask them to let you know about future funder gatherings. Say, "I'd love to have the chance to tell the foundation community about our work. If you hear about any upcoming funder conferences that focus on our issues, would you notify me immediately? Let me know who the conference organizers are . . . and by the way, could you put in a good word for us? Maybe we could send one of our folks to be a presenter at the event."

This strategy requires diligence and persistence. It can take a few years to succeed, but here's the payoff: you're standing at the front of the room talking to a dozen (or twenty, or fifty) people about your work. You're passionate, you're professional, and you're probably scared as hell, but it's working. Everyone is listening carefully, asking thoughtful questions. You can sense their minds opening, and, best of all, they all give away money for a living.

This is a fundraiser's fantasy, right? I can pretty well guarantee that someone present will fund you, though you should anticipate several more conversations and the requisite paperwork before you see a check. The question is, will you invest the time and energy to build the relationships that can put you in front of an audience of grantmakers?

Invite grants officers to visit your facility. This is the traditional "site visit," which typically occurs after you have submitted a proposal. These meetings are often initiated by foundation staff with a note or a call saying, "Your group has been chosen as a finalist for our next grant round, and we would like to come out to meet with you to discuss the project."

However, there is no reason that you can't initiate the contact and invite the grantmaker to tour your facility. Nearly every cover letter I've written ends with the phrase, "If you need more information, or would like to arrange a site visit, please contact me." Sometimes I follow the letter with a phone call to repeat the invitation personally.

"Site visits are about feeling the energy in the office, getting to know who people are as human beings," says Denise Joines. Some funders will go to considerable trouble to meet you on your own turf. In their response to my survey, the staff members of the Common Counsel Foundation—Elizabeth Wilcox, Sue Hutchinson, and Margaret Solle—report, "We don't have a big budget for site visits, but when we're traveling (even on personal vacation), we try to meet with grantees."

Grantmakers take these meetings seriously, and so should you. Bill Dempsey relates, "I'm trying to be better informed to do my job more effectively. I'm coming to understand the importance of context: to go into a community and stay there for a while. My ideal site visit would include the applicant group, community members, journalists, allied organizations, unions, and faith-based leaders."

If your group is selected for a site visit, consider the following points of etiquette:

- *Energize your workplace.* Jeff Anderson of the Oregon Community Foundation offers a fine example: "My favorite site visits are with grassroots organizations rather than in boardrooms—with the kind of groups in which somebody bakes coffee cake and brings it in, and while they're serving it, community volunteers are in the next room banging new shelves onto the walls. However, even the grassroots groups must be well-prepared and focused during the conversation."

- *Give your best show and tell.* At Native Seeds/SEARCH, we always joked that if we could just get foundation staff into our seed bank, they would fund our proposals. Why? The seed bank is a stimulating place, filled with beautiful crops, pungent smells, and lots of interesting textures. Spend a few minutes among the jars of beans, ears of multicolored corn, chiles tied into *ristras,* and dried gourds hanging from the ceiling, and the connections between genetic and cultural diversity become abundantly clear. For people besieged with paper, direct sensory experience is a treat. It helps them understand your mission on an instinctive, emotional level.

  Think about how you can best present the emotional side of your organization. If you run a clinic, a preschool, or a shelter, give funders a chance to tour the facility and talk with the clients. If you sponsor a community garden, don't meet in the office—go to the garden. If you're launching a capital campaign for a new building, go out to the site, unroll the blueprints, and walk around—"The front door will be here with a view of the mountains to the north, the nursery will be over here." In other words, take your ideas—which have been thoughtfully laid out in your proposal—and make them tangible.

- *Invite funders to observe your group in action.* Encourage grantmakers to attend your next public event—rally, performance, news conference, voter education workshop, demonstration, educational forum, fundraising campaign kickoff. The best way to show funders what you do is to show them what you do.

Site visits also entail some risk. After seeing an organization firsthand, funders can be forced to make difficult choices, as Ron White points out:

> I did a site visit on a previous job. We met with the staff first, and the lead staff member was a "poverty pimp" kind of guy. It was obvious that he was a crook; the only question regarding theft was not if, but when. Then we met the community leaders. They had vision, they did the work, what they had built was impressive.
>
> So we went back to the office and debated the question: should we support a corrupt organization with a strong base in the community that was working toward positive ends? It was very divisive. In the end, we made the grant. We decided it was more important to believe that the power of the people would triumph.

To help you get ready for a meeting with a funder, try Exercise 6.2 for some role-playing practice.

Donor-Directed Grants

A number of foundations, especially community foundations, manage what are called "donor-directed funds." These are separate accounts set up by individuals who channel their money through the foundation to charities of their choice. Foundation staff sort through incoming proposals and serve as matchmakers between community organizations and philanthropists by presenting proposals they think will interest specific donors. The foundation also administers the grants and, in some cases, provides a degree of anonymity to the donors.

In general, it's best to stay out of the way and let foundation staff do their jobs. If you know the donor personally or have a good letter of reference, however, you can involve yourself in a more active way. This process is similar to cultivating a major donor, except that you are unlikely to have any direct contact with the prospect. Here's how to proceed:

1. Review the annual reports of the community foundations operating in your area. These reports should include lists of all (non-anonymous) donor-directed funds, and may also indicate their areas of interest. Share these names with your board members, major donors, and other foundations that support your work. Ask them to identify any people they know.

2. Add these prospects to your mailing list. If you can't locate a home address, use the community foundation address. Send a brief letter—if

EXERCISE

6.2

Meeting with the Funder

The purpose of this role play is to help you

- Develop confidence and clarity in your pitch—how you present your work.

- Develop empathy for the person on the other side of the relationship—the grantmaker.

- Improve your listening skills.

Dramatis personae:

- The grantseeker.

- The foundation officer: A staff member whose job is to read and screen proposals, meet with grantseekers as time allows, do "background checks" on applicant groups, and make recommendations to the final decision makers—typically the foundation board.

- The observer: Watches and comments after the role play is over.

    By the end of the exercise, everyone will have the opportunity to play all three roles.

Role play:

Funder: Justice for All Foundation.

Funding priorities: A broad range of social justice, human rights, and environmental conservation interests across North America.

Grant budget: $1,000,000 per year.

Typical range: $10,000-$50,000; funds between forty and fifty groups each year; receives five hundred proposals each year.

Sample grant recipients: Southwest Network for Environmental and Economic Justice, United for a Fair Economy, Grassroots Leadership, National Gay and Lesbian Task Force, Yellowstone to Yukon Initiative, Midwest Academy, Western Organization of Resource Councils, Seventh Generation Fund, Southern Empowerment Project, Californians for Justice, Prison Moratorium Project, Western States Center, Direct Action for Rights & Equality, Amigos Bravos, Council of Canadians, Global Exchange, National Organizers Alliance, Mississippi River Basin Alliance.

Deadlines: Three per year

Next deadline: Six weeks from today

Staffing: One program officer (you're sitting with this person), one half-time assistant

Board: Three family members plus two advisors, one of whom is a well-known community activist. All are concerned about a broad range of community issues, but each has his or her own pet projects and issues. The grantseeker knows one of the board members casually through common activities (you get to pick which one and use or not use this information as you see fit).

Where you meet: The funder's office.

If you are the grantseeker, your goals are to

- Introduce the work of your organization.
- By reading between the lines and asking questions, find out what this person cares about and how your work might fit into the foundation's priorities.
- Get the funder to agree to a next step; this could be:

    Letter: review a summary or introductory letter (letter of inquiry)

    Proposal: review a full proposal

    Site visit: schedule a visit to your community to see your work firsthand

    Board involvement: involve a foundation board member, if appropriate

    Leads: suggest other sources of funding

    Recommendation: call or write other funders on your behalf

    Bonus points: Show and tell (visual aids) will help you make your case more effectively.

If you are the foundation officer, your goals are to

- Learn more about this group without spending a lot of time.
- If you can, identify one aspect of the group, the project, or the presentation that grabs your attention.
- If you like the project, talk with the grantseeker about how it might meet the foundation's priorities (you have complete freedom to make this up).
- If the project or presentation seems incomplete, ask probing questions. In fact, ask probing questions no matter what you think of the group or the presentation.

    Bonus points: Unexpected distractions (phone calls, other people going in and out) are allowed.

If you are the observer, your goal is to

- Watch, listen, take notes, and be prepared to talk about what you see and hear.

    Bonus points: Save your comments for the debriefing period.

To debrief this exercise,

- The grantseeker goes first. She or he says two things about the presentation and the meeting that went well and one thing that could have worked better, with an idea for how to improve it.
- The foundation officer goes next, following the same format.
- Finally, the observer offers comments, following the same format.

Timing:

Each side of this triangle (role play plus debriefing) takes fifteen to twenty minutes. Then all participants rotate to a new role. Total time: forty-five to sixty minutes.

---

possible, signed by the person who knows the prospect—introducing the organization.

3. Make an appointment to talk with community foundation staff long before the grant deadline. Describe your work, request their opinions about its fundability, and ask them to try to make a match once the proposal is submitted. It's appropriate to mention any relationship or contact you have with a specific donor, but do not ask for donor names or addresses at this time.

4. When the deadline nears, send the proposal to the foundation.

5. If you receive the grant, send thank-you letters to both the foundation and the donor. This is the time to ask foundation staff for the contributor's name, address, and phone number. If they won't release this information, mail your correspondence in care of the foundation. In either case, send the donor your newsletter and invitations to any special events you host.

Letters of Inquiry

More and more funders now insist that you send a brief letter—anywhere from one to three pages—before you submit a full proposal. This *letter of inquiry* (also known as a *letter of intent* or *pre-proposal letter*) gives them an opportunity to screen grantseekers without handling large volumes of paper. If the letter appeals to them, they can request a full proposal or even a site visit.

"The pre-application phase isn't meant to be an extra hurdle," says Therese Ogle of Northwest Grantmaking Resources. "It's meant to keep the process simpler for the applicant; if their project isn't of interest to a foundation, they haven't had to prepare a full proposal before getting the inevitable rejection."

Even if it's not required, a brief introductory letter is probably a good idea. As Ed Miller of the Illinois Clean Energy Community Foundation points out, "Although many funders will accept full proposals from out of the blue, successful grantseekers at the foundations where I've worked almost always initiate grant requests with a conversation (especially if we know each other) or a succinct letter of inquiry."

Exhibit 6.1 is an example of a letter of inquiry to a previous funder. This letter, from the Association of Vermont Conservation Commissions, is a marvel of compression. Within the one-page limit designated by the Ben & Jerry's Foundation, the letter describes the group's mission and history of success, tying that success back to an earlier grant from the same funder; lays out the rationale for a successful local project and a plan to replicate it; and provides

EXHIBIT 6.1

Letter of Inquiry to Previous Funder

August 8, 2003

Dear Ben & Jerry's Foundation:

In the environmental social change movement, conservation commissions play the role of citizen-activists. Critical environmental problems cannot be effectively addressed unless the general public becomes conscious of the problems, educated about them, and actively involved in the change process. The role of conservation commissions is to alert, educate, inspire, and involve the general public.

Project: We seek $15,000 to address the problem of loss of farmland in Vermont through a pilot project in which five conservation commissions are given pass-through grants to produce, distribute, and market agricultural producers guides for their towns. By inspiring townspeople to spend their food dollars locally, we also would be supporting the Vermont Department of Agriculture's "Buy Local Campaign: The 10% Difference."

The Huntington Conservation Commission produced a local guide to forest and wood product users in town with great success. They are now working on a similar guide for agricultural producers. They will serve as our model.

In this pilot project, we want to give five conservation commissions $2,000 each to produce and distribute an agricultural producers guide for their towns. Additionally, the concept of buying foods locally would be marketed with additional events, such as an annual potluck with local foods, promotional activities at local farmers' markets, etc. An evaluation of the guides' effectiveness would be built into the project.

Who Would Benefit: All Vermonters and visitors would benefit from keeping our working farmlands. Our agricultural economy is critical to our state. Eating locally grown food with shorter time from harvesting is healthier.

Budget: Pass-through grants to five conservation commissions: $2,000 each for a total of $10,000 (for research, printing, and distribution); AVCC would hand-pick these commissions and act as a technical assistance advisor to assist each commission ($5,000).

We are the Association of Vermont Conservation Commissions (AVCC), a statewide grass-roots organization dedicated to fostering local conservation commissions in their stewardship of Vermont's natural resources. There were nine conservation commissions in 1988, when we turned your $2,000 grant into 18 new conservation commissions by the end of 1989. Over ten years later, there are now 89 conservation commissions or similar committees in our state.

Sincerely,

Virginia J. Rasch, Executive Director

EXHIBIT 6.2

Letter of Inquiry from One Funder to Another

April 17, 2003

John McMurray
Norcross Wildlife Foundation
PO Box 269
Wales, MA 01081

Dear John:

Thanks for your February 2003 letter inviting us to apply. We believe we can help you reach even more grassroots groups than you currently do, and we request a grant of $7,500 to underwrite our small grants, training, outreach, and one-on-one consulting programs.

Like the Norcross Wildlife Foundation, we're proud to support the "scrappy, under-funded and understaffed grassroots fighters." As your guidelines state, "These changes in our grantmaking will enable us to serve a constituency of local grassroots organizations that typically have difficulty raising the modest funds they need to do their critical, focused work 'in the trenches' of environmental conservation." What sets the New England Grassroots Environment Fund (NEGEF) apart is our 501(c)(3) public charity status, which allows us to extend the philanthropic reach of our 20 private and community foundation partners to serve informal activist groups. Many of our grantees operate below the awareness of foundations – often at the neighborhood level – yet they represent the most exciting and vital energy in the environmental movement today. We invite you to join our collaborative and help us reach this important constituency.

Through our small grants program, local and regional groups can apply for up to $2,500 per year. With ten issue categories and more than 40 subcategories, we use the word "environment" in its largest sense – if the issue offers a local or regional environmental handle for activism, we do our best to fund it.

Since 1996, we've made more than 650 grants, distributing $1.15 million across New England. NEGEF reaches the deepest level of the grassroots: nearly half of our grantees are ad hoc, unincorporated groups without IRS tax status or fiscal sponsors. Sixty-seven percent (67%) are all volunteer groups; the remaining organizations have, at most, one staff person. Our grantees are the folks who call Norcross Wildlife Foundation grantees for help and advice, and plug themselves into initiatives managed by these larger organizations. For example,

- The work of the Maine Organic Farmers and Gardeners Association (MOFGA) is enriched through many NEGEF-supported local and regional projects, including Maine Right to Know (genetically engineered foods), Farmington Area Local Foods (locally-grown organic produce), and the Low-Impact Forestry Project, which uses the MOFGA woodlot to demonstrate sustainable forestry practices.
- Over the years we've funded a number of independent programs affiliated with the Northern

EXHIBIT 6.2 *(continued)*

Letter of Inquiry from One Funder to Another

Appalachian Restoration Project (NARP), including the Renewable Energy Assistance Project, the Herbicide Project, and the Vermont Citizens Forest Roundtable. Much of NARP's community organizing takes place through these local grassroots initiatives.

- As Pete Didisheim of the Natural Resources Council of Maine recently wrote, "On a wide range of issues – specifically watershed management, toxic pollution, public land protection and forestry – the New England Grassroots Environment Fund supports place-based, locally-focused voices. We would be less effective without NEGEF and the constituency they support and engage." One of our grantees, Maine Rivers, recently spun off from NRCM to become an independent voice for river protection.

After seven years of working with emerging groups, we've come to understand that money is not enough; activists also need skills, advice, referrals, and opportunities to learn from each other. We provide these through:

o *One on one coaching* by phone and in person
o *Referrals* and *subsidies* to allow grantees to attend professional training programs
o *Training events* geared especially to the needs of all-volunteer and lightly-staffed groups with jobs, families, and limited time
o *Networking opportunities* such as our annual grantee retreat, which draws up to 140 participants for workshops, panels, field trips, and informal sharing.

Over the past eight months, we have provided training to 400 activists around the region, including 200 participants at four NEGEF-sponsored events.

The New England Grassroots Environment Fund is a unique funder-activist partnership. The Fund is governed by a Board of Directors, presently five activists and four funders. Our Grantmaking Committee, comprised of one activist from each of the six New England states and five representatives from NEGEF's funding partners, reviews and recommends funding for the grant program. Our policy requires that community activists comprise a majority of both bodies, which helps to ensure that grassroots organizers have a strong voice in our governance, grantmaking, and program development. Should you be interested, we would encourage your participation on the Grantmaking Committee when a position becomes available.

Budget: Your grant would help us meet our 2003 small grants and technical assistance budget. Our goal is to make 150 grants throughout the region while providing hands-on training and consulting to 400-500 activists. Your gift of $7,500 would fund four small grants to ad hoc groups at $1,500 each, and would support one community training event at a cost of $1,500.

Please contact me if you have any questions. In advance, thanks for your interest.

Sincerely,

Cheryl King Fischer
Executive Director

a basic budget. Notice the simple language and adequate margins. It's a quick, easy read.

The letter featured in Exhibit 6.2 was written by the New England Grassroots Environment Fund, or NEGEF. In this case, one funder (a public charity) is asking another (a private foundation) to support its grant program for grassroots groups.

Here's what makes this letter effective:

- It begins by referencing an existing relationship: "Thanks for inviting us to apply."

- It emphasizes the links between the foundation's priorities and the applicant's programs, even restating the foundation officer's language: "Scrappy, under-funded and understaffed grassroots fighters."

- It defines NEGEF's ability to "extend the philanthropic reach" of private foundations such as the Norcross Wildlife Foundation by providing grants to informal groups that don't have IRS tax status. This crucial constituency of activists, who often work at the local and neighborhood level, is ignored by most funders because they can't count these grants toward their IRS payout requirements.

- It establishes credibility by giving a quick organizational history, providing specific examples of how NEGEF's work has benefited Norcross grantees in the past, and describing its unique decision-making structure.

- It lays out clear program goals and itemizes how the grant money would be spent.

- The tone is positive throughout and the language is easy to understand.

Your job, when writing your own letter of inquiry, is to condense your proposal to the required length. Describe the problem, your qualifications for dealing with it, and your plan of action. This may seem difficult, but it's a terrific exercise in organizing. If you can't effectively outline your project in a page or two (see Chapter Four), you need to rethink the project.

Be Professional, Be Patient

Professionalism begins with homework; do the most thorough and accurate job you can. At a basic level, this means proofreading your letters and proposals, spelling names correctly, keeping track of who works at which foundation, and so forth. "Misspelling of the foundation's name is a definite no-no!" says Sigrid Pickering of the Sweet Water Trust. "I try not to be affected by it, but it does count somehow. It indicates that people are not paying attention. Even after being funded, some grantees get the name wrong in the progress report or final report."

Being a professional means honoring deadlines. "You know what gets my attention?" says Pat Jerido. "Proposals that arrive on time, or even early."

Professionals accept defeat gracefully and move on to the next funder or the next proposal. In researching this book, I was amazed to learn that, upon receiving rejection letters, some people actually dump their frustration on foundation staff.

The staff members of the Common Counsel Foundation spend many hours speaking with grantseekers about funding criteria, and they are understandably annoyed when "applicants who have been declined call to argue. If you want to build a good relationship, lashing out in anger isn't productive. We try to explain in advance that we receive three hundred proposals a year but have funds to grant only thirty, which helps them to understand our limitations."

"I understand that people get frustrated," says Irene Vlach, "but don't forget your manners."

Assuming you can maintain your composure, it's acceptable to call the foundation and ask why your proposal wasn't approved. (Unless, of course, they don't have a listed phone number or specifically discourage phone calls.) It's much easier to do this, and maintain a friendly tone of voice, if you've had previous contact with the foundation officer. You might even receive some encouragement.

Finally, it pays to be patient. "We only look at invited proposals, so expect a 'courtship period' of at least six months," says Terry Odendahl.

"We get to know our grantees first; the process takes six months to a year before we ask for a proposal," Shelley Davis says. "When I worked at the Ford Foundation, the courtship phase was typically one to two years. However, we try to be more aggressive with time-sensitive requests that address changes in public policy."

While you're busy building relationships, don't forget to start working on your proposals. Good relationships are crucial, but sooner or later (sooner is better) you must commit your plan to paper. The nuts and bolts of proposal writing are covered in Chapter Seven.

Creating Your Proposal, Piece by Piece

I hate the notion that it's just about relationships; the proposal counts for a lot, too. It's important to explain in writing what you're going to do. Because it's a contractual arrangement, you have to describe what's going to happen with the money.

—LOIS DeBACKER, Charles Stewart Mott Foundation

Keep it short, sweet, and to the point; proposal reviewers often need to read hundreds of proposals throughout the year.

—ELIZABETH WILCOX, SUE HUTCHINSON, and MARGARET SOLLE,

Common Counsel Foundation

When it's time to put words on paper or type them onto the computer screen, most of us freeze up. Somewhere back in grammar school, we learned that written language is supposed to be formal and proper; consequently, we can't, or won't, write the way we speak. We haul out the big words and try to impress the reader with our vocabulary. We use lots of jargon and technical terms. We create elaborate sentences that are hard to read and even harder to understand.

I once asked a student of mine to describe her group's mission. She said proudly, "Intervention for case management."

"Excuse me?"

"We work with disabled kids and teach them how to use their bodies better."

Can you see the difference? The first sentence sounds impressive but means nothing. The second sentence paints a picture using simple, clear words. After enduring my critique with a smile, she wrote a marvelous mission statement describing what it was like to watch a two-year-old girl pick up a ball and hold it in her hands for the first time. The class was practically in tears. We were all reaching for our checkbooks.

In this chapter, you'll learn how to organize, write, and design a winning proposal.

The Value (or Not) of Good Writing

Among foundation officers, there are conflicting impulses about the importance of good writing. On one hand, given the torrent of paper raining down on them, grant reviewers yearn for well-written, well-organized materials. Joni Craig of the San Diego Foundation for Change sums it up nicely: "I am always impressed by clear, concise responses that directly relate to the questions outlined in the application guidelines. I greatly appreciate proposals that are well organized, easy to follow, use common language, avoid jargon, and have rational budgets that match the narrative request."

"In every grant cycle," says Shelley Davis of the Joyce Foundation, "someone on staff jumps up and says, 'I just got the best proposal. It could be framed.'" She adds, with a hint of sadness, "That's never happened to me."

On the other hand, most funders—especially those supporting grassroots initiatives—are pretty forgiving folks. "We understand that many of our applicants are doing this for the first time," says Cheryl King Fischer of the New England Grassroots Environment Fund, "so we try to be generous in our proposal review."

On this subject, program officers have lots of encouraging stories to tell, especially for novices who are intimidated by the idea of actually writing a proposal.

Bill Dempsey, formerly of the Unitarian Universalist Veatch Program, says, "People doing the best work often don't put the effort into presenting or articulating what they do. I've often changed my mind after visiting the group. They weren't focused on paperwork but rather on building their base. Sometimes we see the other end of the spectrum: the proposal is slick, but when you dig below the surface, there isn't much going on."

Pat Jerido, formerly of the Ms. Foundation, concurs. "We give a lot of leeway," she says. "We're often the first funder for a project or group. I remember one proposal that was partly typed, partly handwritten, which didn't inspire confidence. But we did a site visit and they were doing fantastic, incredible work on HIV/AIDS. On the other hand, a lot of well-written proposals still miss the mark."

David Karoff of the Rhode Island Foundation adds, "People with English as a second language don't know how to do this, so we try to talk with them in advance and go over the application questions. It doesn't matter if the grammar stinks; in fact, it's refreshing. We're getting more proposals from young people, who don't have the B.S. down yet, which is also refreshing. Sometimes we get a proposal that's so polished that you wonder if there's any soul in it."

I once traveled all the way from Arizona to New York to present a proposal I had written, only to run into this concern. The grants officer was extremely interested—she talked with me for an hour and asked many perceptive questions—but felt that the proposal was *too* well written. She needed to get past the mouthpiece (me) and deal directly with the people who were running the project. Several months later, she went to New Mexico to meet the leadership, a group of Native American farmers, and eventually supported the organization.

When you sit down to write your proposals, keep these tips in mind:

- It's OK to use an informal, we're-all-in-this-together tone. Think of the reader as an interested friend.

- Avoid jargon and fancy language. Keep it simple.

- Write the way you speak. If you're having trouble, try talking into a tape recorder, then transcribe and edit your words. If tape recorders make you uncomfortable, ask a friend to write down your spoken words. If you can talk, you can write.

- "Have somebody outside your organization read the proposal before you submit it," says Lois DeBacker. "It may be clear to the author, but it's often hard for someone outside your group to understand."

A number of funders will work with you to edit your proposals and make the language more accessible. "We're willing to look at drafts first and make suggestions," says DeBacker. "My job is to help grantees succeed, so I try to give guidance on what to include. Of course, we hope that the first draft we see is really good, especially when we know the group."

Marty Teitel of the Cedar Tree Foundation adds, "You have what you need to do your job. Now let's talk about how to package it. I need to be aware of your vernacular—that's my burden—but if I can't understand your program on paper, we both have to address that. Maybe we'll create it together."

If you can clean up the vernacular on your own, so much the better. If you need help replacing your jargon with more evocative language, see Worksheet 7.1.

Of course, when you seek editing advice from a grantmaker, you'd be wise to follow it. Shelley Davis says, "We try hard not to invite proposals that we can't support. If you get invited, that's a good sign. We give guidance about what to include, and when people don't follow our advice, it's frustrating. I try not to ask for rewrites, but I've done it."

A thoughtful, well-written application may not be crucial, but it will certainly improve your odds of getting funded. In a crowded field, you want your organization to stand out, and the written word is one of the best tools available. Use it. Without getting too fancy, write the cleanest, sharpest prose that you can. Whack the reader on the nose with clear, direct language.

Here's a fine example from the Seattle Young People's Project:

> The Young Women's Conference has always been free and open to all young women. It is planned for by middle and high school women with the support of adults in the community and at SYPP. Over the last six years our vision of empowering young women has become clearer and stronger. We believe it is empowering to be in an atmosphere where we can be loud, sad, strong, vulnerable, and angry; where we can explore our bodies and sexualities and address racism, internalized oppression, and white privilege; where we can learn self-defense, perform our art, laugh, and make friends; where we can share out experiences, teach each other how to use contraception, dance, and learn community organizing skills.

This proposal for their Young Women's Empowerment Program was written by a nineteen-year-old participant. Can you feel the energy coming off the page? The author slips in a bit of jargon, but with this kind of energy, who cares?

Should You Hire an Outside Grantwriter?

Faced with limited time, insecurity about writing, and other pressing priorities—isn't it interesting how fundraising always ends up at the bottom of the to-do list?—organizations sometimes consider hiring a consultant to prepare their grant applications. For most grassroots groups, this is a bad idea for a number of reasons:

- To write effectively about your organization, an outsider needs to know your work intimately: the issues, the players, the nuances of your strategy. You're paying by the hour, and the writer's research can add up to a lot of hours.

- It's hard for a consultant to feel the same commitment to the mission as staff and leadership do—and it shows. As Pat Jerido says, "The meat and the passion must come from the staff, not a hired grantwriter. Prepare your proposals in house; people can sense when it's false."

Jargon Patrol

Every field, including community organizing, has its own terminology. Sometimes these specialized phrases provide handy shortcuts, but just as often words are barriers to people who come from other fields of learning or have different life experiences.

For example, "stakeholders" refers to all the constituencies and individuals who have a direct interest in a particular social problem, and could therefore play a constructive role in defining solutions. If you understand the term, fine. If not, you're left wondering, "Why are they holding stakes? Are they planting tomatoes in the garden? Is there a vampire in the neighborhood?"

Jargon tends to operate at the intellectual level, which is not the best level for fundraising. As a friend once told me, "Statistics raise eyebrows, but emotions raise money." When we use intellectual shortcuts, we bleed all the emotion—the people, the stories—from our proposals.

Here's a fragment of a sentence from an actual grant application:

"Identify existing impediments to greater utilization of non-structural approaches to floodplain management"

Read it a few times, then rewrite it below it in plain, simple language that everyone can understand:

_____

_____

_____

_____

Difficult, isn't it? I use this exercise from time to time in grant workshops. These are my favorite responses so far:

"Let the rivers run free."

"Buttheads who live in the floodplain need to move." (This one came from a board member of the organization preparing the proposal.)

Buried within the original sentence is a fairly radical concept: for the health of the environment, maybe we should remove some dams and levees *(structural approaches),* let the rivers go where they need to go *(floodplains),* and stop providing government-subsidized flood insurance *(existing impediments)* to people who choose to live in flood-prone areas.

Because the author has wrapped this provocative idea in such technical language, it reduces the impact of the idea, perhaps intentionally. Big words provide good places to hide.

What words or catchphrases do you use regularly in your work? Would they qualify as jargon? Write them down here:

_____

_____

_____

_____

_____

_____

_____

_____

Do these words do justice to the importance of your issue? Do they capture the passion and the commitment of the people involved? Do they tell a compelling story? Is the meaning clear to people from different backgrounds?

If not, what are your alternatives? Write down words or phrases that might do a better job of reflecting the energy and emotion that people bring to the work:

_____

_____

_____

_____

_____

_____

_____

_____

Remember, jargon words are usually shortcuts. It's worth spending a few more words to tell a good story. With skill and practice, these stories can define what you do, which will allow you to save words when discussing your constituency, internal decision-making processes, and the like.

_____

- Whoever writes the proposal ends up shaping the work plan in subtle or not-so-subtle ways. Do you really want a consultant making those kinds of choices about your work? This problem can be addressed with close supervision and editing, but if you're too busy to prepare your own grant applications, you're probably too busy to provide close supervision to a contractor.

- Ideally, the proposal writer is also reaching out and building relationships with the funding community. It's awkward for a consultant to fill this role, especially if he or she is engaged with multiple nonprofits.

- Why deny yourself the opportunity to improve your skills? If you can learn to raise money effectively, you will never lack for a job (and you'll have more power within your group).

If you do choose to hire a consultant, consider the following guidelines:

- Look for a person who has a basic understanding of your issues, your constituency, and so forth. For example, if you're working on a living wage campaign, be cautious about contracting with a consultant who specializes in grants for scientific research.

- Check references and review writing samples. If they don't check out, find somebody else.

- Most consultants work by the hour or by the job. If you're paying by the hour, negotiate a limit on the number of hours. It is the contractor's responsibility to finish the work for the agreed price, even if it takes longer than expected. Paying fundraisers (including grantwriters) a percentage of what they bring in is considered bad practice in professional circles, so don't do it.

- Develop a clear written agreement that outlines the scope of work, deliverables, deadlines, and all costs, including consulting fees and any relevant expenses.

- Set aside time to be available to the grantwriter to answer questions and review drafts.

Layout: Creating a Good-Looking Proposal

The basic principles of layout can be summed up with the cliché "less is more." Follow these guidelines:

- The less type on the page, the easier it is to read.

- The less clutter on the page, the easier it is to understand.

David Karoff identifies the most common layout problems as "cheating on the [specified] font size and the margins or using single spacing. We'll read anything, but we have to be able to actually read it."

You don't need to be a graphic artist to create an attractive proposal. Just keep in mind the following points:

Follow the guidelines. Forgive me for repeating myself, but you need to request, read, understand, and follow the application guidelines, which vary from grantmaker to grantmaker. Many foundations publish specific instructions, including the length and format of proposals. Some foundations and corporations, and virtually all government agencies, require you to fill out forms, or request that you use their outline in presenting your proposal.

"Follow the directions on the application," says Zoë Rothchild of the Northwest Fund for the Environment. "This may seem obvious and minor, but it really is crucial. If we ask for no more then a three-page narrative, then we mean no more then a three-page narrative. While we don't like creating seemingly meaningless hoops to jump through, there are complex reasons behind every question we ask and the way we ask it." Jeff Anderson of the Oregon Community Foundation also notes, "Don't leave out some of the required materials and force the foundation to work harder to keep your application active."

My experience has been that most grantmakers will try to accommodate you within their guidelines, especially if you make a genuine effort to comply. A number of foundations affiliated with the National Network of Grantmakers accept a common application form (see Resource A), which makes life a bit easier for grantseekers.

Leave lots of white space. Use margins of at least one inch on all sides of the page; a bit more is helpful. It's OK to use single spacing for the text, but if you do, add an extra space between paragraphs. All the proposals featured in the next chapter use this format. A combination of single and double spacing can also be effective.

Use twelve-point (or larger) type. Twelve-point type is the standard size for most computer fonts. Do not switch to a smaller type size to squeeze more words onto the page—figure out a way to tell your story with fewer words.

Grantmakers consistently cite tiny type as one of their pet peeves. "I'm really annoyed by tiny print," says Ron White, formerly of the Tides Foundation, "which is a testament to my advancing age. People say, 'We'll just shrink the print.' That's a big mistake."

Use running heads, not just page numbers. A running head is a word or phrase that appears on the top of each page; it can include the page number and an identifying phrase. (Look at the top of this page.) This is a courtesy to the reader and a big help to the photocopy staff at the foundation office. All word processing programs can create running heads for you.

Break up the page. Nothing tires the eyes more than repetition. If your pages all look the same, the reader's eyes start to wander, and his or her mind won't be far behind.

Use bold text, underlining, italic text, bullets, lists, and indented paragraphs to build visual variety into your pages. These techniques, used judiciously, also guide the reader through your grant application, highlighting the most important points.

Don't justify the text. "Justification" means that the words line up on both sides of the page. This works fine in narrow columns, like a newspaper, but it's harder to read across the width of a standard page. Leave the right side of your text "ragged."

Use graphics where appropriate. Some information just can't be reduced to words or is better presented in other ways. In these situations, graphs, charts, maps, photos, and even artwork can be incorporated directly into the proposal. Most word processing programs allow you to wrap text around tables, photos, and so forth, which makes for a good-looking, easy-to-read proposal. An example of text wrapped around a graphic appears in Exhibit 7.1. AGENDA (Action for Grassroots Empowerment & Neighborhood Development Alternatives) uses a bar graph to show the growing disparity of income among California families.

In its grant report, Native Seeds/SEARCH includes photos of volunteers working on the farm, as shown in Exhibit 7.2. Note the informal, friendly tone of the writing that accompanies this photo.

The Wildlands Project incorporates a map that defines its "Spine of the Continent" conservation program. Their proposal is shown in Chapter Eight.

Print your proposal on standard 8½-by-11-inch paper. Stick with white or off-white paper; several funders now ask you to use recycled stock. Laser or ink-jet printers are best because they produce the cleanest, darkest type. If you don't have access to a high-quality printer, many photocopy shops will rent you time on theirs; they generally charge by the page.

Single-sided or double-sided? It's becoming more acceptable to print your proposals on both sides of the page to save paper. In fact, some funders now specify that you do so. Read the guidelines carefully and if you're still not certain, call and ask. When in doubt, do it the old-fashioned, wasteful way: print on one side of the page.

Clip, don't staple. Once your proposal lands in the foundation office, it will likely be photocopied for distribution to board members or other grant reviewers. Unless given other instructions, use a paper clip to hold the pages together. Do not use staples, folders, or plastic covers.

EXHIBIT 7.1
Use of Graphics in a Proposal

Los Angeles, like urban centers across the United States, continues to face the serious challenges of economic, political and social inequality, which are systemic in nature and require systemic solutions. During the past twenty years the United States, and the world, has undergone dramatic structural changes, both economic and political. The impact of advances in technology, changes in the structure and operations of corporations, and globalization are felt everywhere. These changes fed a decade (the 1990s) of record "economic growth" in the United States and elsewhere, but the

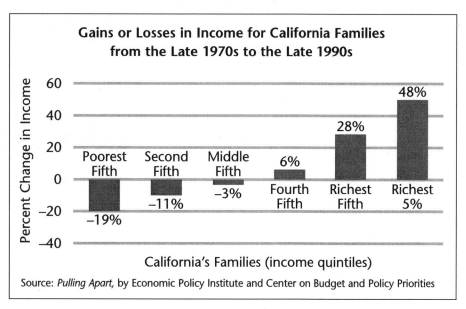

majority of the benefits of this "growth" went to large corporations and wealthy families. Growing numbers of people are experiencing an *ongoing* structural decline in economic and social opportunities, as well as *ongoing* major barriers to meaningful and effective civic participation.

Keep it brief. Grant guidelines generally include page limits; honor them. However, if the guidelines say, "No more than ten pages," you can certainly use fewer than ten pages, as long as you include the required information. As the staff members of the Common Counsel Foundation say, "We admire four-page proposals!" By reducing your pitch to its essentials, you will become more effective at both raising money and getting your message across in the community.

The remainder of this chapter describes the basic components of a grant proposal. The requirements for format and content will vary according to the grantmaker, so use this section as a general guide. If your prospective funder doesn't suggest a specific format, it's acceptable to combine and rearrange these sections, but make sure all this material is contained somewhere in the proposal.

EXHIBIT 7.2
Use of Graphics in a Report

It was like that all summer—folks came, they helped, they left. Students from Patagonia High School spent almost six weeks helping us cover young corn shoots ("shoot bagging") as they emerged, protecting them from being pollinated by anything except us. Kevin also spent eight weeks with us on an internship sponsored by his employer, Patagonia, Inc. Kevin inherited the "Johnson grass obsession" from our first summer camper, Mark Shipley, who also left the remnants of his twenty-five-pound bag of peanuts and more jars of sauerkraut than would fit in his backpack. Thanks to all the volunteers

Interns at work: High school students from Patagonia

(too numerous to name, especially if you didn't sign in!) who came from Patagonia, Tucson, and even some from Phoenix (a three-hour drive, at least). As far as I know, however, Abel Duffy came the farthest distance—all the way from Mimbres, New Mexico—to volunteer with us. Among the many who helped with the overwhelming task of pollinating 154 different corn accessions were a musical composer, an ex-Buddhist monk, (many) yoga instructors, a conservation biologist, a lawyer for a local mining company, a homesteader, an organic juice bartender, a legal assistant, a graphic arts student from Denmark, a university professor, an anthropologist, and many, many more folks from a wide diversity of backgrounds and interests.

The Components of a Grant Proposal

Most proposals should include the following building blocks:

- Cover page and executive summary
- Organizational history, structure, and constituency
- Problem statement
- Program goals and objectives
- Strategy and implementation (methods)
- Timeline
- Evaluation
- Personnel
- Budgets
- Attachments
- Cover letter

Cover Page and Executive Summary

Put your cover page on letterhead and address the funder directly at the top of the page: "A proposal from the Peace and Justice League to The John Q. Public Foundation." Do not exceed one page. Include the following elements:

- Title of the project

- Submission date

- Beginning and ending dates for the project

- Total project budget

- Amount requested

- Contact persons and phone numbers for your organization

- A brief summary, sometimes called an executive summary, describing the need and your proposed activities to address the problem

Take at look at the following summary from the Youth Empowerment Center. A foundation officer could read this page and understand the group's mission, goals, constituency, number of youth who will be involved, and evaluation strategy. For people who review hundreds of proposals, a brief, well-organized cover page like this one is a huge help.

YOUTH EMPOWERMENT CENTER

FUNDING REQUEST TO THE W. CLEMENT AND JESSIE V. STONE FOUNDATION

"When looking at its contribution to communities, organizing may be one of the few areas of youth work with such a long and undisputed history of success. Nearly all the social movements for civil rights, peace, health, and environmental justice had young people both on the front lines and in positions of leadership."

—KIM McGILLICUDY AND ANNETTE FUENTES,
Funding Youth Organizing: Strategies for Building Power and Youth Leadership, written for the Funders Collaborative on Youth Organizing

PROPOSAL SUMMARY

Youth Empowerment Center (YEC) is an innovative umbrella organization of youth-serving projects that put youth organizing and youth culture at the center of our practice. **Our mission is to build the capacity of youth and youth groups and to empower young people to engage in organizing campaigns that create and shape public policy.** We fulfill our mission through services and activities ranging from youth organizing to training, from networking to hip-hop dance and spoken-word classes.

This proposal for general support to the W. Clement and Jessie V. Stone Foundation outlines our work to support Bay Area youth organizing in 2003. We respectfully request a one-year grant of $20,000 for the time period March 1, 2003 to February 29, 2004.

YEC seeks to address the poverty, racial inequality, inadequate education system, and criminalization that many young people face. Our main goals are to:

1. Nurture young people's visions for social change in their communities.

2. Engage low-income youth and youth of color in organizing efforts to shape public policy that directly affects their lives and their communities.

3. Develop the skills of youth organizers through organizer training and civic education.

4. Maximize the collective impact of Bay Area youth groups to affect public policy.

5. Influence public policy on education and juvenile justice issues to be more youth-oriented through organizing and advocacy.

6. Provide a strong organizational infrastructure for youth empowerment projects.

We seek to achieve our goals through youth organizing and youth arts training, as well as by supporting youth groups through technical assistance and networking. We plan to train over 700 youth and work with over 15 youth groups to help shape public policy that affects young people directly. We also plan to help reduce the rate of incarceration of young people by pressuring the Alameda County Board of Supervisors to implement the Juvenile Detention Alternatives Initiative.

Our evaluation plan takes into account the satisfaction and impact of our constituency on three levels: (1) individual youth evaluations of workshops and classes; (2) evaluations from groups that we work with; and (3) internal evaluations by our staff of our overall program work.

YEC has a young, enthusiastic, and committed staff who come from diverse backgrounds. Our staff has training and experience in community, labor and youth organizing, independent media, spoken word, music and event production, working with homeless and formerly homeless youth, and working with gay-lesbian-transgender-queer-questioning youth.

Organizational History, Structure, and Constituency

Describe your mission, your constituency, your goals, your accomplishments. Why do you deserve support? This is your opportunity to brag. Emphasize aspects of your work that have a direct bearing on your ability to develop and manage the proposed project.

In outlining the history of your group, don't overdo it. If you can't do justice to your accomplishments in a page or two, include your best brief description in this section of the proposal, then attach an appendix outlining your track record in more detail.

As you read the following example from Alabama Arise/Arise Citizens' Policy Project, notice the tone of the writing. It's consistently positive and refreshingly informal, especially for a group that does policy analysis. The authors refer to their organization in the first person—"We," "Our"—which reinforces the informal tone. (Discussing your work in the first-person voice is always a good idea.) They also convey a lot of information without unnecessary details. After reading this page, we know a number of things about them and their work:

- Public policy challenges in Alabama that set the context for their work

- What makes them unique: the combination of organizing and policy analysis

- Their most successful campaigns of the past decade, adding up to a significant track record

- How the membership participates in choosing and defining the issues

If you can cover this much ground in such a small space, you're sure to impress foundation staff and improve your odds for success.

ALABAMA ARISE—ORGANIZATIONAL HISTORY

Arise has weighed in on major issues—tax reform, education reform, welfare reform, and health care—always from the perspective of what these issues would mean for low-income Alabamians.

- During the statewide tax reform efforts of 1991–92 we held 28 tax reform workshops, and we have continued to bang this drum. Ask a group of citizens about Alabama's income tax threshold, and they're likely to know that it's $4,600, lowest in the nation. Ask about sales taxes, and they know that Alabama taxes infant formula for babies, but exempts formula for calves. Ask about property taxes, and they know we have the lowest tax rates in the nation, and that timber land here is taxed at less than $1.00 per acre per year, while Georgia taxes the same kind of land at over $4.00.

- On education reform, we spoke out for school-linked health and social services (the proposed package included $42 million to put $100,000 in these services at each of 420 schools) and helped to explain the notion of equity funding. After Gov. Fob James's watered-down reform plan passed, we published a study showing that the per-pupil spending gap between the best- and poorest-funded systems had been reduced by only 20 percent.

- We almost single-handedly changed the conversation on welfare reform from Gov. James's punitive talk of pregnant teens and runaway budgets to a consensus discussion of jobs, child care, and transportation, which were the barriers we had identified in listening sessions. We pointed out constantly that no one would have a baby just to gain $29 a month in additional benefits, and we showed that welfare spending was only 0.59 percent of the state budget.

- Arise helped build support for the Children's Health Insurance Program (CHIP) and ultimately Alabama became the first state to implement coverage. While our executive director served on the Governor's Task Force on Uninsured Children, we helped build the case for higher Medicaid dental reimbursements, which Gov. Siegelman soon ordered. The result was greater access to dental care for children on Medicaid.

One of our most striking accomplishments is the wedding of policy analysis and organizing under one umbrella. Having three policy analysts and four organizers with good working relationships means that the policy analysts are better grounded in the concerns of the membership, and the organizers are better equipped with credible policy analysis. We are able to moderate the stereotypes of the pointy-headed policy analyst and the ill-informed organizer, and we intend to continue to maintain this balance on our staff.

We also extend the policy-organizing marriage to our membership. Member volunteers serve on **issue caucuses**, which study issues, give feedback to our policy analysts, and make policy recommendations to our Board and membership. Each caucus is staffed by both a policy analyst and an organizer. Caucuses on tax reform, transportation, health care, and welfare reform are currently active, as are coalition steering committees for a moratorium on the death penalty, felon refranchisement, Medicaid reform, and tax reform. Our other membership structure is the **regional cluster,** in which local members assume responsibility for Arise's education, advocacy, and growth in their communities. We now have nine active clusters. Policy analysts, organizers, and caucuses work together to develop workshop models in a popular education format so that we can engage people's hearts as well as their heads. We expect people to walk away from a workshop with the ability to carry on an intelligent two-minute conversation on an issue, because that is as much time as we get to make our case.

Arise has achieved a reputation for timely, credible, accessible policy analysis and for having a widespread membership active in advocacy. Reporters and editors depend on our opinions on a wide range of poverty-related policy issues. It is gratifying to watch as our reputation creates a steady flow of groups and congregations interested in joining.

If you're working with a new organization, you will probably have fewer accomplishments to brag about. To solve this problem, you might combine your organizational history with the personnel section of the proposal and discuss the relevant experience of your leadership and project organizers. Some of their personal know-how and commitment to the cause will transfer to the group as a whole. (Of course, if the guidelines require separate sections on personnel and organizational history, follow instructions.)

If the funder wants information about your structure and decision-making process, describe it as simply as possible. Consider this another opportunity for creative use of graphics.

The flow chart from Communities Against Rape and Abuse, or CARA (Exhibit 7.3), shows how decisions are made in that group. (You need to know that a CAT is a "community action team," a program advisory board made up of representatives from the community.) It's an elegant solution to a thorny problem—how to discuss your process without descending into the boredom of subcommittee descriptions, agenda preparation, who brings the food, and the recurring debate about who gets to hold the gavel.

Finally, a word about sequence: With some proposals, it makes more sense to go straight from the cover page into the problem statement and save the organizational history for later. The document should flow. Use your best judgment as to order.

Problem Statement (also called a Needs Statement or Background Statement)

What's the current situation? How did it get that way? On the assumption that you are trying to solve a problem, you have to define it first. What's the relevant background on the issue, the constituency, the local scene? Why is your proposed action necessary?

"Specifics and facts get my attention," says John Powers of the Educational Foundation of America. "Not that the writer writes from anger, but writes the facts so that the reader gets angry at what's being battled." It's not enough to say that your neighborhood is threatened by air pollution. Describe the specific circumstances and perhaps a typical story or case history. Then, and only then, will your efforts to hold the polluter accountable resonate with the reader.

EXHIBIT 7.3
Visual Display of Organizational Structure

COMMUNITIES AGAINST RAPE AND ABUSE DECISION-MAKING STRUCTURE

Program-Specific Idea

Ideas are usually gener- → Program Coordinator → Community organizer
ated by community determines whether and CAT review idea and
organizer and CAT make final collective
members • Idea is within budget decision

• Idea is within organizational capacity

• Idea fits the values of
the organization

Organization-Specific Idea

Idea is fundamental, such → Board of Directors → All organizational mem-
as changing mission state- determines whether bers (staff, CAT members,
ment or dissolution of board members, and
organization • Idea makes sense finan- activists) make final col-
cially and legally lective decision

• Idea is within organizational capacity

• Idea fits the values of
the organization

Consider the following problem statement from Manchester Area Residents Concerned about Health, or MARCH.

MANCHESTER AREA RESIDENTS CONCERNED ABOUT HEALTH—PROBLEM STATEMENT

We are a group of residents that first came together about two years ago due to a concern about a company operating in our neighborhood. This company, Tilcon Connecticut, has been operating an asphalt plant on North Main Street for over forty years, next to houses and very close to senior housing, daycare centers, and an elementary school. Throughout this time, we have suffered noxious smells, burning eyes and throats, and sleepless nights due to the asphalt plant. . . . In the summer, the smells are so bad that we are forced indoors and have to keep our windows shut. Soot builds up on the insides of our windows. Eileen, one of our core group members, has had to put her children's jackets over their heads as they ran from the car to the house to avoid vomiting from the odors.

We first got organized when we learned of a proposal to add a concrete plant to the asphalt plant's operation. This made us mad and so we rallied at a public hearing . . . forcing the town to deny the concrete plant's permit. This was our first victory. The battle over the concrete plant continues as Tilcon appeals the decision.

Since then, we have formed our group, Manchester Area Residents Concerned about Health (MARCH), to not only stop the building of the concrete plant but to shut down the existing asphalt operation. We are fighting for our quality of life and our health. Our research uncovered that not only is Tilcon part of an international conglomerate with billions of dollars behind its name, but that the awful smells that permeate our neighborhood actually contain known human carcinogens.

We have mounted a public education campaign to educate our neighbors about the plant and its dangers, and to push for closure of the plant. This has included meetings with elected officials, public meetings, resident education, and work with the media.

Under pressure for answers, the Department of Environmental Protection finally conducted an inspection of the plant last September and found several violations. The DEP cited Tilcon with operating a burner that is larger than allowed, potentially increasing sulfur dioxide emissions by 9.7 tons per year in violation of its permit. The plant was also charged with exceeding its permitted hours of operation, having its smokestack too close to the property line, and emitting excessive amounts of formaldehyde.

We asked the DEP to levy the maximum fine on the company, which we calculated to be $227 million. In a huge victory, the DEP responded by ordering the asphalt plant to be shut down.

However, Tilcon is determined to be a bad neighbor. A few months ago they resumed operations in defiance of the DEP order to shut them down. They are currently risking fines of up to $25,000 per day and are banking on the fact that they will win their appeal and so not have to pay.

Therefore, we realize we need to "up the ante" and have vowed to fight until the plant is closed permanently. We have a lawyer to represent us pro bono in this matter. We have redoubled our efforts to keep this issue in the public spotlight and are planning another large neighborhood meeting to rally the troops. We are seeking funds to help with the resources we need to do this.

The proposal outlines a classic community-organizing battle: neighborhood group versus big corporation. What makes this piece effective is the simple, nontechnical language that combines factual data (9.7 tons of sulfur dioxide emissions per year), compelling visual images (soot on window panes, children with coats over their heads), and strongly felt emotion: "We are fighting for our quality of life and our health."

David versus Goliath stories are compelling on several levels, especially when David wins a round by pressuring state health officials to do the right thing. This section ends with a hint of suspense: will the good guys win? The answer lies with the reader (funder), who can influence the outcome with a timely grant.

You'll have a strong chance of success, says John Powers, "When the reader is persuaded that the applicant organization is capable of improving the circumstances, and the only missing link is the funding—the fuel. The reader can provide that fuel to power your project."

Judicious use of statistics can help to quantify the problem, especially if you combine the numbers with stories about real people and real places. The following problem statement from the Michigan Land Use Institute describes the way that school relocation and expansion choices encourage sprawl. Notice how the broad concerns addressed in the proposal are embodied in stories about two specific communities, Traverse City and Charlevoix. The authors also cite statistics—smaller schools provide better education, only 4 percent of students at the outlying high school use public transit—to strengthen their case.

MICHIGAN LAND USE INSTITUTE—PROBLEM STATEMENT

Neighborhood schools allow children to walk down tree-lined streets, interact with community members, patronize local businesses, and cultivate a sense of independence. These interactions tie children to their community—and the community to its children—in many invaluable ways. Neighborhood schools are also smaller in general, which offers students more opportunities to foster relationships with teachers and other students, as well as to participate in activities. A recent North Carolina study found that a school's learning environment suffers when the number of students exceeds a certain, optimum level. The study recommended that elementary schools average 300–400 students, middle schools 300–600 students, and high schools 400–800 students.

Yet many school expansions result in larger schools far from neighborhoods. In Traverse City, for example, a new high school on the west side of town houses 1,350 students in grades 10 through 12. Along with the higher numbers and longer distances come greater costs for both school districts and parents. The Traverse City school district no longer can afford to provide transportation for high school students. Many who attend the city's original, east-side high school can walk, ride bicycles, or use city buses. Traverse City West Senior High School, however, is too far for walking and bike-riding; fewer than 4 percent of west-side students use the city bus.

School districts often build new and larger schools far from existing neighborhoods and services because of a real or perceived need for space to accommodate such amenities as major athletic fields and parking lots. But a recent example in Charlevoix tells the increasingly common story of new community costs that can follow such school relocations. In 1999 the Charlevoix School Board developed a plan to move its high school from downtown Charlevoix to a 75-acre parcel in Marion Township's agricultural preservation district. School officials decided not to renovate Charlevoix's existing high school, citing a preference for a single-floor facility and a need for athletic fields and parking space. Relevant to community growth concerns, however, was the fact that an $18.5 million bond for the project would underwrite a three-mile sewer and water extension to the new site. Local manufacturers and a developer planning an 80-unit subdivision near the school supported the idea. But other citizens argued that the publicly funded utilities would subsidize a new wave of growth around the school and across farmland that local citizens are trying, through other land-use planning and conservation means, to protect.

Conflicts such as these are increasing in communities across Michigan as school districts respond to population pressures and as citizens react to growing evidence that sprawl costs more than many want to pay. Water quality suffers as pavement spreads, promoting flooding and pollution runoff by preventing rainfall from filtering naturally through the ground. Traffic congestion taxes family budgets and patience as Soccer Moms shuttle kids to and from school, sports, and other activities strung out across a strip development landscape. Locally owned businesses literally fall by the wayside as high-speed commerce demands the neon-name recognition and marketing savvy that only big-box franchises can afford.

When writing your proposal, try to define the problem in such a way that it's clear that your group can actually do something to solve it. Shape problems into community organizing issues, then show how you will organize to address them. This approach links your background statement to the strategy section, where you'll lay out your organizing plan.

In this proposal, action steps include additional research, community forums to discuss the findings, policy recommendations, and hands-on technical assistance for communities dealing with school relocation issues. The rationale for each of these steps is introduced in the problem statement.

Program Goals and Objectives

What do you hope to achieve with your project? Without clear goals and definite, measurable objectives, you will have a much harder time winning grants (and knowing when your organization has achieved success).

Goals restate the need your group seeks to address. Here's an example for the fictional Metropolis Food Bank: "We aim to end hunger in Metropolis by the year 2010." Depending on the nature of the project, your goals may be covered in your organizational history portion, but it's helpful to restate them in this section of the proposal.

Objectives are outcomes. The most clearly stated objectives can be measured: "We plan to provide food service to five thousand families this year." These should not be confused with methods (see the next section), which describe how you will meet these objectives. In the food bank example, methods could include distributing government surplus foods, gleaning crops from local farms, giving out holiday food baskets, and organizing a meals-on-wheels program.

Some grantwriting instructors emphasize the need to describe your goals, objectives, and methods separately in your proposal, and they've created exercises and workbooks to help you sort those out. While I support this impulse in the interest of clarity, it makes me a bit nervous. I'm reminded of kids who don't want their peas and mashed potatoes to touch each other on the dinner plate. I've seen people waste a lot of time fretting about these categories.

As discussed in Chapter Four, the best proposals serve as road maps to help you get from here (your problem) to there (your solution). The goal is your destination, objectives serve as mileage signs you pass along the way to help measure your progress, and methods are your modes of travel. You're the driver, so the map should be drawn in your own handwriting. Many fine proposals describe the applicant's goals, objectives, and methods in one discussion. If it works—if the reader understands where you're going and how you plan to get there—then you've done your job.

Some proposal writers choose to organize their work in outline form: under each goal are several objectives, and beneath each objective are several methods and tactics relating to that objective. Here's a fine example from the OutVote Project of the Milwaukee LGBT Community Center, which works to increase voter participation among the city's lesbian, gay, bisexual, and transgender community.

**MILWAUKEE LGBT COMMUNITY CENTER—
PROGRAM GOALS AND OBJECTIVES**

Goal I: Increase the numbers of self-identified LGBT voters in elections, particularly for state and local legislative bodies that have critical impact on the lives of LGBT people, through a nonpartisan voter registration and "get-out-the-vote" (GOTV) campaign. The campaign will target the Spring 2003 Supreme Court, circuit court, and special elections, as well as the Spring 2004 Milwaukee Mayoral and County Executive races. The Spring 2004 races will feature the first competitive election for Mayor since 1988, and a hot contest for County Executive. Work in 2003 through Spring 2004 will also lay the groundwork for the Fall 2004 elections, where national organizations are already targeting Wisconsin as a battleground state in the Presidential contest.

Objective 1: Expand the universe of LGBT identified voters from 2,800 to 5,000 by April, 2004.

The LGBT Center's voter file of LGBT-identified constituents (with voting history and districts) created for the OutVote 2002 campaign will be expanded with tactics including:

A. Registering nonvoters in a campaign at LGBT bars in Milwaukee (new for 2003). This will require deputizing more volunteer voter registrars.

B. Collecting "I pledge to vote" cards distributed at a greater number of places where LGBT people congregate.

C. Collecting these voter pledge cards at dozens of LGBT community events, including PrideFest and AIDS Walk Wisconsin.

D. Improving the on-line voter pledge drive by increasing Web traffic with visits to chat rooms and possible Web advertising.

E. Acquiring constituent names from one to three allied LGBT organizations to add to the voter file.

This section is effective for a number of reasons:

• The goal is broad, but also clear and achievable.

• The objective is measurable—increase LGBT voters from 2,800 to 5,000—and time-limited—by April 2004. (The full proposal outlines several objectives; I've included one here.)

• The methods (tactics) are specific and provide a variety of outreach and organizing opportunities.

Many community organizations struggle to develop measurable objectives. There are several reasons for this—after all, certain aspects of social justice work are hard to measure—but the most troubling may be a desire to avoid accountability. A grant is a contract; by putting numbers on paper, you commit your organization to certain targets. After the grant period ends and the money is spent, you will be judged, in part, on how well you met those numerical goals.

The following excerpt from the Bus Riders Union, a project of the Labor/Community Strategy Center, tackles this problem head on. By attaching a number to each objective, the authors are saying, "We know our work, we know our constituency, we know what's feasible, and we have the energy and the skill to accomplish what we set out to do." This takes guts. The numbers inspire confidence.

BUS RIDERS UNION—PROGRAM GOALS AND OBJECTIVES

2003 Objectives (a more detailed organizing plan for these objectives is further below)

- **200 expansion buses to reduce overcrowding.** We will use the U.S. Supreme Court victory to jumpstart the Special Master's mediation on the bus overcrowding provisions of the Consent Decree to win those buses in order to meet the requirement of "no more than eight people standing on a bus" during peak hours.

- **500 expansion buses for new service.** While these will be won over the next several years, we will begin to use the Supreme Court victory to develop a three-year legal and organizing campaign around another Consent Decree pillar—the requirement for new, expanded county-wide express bus service.

- **200 new, unionized mechanics and drivers hired.** While this would be a major economic justice victory, it represents only 15 percent of the new hires that will result if we can win all the overcrowding and new service expansion buses over the next several years.

- **Stop fare increases and service cuts; fight for a $20 pass and 50-cent fare.** The MTA kicked off 2003 with its most aggressive efforts in eight years to raise fares and make massive service cuts. This is another result of the Supreme Court victory in that the MTA now realizes it will have to find major funds to meet legal requirements to expand the bus system, and yet it loathes to cut any of its cash-cow rail projects. The fare reductions will be multiyear objectives, as we build the mass base and popular expectation that increased fare subsidies are both a right and winnable goal.

- **Recruit 100 student members; win a $10 accessible student pass.** Again, while we will recruit this number of new youth members in the next year, winning the pass reduction will be part of a multiple-year campaign that has tremendous organizing potential.

- **Recruit 50 new Korean members.** Our new (and first) Korean staff organizer, Daniel Kim, as well as the one or more Korean organizers-in-training recruited to the organizing school from July through December, will be able to solidify the BRU's new Korean membership, leadership, and trilingual organizational culture.
- **Recruit 300 additional new BRU members.** Expanding BRU membership will be critical to winning the other objectives listed here for 2003 and beyond.

These objectives address two important aspects of their work: their issues—buses, jobs, fares—and building the strength of the organization—membership recruitment, constituency development. By explicitly setting internal goals, the Bus Riders Union shows a lot of savvy. Any organization can take on a transit agency, but only a strong, self-sufficient group can take on a big metropolitan transit agency and win. By setting benchmarks for membership growth and leadership development, the BRU is positioning itself for the long haul.

Strategy and Implementation (also called Methods, Tactics, or Activities)

Now that you've defined what you're going to do, how are you going to do it? This is the nuts-and-bolts portion of the proposal where you explain your detailed plan for creating change. Show the funder that you've thought through all possible action scenarios and that you're prepared to control the project and not be controlled by it.

For many funders, this section can make or break a proposal. "You know what concerns me?" asks Hubert Sapp, currently of the Hartford Foundation and former director of the Highlander Center. "A big fat package with no strategy. There's nothing to hold it together." Shelley Davis adds, "It's important to be able to articulate your strategy. When you don't do it well, it's harder [for me] to advocate on your behalf."

As mentioned earlier, it's acceptable to combine your goals, objectives, and activities into one section. For example, see the work plan from Strategic Actions for a Just Economy in Exhibit 7.4. It encompasses goals, objectives, and strategies in one piece. Notice that under "Activities/Strategies," the authors mix objectives ("Organize ten new tenant associations," "Help five hundred residents establish bank accounts") with a summary of how they will achieve these objectives—and it works.

EXHIBIT 7.4

Strategic Actions for a Just Economy Work Plan

GOALS, OBJECTIVES, AND STRATEGIES: 2003–2004 WORK PLAN

The following work plan describes SAJE's goals, activities and strategies over the next two years.

Goals	Activities/Strategies
Stop displacement and increase community control. Preserve affordable and healthy housing in the Figueroa Corridor by stopping the trend towards gentrification and displacement and creating a truly income-integrated community.	• Hold weekly tenants rights workshops. • Provide legal assistance and representation for unfair eviction cases. • Organize ten new tenant associations. • Establish Displacement Free Zone. • Research and implement strategies to take buildings off the speculative market (through land trusts, non-profit and resident ownership). • Investigate potential of high profile litigation against a major slumlord. • Systematically bring together dust wipe samples and blood tests collected by Esperanza's health promoters with photos and letters generated by organizers; ensure that all children in buildings we are working in are tested for lead.
Change city redevelopment policy to provide protections and substantial benefits to poor and homeless residents. Create a redevelopment policy that can serve as a model for the entire city and nation.	• Organize a strategic media campaign to advance our Share the Wealth platform city-wide. • Develop joint strategy and plan of action with homeless residents through work with the L.A. Coalition to End Hunger & Homelessness, the L.A. Community Action Network, and the Downtown Women's Action Center. • Organize six tenant unions in the City Center redevelopment plan area; train leaders in organizing and negotiating skills and provide popular education on policy alternatives. • Create political and media pressure for the community redevelopment agency to settle its lawsuit with the L.A. Coalition to End Hunger and Homelessness in a manner that advances our policy agenda. • Link redevelopment issues to displacement issues through our media strategy. • Force CRA and planning commissions to have dialogue with residents, the Coalition, and organizational allies.
Establish the Figueroa Corridor Community Jobs Program. Residents of the Figueroa Corridor will begin to prepare for the 2,500 living wages jobs negotiated with the L.A. Arena Land Company, as well as other employment opportunities.	• Establish a Figueroa Corridor Jobs Collaborative designed to connect current low-income residents with jobs generated by the L.A. Arena Land Company agreement. • Pilot the Figueroa Corridor Jobs Program. • Integrate financial literacy and home ownership training into the Figueroa Corridor Jobs Program.

EXHIBIT 7.4 *(continued)*

Strategic Actions for a Just Economy Work Plan

Goals	Activities/Strategies
Increase financial opportunities for immigrants, people on welfare, and other low-income people in the Figueroa Corridor. Residents will establish bank accounts, financial management skills, and savings vehicles that will prepare them for home ownership and educational opportunities.	• Provide financial literacy training and outreach to two thousand people, beginning with organizational members of the Figueroa Corridor Coalition such as HERE Local 11, Esperanza Community Housing, St. John's Well Child Center, and the St. Francis Center. • Help five hundred residents establish bank accounts that will assist them in moving from fringe to mainstream banking. • Ensure that electronic benefit transfer policy is fair and affordable to people on welfare. • Integrate financial access into jobs and housing efforts. • Coordinate access to IDA accounts for housing and educational opportunities.
Implement the L.A. Land Arena agreement in a manner that builds community economic development and organization in the Figueroa Corridor.	• **Jobs**—Use the L.A. Land Arena's $100,000 commitment to build and pilot a Figueroa Corridor community jobs program. • **Housing**—Direct benefits of agreement to displaced residents and our Displacement Free Zone neighborhood. • **Parks**—Monitor development of at least one park in the Figueroa Corridor. • **Parking**—Develop L.A.'s first poor people's permit parking to benefit our members who live across from the Staples Center. • **Displaced residents**—Reopen the cases of fifty families who were displaced by the original Staples Center and obtain long-term affordable housing for them.

This chart is a model of brevity. In a little more than one page, it outlines the full range of their ambitious, dynamic programs. We know what they plan to do, how they plan to do it, whom they plan to do it with, and what results they expect to achieve. Study this model. If you can describe your own work this succinctly, you will endear yourself to grant reviewers.

Timeline

It's useful to include a timeline indicating when your objectives will be met. A straightforward list of deadlines or benchmarks will also give you an easy way to measure your progress once you begin the project. You can build your timeline into your strategy section or create a separate timeline that stands alone.

Two examples follow. Each proposal outlines a year's worth of activities; I've included a portion of each. The first is from the Little White Buffalo Project, which works to ensure that urban Native American youth are connected to their Lakota language and culture.

LITTLE WHITE BUFFALO PROJECT—TIMELINE

NOVEMBER THROUGH FEBRUARY

Work on storytelling project with participating youth. Have a program potluck and monthly incentives. Have one beaded earring and one shawl-making workshop. Continue with after-school program with a short holiday break from physical program; this time is used for concentrated administration. Provide youth with holiday food baskets for both holidays. Seek out resources to provide youth with winter coats. Host a Traditional and Cultural Foods workshop. Implement holiday youth and elder adoption project. Host a community feed and *wacipi* (powwow, or dance). Research grants and continue fundraising. Enhance program development, perform administration and bookkeeping maintenance. Seek out technical training.

The second timeline was prepared by the Montana Wilderness Association, which was founded to help protect Montana's wildlands.

MONTANA WILDERNESS ASSOCIATION—TIMELINE

JANUARY 1–MARCH 31, 2003

- Recruit and educate members and activists for participation in the Travel Plan process on Lewis and Clark National Forest.
- Broaden support for limiting motorized use on the Rocky Mountain Front through public outreach.
- Collaborate with Blackfeet Nation tribal leaders and members to build support for protecting lands along the Front, including the Badger–Two Medicine area.
- Develop media contacts and educate those contacts regarding current threats; meet with editorial boards of local and regional newspapers.
- Develop informational materials and publications; circulate among members of coalition and supporters and collaborators.
- Execute intensive organizing effort to educate and mobilize membership.

Both excerpts are competently done—they're comprehensive, specific, and ambitious. Simply by putting tasks on a calendar, these groups demonstrate their commitment to follow-through. They also enjoy a competitive advantage, since most grantseekers lack the focus or courage to map out an entire year. The two presentation strategies are nearly identical, with one difference: the layout. As you can see, the bulleted list is easier to navigate. Always look for opportunities to break up the page and create more visual variety for the reader.

Evaluation

How will you know if you succeed? How will you measure your success or failure? How will you use what you've learned? Your evaluation section is the place where "the difference" that you've made is defined, counted, and weighed.

Your evaluation plan should be designed to measure the success of each of your objectives, so it's useful if the objectives are stated in measurable terms. Design your project to generate some numbers when the grant period is over: people served, increase in membership, performances staged, neighborhood houses renovated, newsletters distributed, acres protected—whatever relates to your program goals. Find a way to quantify the results of your work.

It's OK to include a few subjective items, but if all your evaluation points are subjective—"We will work to make people feel more secure"—you'll have a difficult time judging your success. Of course, you can always survey your constituents about how they're feeling when the project is over; just make sure to set numerical goals for the number of questionnaires you distribute and collect.

An excerpt from the Western Prison Project follows. By putting a lot of thought into creating evaluation criteria, the authors have made a good start.

WESTERN PRISON PROJECT—EVALUATION

We will assess our work by looking at both our process and our specific outcomes. In this way, we can measure our success at meeting our objectives, assess our responsiveness to our core constituencies, and help lay the framework for future activity.

Criteria for assessing our outcomes include:

- The number of groups participating in the Oregon Criminal Justice Reform Coalition
- The number of individuals participating in the action alert network in Oregon
- The number of criminal justice reforms instituted in Oregon as a result of our efforts

- The number of new members joining the Western Prison Project
- The number of organizations that join the regional coalition and work on at least one prison-related issue
- Increased skills demonstrated by participants in WPP trainings
- Number of former offenders and their families registering to vote as a result of the VOICE project

Criteria for assessing our process include:

- Did we develop internal structures and processes that facilitate participation in the organization by all of our targeted constituencies?
- Were our outreach strategies effective in recruiting new members/activists/ organizations into our work?
- Were our outreach strategies accessible and meaningful, as defined by our target constituencies?
- Were we successful in building the skills of our base and developing new leaders throughout the region?

Here's where the proposal falls short: while it's nearly impossible to quantify process—so no numbers are included there—this proposal hedges a bit on quantifying outcomes. For example, success will be measured by "The number of groups participating in the Oregon Criminal Justice Reform Coalition." As a grant reviewer, I'd want to know how many groups would be a good result—ten? twenty? fifty? The proposal doesn't give us any indication.

When you set your own evaluation benchmarks and include the numbers, funders must judge your work on your own terms. You control the definition of success. If you neglect the numbers—indeed, if you skip the evaluation component entirely—then the grantmaker has a lot more leeway in assessing your success or failure. Do you really want someone outside your group setting the standards for how you'll be evaluated?

Personnel

Provide one-paragraph biographies of the main project organizers or key volunteers. Some foundations request full résumés, in which case these biographical sketches are unnecessary.

A simple but effective personnel section can be found in Chapter Eight as part of the Hate Free Zone Campaign of Washington's proposal to the Threshold Foundation.

Budgets

Unless you're submitting a request for general support, you'll need two budgets: one for the featured project, another showing the annual budget for the entire organization. For some grant reviewers, the budgets are the most important pages in the grant application. Many otherwise fine proposals don't get funded because the financial documents are unclear or unrealistic.

"We find that a lot of groups need help with the budget," says Gaye Evans of the Appalachian Community Fund. "Most people working in nonprofits and community organizing don't have a background in financial management. We offer help, but it's rare that groups take us up on it." Ron White adds, "Sometimes the numbers don't add up. You'd be surprised how often this happens—perhaps in 15 percent of the proposals I see." Note to proposal writers: Always double-check your math.

Budgets should include two sections: expenses (how you're going to spend it) and revenue or income (how you plan to raise it). It's acceptable to round most line items to the nearest $100 or $500, though you can certainly estimate costs to the nearest dollar if that seems appropriate. For most projects, ten to fifteen expense lines are plenty. I've seen small budgets handled adequately with five or six line items.

In many cases, you'll need to piece together funding from a variety of sources to pay for the total cost of a project. Let the grantmaker know the status of your fundraising: how much project revenue is in hand, pledged, and sought.

Because some of your proposals will be turned down, it's acceptable to show that you've applied for more funding than you need; be sure to include a sentence at the bottom of the budget page stating that you don't expect to receive full funding from all sources. Rather than make you look greedy, this indicates you're serious about raising enough money to complete the work.

If you're applying for partial funding from a specific funder—for example, you're seeking $10,000 toward a $25,000 project budget—the foundation might want to know which line items it is being asked to underwrite. The project budget from the Canadian Parks and Wilderness Society's Yukon Chapter, shown in Exhibit 7.5, suggests a nice format for handling this type of request. However, assigning line items can really complicate your bookkeeping, so avoid it if possible.

Many grantmakers are also interested in your long-range fundraising plan. What happens to the project at the end of the grant period? Is it designed to achieve a goal and shut down? If not, will you seek alternate funding, absorb the project costs into your general budget, or let it die? Grants are known as "soft money" because they are seldom renewable. Even if you don't submit a long-range funding plan with your proposal, it wouldn't hurt to develop one for internal use.

Next, let's talk about the big picture: your organizational budget. Always submit an organizational budget for the current year, based on projected

EXHIBIT 7.5

Canadian Parks and Wilderness Society Project Budget

Task	Budget Amount	Proposal to Brainerd	Other Funding Sources
Contract local consultant to work with the community to set up and design the economics study	$1,500		$1,500 (CPAWS-Yukon, in hand)
Contract economist to design the study and oversee the survey and report production	$20,000	$5,000	$10,000 (CPAWS-Yukon, in hand) $5,000 (proposal to Yukon Gov't invited)
Contract community assistant in Haines Junction to assist with survey	$3,500		$3,500 (Walter & Duncan Gordon Foundation)
Produce and distribute two hundred copies of the report	$2,500		$2,250 (CPAWS-Yukon, in hand) $250 (Walter & Duncan Gordon Foundation)
Travel and project expenses, administration	$2,500		$2,500 (CPAWS-Yukon, in hand)
Total Project Budget	**$30,000.00**	**$5,000**	**$25,000**

income and expenses. If appropriate, include a brief budget narrative describing any line items that might seem curious to an outsider.

Many funders also ask to review the previous year's financial statements; these are drawn from real numbers, not projections.

If your organization raises and spends more than $500,000 a year, consider getting an audited financial statement. You can hire a certified public accountant (CPA) to review your books and verify that you're handling the money in an appropriate way. Some CPAs specialize in working with nonprofits, and as part of the audit will give you advice about how to improve your bookkeeping. Your audited financial statement can then serve as "last year's budget" when you include it with your grant proposals.

Audits normally cost $3,000 to $10,000, but you might be able to negotiate a discount if the accountant is supportive of your work. According to trainer and author Terry Miller (1992, pp. 113-114), if you receive federal grants (or federal money passed through your state or local government), you should expect to pay twice as much for an audit, since government accounting standards are so rigorous. In fact, Miller suggests that you hire a CPA before applying for federal grants to review your accounting procedures and make sure you can handle the reporting requirements.

Exhibit 7.6 presents an annual budget from Big Creek People in Action. Several aspects of this budget caught my attention:

- The variety of ways they raise money: from government, foundations, corporations, faith institutions, individuals, events, and other sources, too. They're trying everything! Just by looking at the budget, you can tell this is an energetic, creative organization.

- The "status" column is divided into four categories, which indicates good planning and at least a basic level of record keeping.

  - *Received:* money in the bank.

  - *Committed:* they have a written agreement—a contract, grant letter, or other document. (For budgeting purposes, oral commitments don't count.)

  - *Pending:* the application has been submitted; no decision yet.

  - *Projected:* the proposal deadline is on the calendar and the application will be submitted.

- They saved enough money to carry over $37,500 from the previous year. This probably represents restricted grant money for projects not yet completed, but it's still evidence of careful financial management.

- Based on expenses, they are clearly doing a lot of work with a limited amount of money. A bit more detail here might be useful. For example, it would be helpful to know which employees are full time or part time, since it is unlikely they can hire eleven full-time people for $171,000 per year.

Attachments

Funders sometimes require you to include extra materials with your grant proposal. The most commonly requested items are the following:

- A copy of your Internal Revenue Service tax-exemption letter or Canadian equivalent. (If you don't have tax-exempt status and are using a fiscal sponsor, attach their IRS letter and a note on their letterhead, signed by the sponsor, explaining that they will be handling the money.)

- A list of your board members or brief biographical notes about your board.

- A current brochure or newsletter.

EXHIBIT 7.6

Big Creek People in Action Annual Budget

FY2002-03 PROJECTED INCOME

Funding Sources	Amount	Status
Government grants and contracts	**$78,248**	
WV DOE 21st Century Learning Center	$47,911	Projected
WV Office of the Attorney General	$14,947	Pending
WV DOE Nutrition Program	$3,470	Projected
McDowell County Commission	$10,000	Projected
WV Department of Agriculture	$1,000	Committed
WV Division of Culture & History	$917	Projected
Foundations	**$50,500**	
Bonner Foundation	$7,500	Received
Appalachian Community Fund	$7,500	Projected
ACF/Seize the Moment	$8,500	Received
Tides Foundation	$25,000	Received
WV Literacy Foundation	$1,000	Committed
WV Laubach Literacy	$1,000	Committed
Corporate	**$1,600**	
Verizon	$600	Projected
Wal-Mart	$1,000	Committed
Religious Institutions	**$11,050**	
Commission on Religion in Appalachia	$6,300	Committed
Christian Appalachian Fund	$4,750	Projected
Individual Contributions	**$9,681**	
General Donations	$1,500	Projected
College, Church & Other Work Groups	$8,181	Projected
Special Events	**$7,170**	
Fall & Spring Festivals	$2,418	Projected
Music Festival	$2,982	Projected
Facility Rental	$1,770	Projected
Other Income/Fee-for-Service	**$85,078**	
WV DHHR/Child care	$36,674	Projected
Child Care/Private Pay	$2,072	Projected
Just Connections/LSA & ACA	$26,500	Received
APPALREAD	$1,500	Projected
WV Humanities Council	$1,854	Committed
Safe & Drug Free Communities	$5,067	Committed
Other—Interest, Reimbursements, etc.	$11,411	Projected
2001-02 Carryover	**$37,500**	Received
Total	**$280,824**	

EXHIBIT 7.6 *(continued)*

Big Creek People in Action Annual Budget

FY2002-03 PROJECTED EXPENSES

Line Item Expense	Amount
Personnel Wages & Fringe Benefits	**$171,276**
Executive Director; Bookkeeper; Strong Families Program Director; Early Education Teacher; two Assistant Teachers; Substitute Teacher; Driver/Maintenance; Learning Coordinator; Youth Coordinator; Community-Based Research Coordinator	
Renovation/Repairs	**$10,000**
Program Costs	**$99,548**
Travel	$5,975
Training	$2,000
Equipment	$5,172
Supplies	$22,763
Telephone/Fax	$5,023
Postage/Delivery	$742
Rent/Utilities	$9,992
Maintenance	$3,833
Memberships	$90
Licenses, Permits	$135
Advertising	$600
Insurance	$3,206
Financial Management-Audit	$3,150
Special Events	$6,546
Collaborative Projects:	$30,321
APPALREAD, CWEP/JOIN, Just Connections, Arts & Culture, Education Extension	
Total	**$280,824**

The key phrase is "requested items." If you take one final message from this chapter, let it be this: include only what they ask for, because foundation officers hate to receive big piles of unsolicited stuff. The staff members of the Common Counsel Foundation get frustrated, they say, "when groups send thick, glossy, expensive materials that may be thrown away . . . especially environmental groups." Adds Joni Craig, "Attachments are extremely annoying—especially when you have to prepare dozens of applications for duplication and some have trifold brochures, videos, newspapers, and other awkward materials. You can't exactly drop them off at a copy shop that way, and removing all the unsolicited stuff is extremely time-consuming."

Let me repeat: do your homework and send only what's requested. Occasionally, you will be given the option of enclosing whatever you think is most relevant. Be judicious. In my experience, there are a few very effective attachments:

One or two recent press clippings. Select articles and editorials that have a direct bearing on your proposed project. Do not send your entire news file. As an alternative, you can summarize your best press on a one-page "quote sheet," as Alabama Arise/Arise Citizens' Policy Project has.

ALABAMA ARISE—ATTACHMENTS

THE VIRGINIA PILOT—2/21/2003

In Alabama they're asking, "How would Jesus tax?"
"Suddenly in Alabama it's a sin to soak the poor while shielding the wealthy. Until this year, that wasn't a sin; it was the longstanding official state policy."

WALL STREET JOURNAL—2/12/2003

"For nearly a century, reformers have tried in vain to change this state's antiquated tax structure. The Alabama code requires families of four earning as little as $4,600 to pay income tax, the nation's lowest threshold. It charges a higher sales tax on baby formula than on cattle feed and permits timber interests to pay relatively meager property taxes compared with homeowners."

BALTIMORE SUN—EDITORIAL 6/16/2003

"Every state in the union is facing difficult, if not disastrous, financial problems. But one of them, Alabama, has chosen to use the emergency as an opportunity."

CHICAGO SUN TIMES—6/14/2003

There's no excuse for failure to reform state tax system
"Where can Illinois look for guidance on generating the political will to solve its problems? For starters, try Alabama."

THE NEW YORK TIMES—6/10/2003
(REPRINTED IN *THE COURIER-JOURNAL—6/15/2003*)
Editorial Observer; What Would Jesus Do? Sock It to Alabama's Corporate Landowners

"If Riley's crusade succeeds this summer, Alabama may offer the nation a model for a new kind of tax system: one where the Devil is not in the details."

THE NEW YORK TIMES—6/3/2003

G.O.P. Chief's Idea for Raising Alabama: Taxes

"In one fell swoop, it seems, Mr. Riley is trying to overhaul what many here in Montgomery acknowledge is one of the nation's most dysfunctional state governments, and drag Alabama's finances, schools and prisons into the 21st century—if not, some might say, the 20th."

Testimonials or letters of support. Material from your clients or cooperating organizations can be excerpted and used in the body of your proposal, as the Hate Free Zone Campaign of Washington has done (see Chapter Eight). You can also create a "quote sheet" for testimonials. Here's an example from SouthWings; their motto is "Conservation through aviation."

SOUTHWINGS—ATTACHMENTS

A SAMPLING OF WHAT OTHERS HAVE SAID ABOUT SOUTHWINGS:

"We are so thankful to SouthWings for the work you do, to bring attention to the profound destruction of the forests in this region. I found myself weeping over the earth, looking down. Thank you for carrying us up. Thank you for hanging on to your hope."

—Janisse Ray, author, Georgia

"SouthWings has allowed us to see more in two and a half hours than we would have been able to do on foot in ten years. Now we have a better understanding of where the problems are coming from. A great way to get the big picture!"

—Ken Robinson, Friends of Hurricane Creek, Alabama

"I never would have located the exact point of these discharges without SouthWings' help."

—Leaf Myczack, Tennessee Riverkeeper

"The article would have fallen flat without the perspective of flight."

—Ted Williams, *Audubon* Magazine

Exercise 7.1 provides some ideas for how to solicit good quotes and statements of support.

Collecting Testimonials

Among your many fundraising assets, the voices of your constituents are perhaps the most potent. Nothing in fundraising trumps a good story. To be effective grantseekers, we must collect stories and retell them with passion and commitment.

Here's a suggestion: Go to the people you work with—your members, leaders, collaborators, constituents, allies, neighbors, the folks who benefit from your work—and ask them a question:

"What difference does our work make in your life?"

Feel free to rephrase this question any way you like, but the essence must be: How do people feel about the work, and how do they perceive the benefits of the work?

Write down or record the responses. If you hear a compelling story, ask permission to use it. Insert these quotes into your grant proposals, brochures, news releases, annual report, membership appeals, and so on. For an example, take a look at the Hate Free Zone Campaign of Washington proposal in Chapter Eight.

Grassroots Grants, 2nd edition, by Andy Robinson. Copyright © 2004 by Andy Robinson.

Maps. Maps are especially useful for organizations whose work can be represented geographically. For example, a map is incorporated in the Wildlands Project proposal in Chapter Eight. You can use maps to visually present a variety of issues—for example,

- Neighborhoods in your community that are dealing with substandard housing, or air pollution from the local factory, or discriminatory lending ("red-lining"), or gentrification.

- Public lands you are working to protect from logging, mining, motorized recreation, and the like.

- Private land you plan to purchase for your daycare center, or affordable housing project, or environmental education center, and how this location relates to the needs of your clients.

- Loss of farmland due to unregulated development.

- The ways in which public transit does a poor job of serving low-income communities.

Photographs, where appropriate. Choose action pictures that demonstrate your work—volunteers cleaning up an abandoned house, protesters picketing the public utilities commission, children studying wildlife in the woods. Skip the boring snapshots of your annual awards dinner or board members sitting around a table. Though most funders don't want your videos, they often encourage photos, which take a lot less time to view. Figure out ways tell your story visually.

Cover Letter

The cover letter (not to be confused with the cover page and executive summary) is the first thing that emerges from the envelope, but the last thing you write. This letter serves as a friendly introduction and helps to establish rapport between you and your foundation contact. When you write it, make sure to follow these steps:

1. Remind the reader of any previous communication or relationship between your organization and the funder. Here are some typical opening sentences:

   "Thanks for taking the time to meet with me to discuss our community organizing programs."

   "Last year, your foundation provided a $____ grant to underwrite our successful community outreach efforts. With the enclosed proposal, we seek your renewed support."

   "We submit this proposal with the encouragement of Ms. Goodpeer, who thought you might be interested in our work."

2. State how much money you're requesting.

3. Describe—briefly—the mission of your organization and why the featured project is essential to your work.

4. If you wish, explain how your proposal meets the foundation's guidelines and interests. If you've done your homework and carefully screened the funder, the fit should be self-evident. Nonetheless, some foundations want to hear you talk about why you chose them.

5. Offer to provide additional information, if needed, and suggest a site visit at which foundation staff and board can see your work firsthand.

Keep your cover letter brief. One page is preferable, two pages are acceptable. Never include any important information that is not covered elsewhere in the main proposal. Here's why: Your proposal will likely be photocopied for distribution to the grant reviewers; don't assume that the letter will be copied and passed along as part of the package.

EXHIBIT 7.7

Sample Cover Letter

CANADIAN PARKS AND WILDERNESS SOCIETY

YUKON CHAPTER

January 15, 2001

Ms. Ann Krumboltz,
Brainerd Foundation,
1601 Second Avenue,
Seattle, Washington, 98101

Dear Ann,

Thank you for inviting the Yukon Chapter of the Canadian Parks and Wilderness Society to submit a proposal to the Brainerd Foundation for project support in the Year 2001. We have identified three priority projects for our grant proposal:

- Facilitate northern conservation leadership training and Environmental Non-Government Organization capacity building, in cooperation with TREC;
- Develop a local CPAWS-Yukon web site to feature public education on northern conservation, along with our specific conservation research, maps and protected area proposals;
- Undertake a study of the economic impacts of Kluane National Park on the community of Haines Junction, and use the results to foster support in other communities for implementing the Yukon Protected Areas Strategy.

These projects are in support of the core CPAWS-Yukon mission:

- To protect the Yukon's wilderness and wildlife through an interconnected system of protected areas;
- To promote awareness, understanding and enjoyment of the inherent values of Yukon wildlands through education and experience;
- To encourage all levels of government to fulfill their conservation and protected area commitments;
- To work in co-operation with other organizations and individuals in meeting conservation goals.

Our three project proposals are described separately in order of priority, with a common appendix outlining our organizational status. For each of the three projects, we are requesting matching funding from the Brainerd Foundation to supplement in-hand and pending funds.

Thank you for considering this proposal.

Yours sincerely,

Juri Peepre
Executive Director, CPAWS-Yukon

Box 31095, Whitehorse, YT, Y1A 5P7 (Mailing)
209 Lowe Street, Whitehorse, YT, Y1A 1W5 (Delivery)

Phone: 867-393-8080
Fax: 867-393-8081
Email: cpaws@yknet.yk.ca

A cover letter from the Canadian Parks and Wilderness Society's Yukon Chapter appears in Exhibit 7.7. Notice how in just one page, this letter thanks the funder for inviting a proposal, summarizes the proposed projects, links them directly to the organization's mission, and lets the reader know that partial funding has already been raised for these projects. The tone is straightforward and professional. The only thing missing is a clear "ask"; how much is the total request?

There you have it: all the pieces of a successful grant proposal. In Chapter Eight I'll analyze four complete proposals and discuss what makes them work.

chapter

8

A Tour Through Four Winning Proposals

What grabs my attention? Strong goals and a strategy that makes sense; identifying your audience and thinking through the best approach for reaching them and getting them to act.

—ANN KRUMBOLTZ, Brainerd Foundation

Clarity plus entertainment is the best combination.

—DAVID KAROFF, Rhode Island Foundation

We all need role models. On the following pages you'll find four successful proposals. They're each different in tone, writing style, constituency, issue, and format—and they all work. As you will see, there are many "right ways" to do this job.

These proposals are well written and well organized, but, just as important, the projects they describe are interesting and provide good fundraising handles. Therefore, my comments address both what makes the proposals effective and what makes the programs compelling.

"A good portion of grantmaking is subjective," says Irene Vlach of the Lazar Foundation. "It's not a science, it's an art. There's no black and white." If grant reviewers are operating, to some degree, on instinct, then we grantseekers need to develop the same kinds of instincts. To serve as true feasibility testers, we must have the skill to judge the fundability of the work before investing a lot time writing the grant application. In other words, why create a technically superb proposal for a dull, seen-it-before program? More than likely, it won't get funded.

By analyzing the applications in this chapter, you can begin to develop your own sense about what makes a proposal effective. I will walk you through each one, page by page, offering praise and suggestions for improvement. As you read, keep track of your reactions. What gets your attention? What makes you uncomfortable? Do you have questions about the group or the project that haven't been addressed? What can you borrow and adapt for your own work?

APPLICATION FORM

DATE: August 26, 2002
NAME OF APPLICANT ORGANIZATION:
    URBAN GARDEN RESOURCES of WORCESTER (UGROW)
    A program of The Regional Environmental Council (REC)
CONTACT PERSON: Jonah Vitale-Wolff
DAY PHONE: (508) 799-9139
EVENING PHONE:
FAX: (508) 799-9147
ADDRESS:
172 Shrewsbury Street 3rd Floor
Worcester, MA 01604
EMAIL: ugrow@recworcester.org

AMOUNT OF THIS REQUEST: $2,500

TOTAL PROJECT BUDGET: $40,475

TOTAL ORGANIZATIONAL BUDGET: $127,300

PROJECT PROPOSAL

Urban Garden Resources of Worcester (UGROW) is a grassroots program that began developing community gardens throughout the city of Worcester in 1995 under the leadership of Nancy Wilcox, a long time gardener who had a knack for inspiring and teaching others. There were four garden sites the first year, and word quickly spread. In 1997 the Greater Worcester Community Foundation encouraged GROW, as it was named at the time, to merge with the Regional Environmental Council in order to take advantage of complementary skills and resources. REC was an established organization with administrative systems in place and a connection to the community. UGROW continues as a project of REC with a separate mission statement and separate budget. UGROW currently has a presence in two dozen sites with over 300 gardening participants, hundreds of excited volunteers, and an advisory committee composed of people representing a diverse cross section of Worcester's communities.

UGROW focuses its energy on inner-city and underprivileged communities that would otherwise lack the access to greenspace or resources to start community gardens. Community activists and UGROW have worked together to successfully reclaim, revitalize and transform derelict vacant lots into publicly accessible green space that once were site of litter, drug activity and violence. Inner-city neighborhoods, public-housing groups, youth groups, mentally and physically disabled, schools, and elderly housing define communities that compose the UGROW network. UGROW links all of the gardens in a cohesive network encouraging exchange of skills and ideas.

Urban Garden Resources of Worcester (UGROW)

I'm not a big fan of acronyms, but UGROW is a great name. Some groups begin with the acronym and then struggle to find the words that fit; this name feels more natural.

This proposal was submitted to the New England Grassroots Environment Fund, also known as NEGEF. It follows NEGEF's standard format, which at the time limited applications to four pages. In the interest of preserving privacy, the home phone number of a board member has been deleted.

Project Proposal

Like most effective proposals, this one begins with a story. It's a founding story about someone "who had a knack for inspiring and teaching others." Note the informal narrative style—you could almost substitute the words "Once upon a time . . . "

It's interesting that this merger was recommended by a local foundation. After five years, the experiment has proved a success. The pitch here is efficiency through sharing "complementary skills and resources," which indicates that the grant will be used efficiently.

Given Worcester's size (not too big) and UGROW's budget (really small), the scale of their work—two dozen sites, three hundred gardeners, and so forth—is impressive. From a funder's perspective, this looks like a lot of impact for a modest price.

Referring to their work in the third person—"UGROW" instead of "we"—is a bit disconcerting, especially in such an informal proposal. The transition could be, "At UGROW, we focus . . . "

Strong language—"reclaim, revitalize, and transform"—is linked to strong visual imagery. This phrase could serve as their motto.

By listing the many constituencies involved with UGROW, the authors begin to establish the scope of their work, build credibility, and define themselves in terms of collaboration.

The grant will be used to partially fund the position of the UGROW Coordinator, who will:
- Provide *technical support* with education on organic agriculture and garden design.
- Organize *public educational events* that network gardeners, activists, funders, and public, such as Spring Forum and Fall Harvest Festival to share resources, skills, and ideas.
- Coordinate *garden stewards* and assist in community organizing.
- Grow and distribute *organic seedlings* to both new and existing gardens.
- Produce a quarterly *newsletter*, "Seasons in the City", written as a collaboration of volunteers and gardeners.
- Coordinate *volunteer labor* and garden workdays, including the local carpenter's union to build raised container beds, university students, and local organizations.
- Provide *soil testing* for new garden sites and periodic testing thereafter.
- Coordinate *compost* deliveries from the city.
- Coordinate *water* hookups.
- UGROW is the sole coordination entity of community gardens throughout Worcester, and continues to expand through supporting *two new garden sites* each year.

Project Outcomes

UGROW's approach to community gardening continuously benefits the natural environment and the communities living within. UGROW aims to support two new gardens each year. This is an ongoing process that transforms derelict vacant lots into safe, productive land.

UGROW encourages chemical-free agriculture to produce healthy, locally grown food. UGROW promotes and educates about organic agriculture to reduce the negative effects of poisonous pesticides and fertilizers on humans and the natural environment. Locally grown food also diminishes the need for food to transported thousands of miles that depend on fossil fuel. Vegetation in gardens contributes to lessening air pollution, which combats the problem of respiratory problems for inner-city populations, and reduces toxics in the environment.

UGROW offers four effective means for addressing the issue of lead in soils, depending on the severity. These include (1) intense composting, supported by city, (2) phyto-remediation using plants, (3) providing landscape fabric, and (4) building raised containers beds, with support of the local carpenter's union. As pat of UGROW education initiative, community gardeners are educated about the risks associated with past practices that lead to soils with lead.

The longer community gardens exist the more communities benefit and grow into a cohesive community group. Community gardens create safe public green spaces that are free of drugs, litter and violence that plague vacant lots in the inner-city. The gardens provide a space for participants to have regular physical activity. This is particularly important for seniors that run the risk sitting idle. The space also serves for community members to interact and develop solidarity around local issues. Successful garden groups become cohesive community groups that organize neighborhood cookouts, have art in the garden, and integrate children through hosting after school and summer programs.

UGROW also encourages cultural diversity and awareness through: (1) providing culturally specific plants, and (2) organizing gardens in inner-city neighborhoods of largely immigrant

The list of how the grant will be used accomplishes at least two tasks:

- It shows the scope of their work, which is incredibly comprehensive for such a small group.

- It provides a job description for the coordinator. (This raises a crucial question—can one person really do all this?)

Notice the active verbs (organize, coordinate, grow, distribute) and the simple layout tricks: indentation and careful use of bold text.

The involvement of the local carpenters' union is a nice touch. It demonstrates broad outreach, a commitment to social justice, and the good sense to know where to look for skilled labor. (Could the union could be approached for a contribution? They're not included on the donor list.)

Up to this point, I've been wondering if any other groups organize community gardens in Worcester. It appears that UGROW has the niche all to themselves, which further strengthens their pitch.

Project Outcomes

In this section, the authors describe at least four different ways that community gardens benefit people and the natural world:

The environment. This brief paragraph really nails the environmental case for urban gardens as a way to reduce greenhouse gases and the use of chemicals. As a result, they're also beneficial for humans.

Human health. The discussion of lead in the soil is also terrifically brief and simply written. The writers lapse into a bit of jargon ("phyto-remediation"), but imagine how technical this paragraph could have been.

Community building. It's not really about the food, is it?

A specific neighborhood example—a story—would make this discussion even more effective. In one paragraph, the authors could take us through the steps of how a group of neighbors got together to reclaim the lot, clear the junk, plant their gardens, and tend them all summer. Finally, they threw a big multiethnic, multigenerational harvest party in the fall with food from several cultures. This transformation process is hinted at, but a story would have even greater impact.

Cultural preservation. Since food is culture, then gardens are important for passing traditions between generations. Once again, the writing here is simple and evocative.

populations. Vietnamese and Latino cultures in Worcester come from largely agrarian-based societies in which growing food is part of everyday life. The urban landscape of Worcester poses a challenge for maintaining this integral component of cultural identity. Community gardens act as a space for multigenerational exchange of cultural ideas, skills and knowledge.

As a result of the UGROW program, more Worcester residents in marginalized communities are able to enjoy the benefits of gardening while making their communities safer, healthier, and more livable. UGROW works to gauge these benefits through: (1) encouraging feedback from gardeners through informal interviews and questionnaires, (2) the number of requests for support and new gardens, and (3) the geographical area covered by community gardens in Worcester, supported by city technicians mapping gardens with GIS.

PROJECT BUDGET

Expenses
Personnel	$33,000
Project Expenses	4,000
Administrative Expenses	3,475

Total amount your organization spent last year: $31,000

Number of employees, full and/or part-time:

Jonah Vitale-Wolff, UGROW Program Coordinator
Peggy Middaugh, Executive Director

Principal sources of support

Source	Anticipated Income Sources for 2003	2002 Support
Foundations:		
Greater Worcester Community Foundation	$10,000	$10,000
Stoddard Charitable Trust	5,000	5,000
Fletcher Foundation	5,000	5,000
UMASS Memorial	5,000	5,000
French Foundation	4,000	4,000
Other	5,575	5,575
TOTAL	$34,575	
Membership	4,000	
Major Donors	2,000	
TOTAL	**$40,575**	

This would be a fine place for a quote from a recent immigrant, describing in his or her own words what the garden means to the community.

This paragraph describes a rudimentary evaluation plan. The addition of a few numerical objectives—for example, how many requests for support would be a good result?—would make this piece stronger.

Project Budget

How do the personnel costs break down? Two employees are listed; how many hours for each are included in the budget?

Principal sources of support. It's a bit of a concern that 75 percent of their budget comes from foundations and corporations. On the other hand, a number of funders participate, which reduces the danger that the loss of a single grant will doom the project. Looking at the revenue data, several questions come to mind.

- Why isn't the funder reviewing this proposal—the New England Grassroots Environment Fund—included on the list of "anticipated income sources?"

- What's the mysterious "other"? A little more detail would be helpful.

- I also wonder about their potential for earned income. Maybe program fees? How about an urban farm stand? What about consulting income—would community garden organizers in other cities pay for their expertise? This is a lot to ask of a small staff, but anything they can do to reduce reliance on grants would be a good thing.

ORGANIZATION PROFILE

UGROW's mission is to facilitate collective grassroots efforts to reclaim greenspaces, empower neighborhoods, and strengthen community spirit, all while growing healthy food. We have been working for close to ten years supporting existing and new community gardens with groups in the inner city, such as neighborhood groups, public housing, seniors, mentally and physically disabled, youth groups, and schools. Established gardens often become a focal point of community activity, hosting regular events and meetings. UGROW promotes chemical-free diversified agriculture through educational events, such as the annual Spring Forum and Fall Harvest Festival, regular garden visits, workdays, and the quarterly newsletter. Gardens in the UGROW network have access to essential resources including compost, soil testing, building materials, water hookups, organically grown vegetable and flower seedlings, seeds, and volunteers. UGROW is able to provide these resources through partnerships with city agencies, universities, neighborhoods centers, and Community Development Corporations.

Membership

UGROW works as a program under the umbrella of the REC, but with a separate budget. The membership of the REC is 300 members.

Volunteers

Volunteers are involved with UGROW in several capacities:
(1) *Interns* from local public schools and universities work regularly with the program coordinator, including taking on particular tasks and projects, and commit 10-20 hours a week for several months.
(2) The *UGROW Advisory Committee* is composed of fifteen people from the Worcester community who commit to one meeting a month and associated tasks and projects.
(3) Some volunteers take on particular projects, such as working with youth, coordinating the newsletter, or doing art in the gardens.
(4) Hundreds of volunteers from local universities, churches, businesses, and households are involved with gardens through participating in workdays, including large Earth Day cleanups at potential future garden sites.

✓ Incorporated as a nonprofit in the state
✓ 501(c)(3) status with the IRS
✓ Checking or Savings account in group's name

Organization Profile

This is concise and well-written, but notice how—even in a proposal as brief as this one—we know most of this information already from the first three pages.

This paragraph also introduces a new group of collaborators that we haven't seen before. The first list, on page one, emphasized grassroots constituencies. This one indicates that they also work with larger, established agencies, which further establishes their reach and credibility.

Volunteers

This discussion is specific and clear. It would be strengthened by numbers in each category: how many volunteers, how many donated hours, and so forth. These numbers are another way of gauging community support.

NEGEF supports a range of organizations, including many informal groups without tax status. These questions allow the funder to collect data about grantees and prospective grantees.

Hate Free Zone Campaign of WA
Proposal to the Threshold Foundation—Coexistence & Community Committee
January 15, 2003

Please accept this proposal for $20,000 in general operating support from Threshold Foundation Coexistence & Community Committee.

Narrative

Mission, Purpose and History. Hate Free Zone Campaign of Washington is a grassroots, nonprofit organization founded one week after the September 11, 2001 attacks in direct response to the backlash against immigrant communities of color, primarily Muslims, Arab Americans, East Africans and South Asians. Initially a volunteer effort that was to focus on hate crimes and discrimination by individuals against other individuals, the organization has grown into one of the foremost immigrant and human rights groups in Washington State with seven full-time staff, over 75 committed volunteers and 20 partner organizations, under fiscal sponsorship of The Tides Center. *We are currently the only organization in Washington State providing services to immigrant victims of hate crimes and discrimination.* On Human Rights Day 2002 (December 10), in recognition of our work, the City of Seattle awarded its highest citizen award for human rights to Hate Free Zone Campaign of Washington, an exceptional accomplishment for us as a young organization.

HFZ Campaign's mission is to establish Washington State as a place where all individuals can feel safe, secure and welcome, regardless of race, religion or ethnicity, and where acts of hatred and discrimination will not be tolerated. In order to achieve our mission, HFZ has four primary goals that we believe are essential to the institution of systemic change: 1) to advocate politically against policies and actions that threaten immigrant communities; 2) To provide direct support to targeted communities; 3) To provide anti-bias education and training to youth, the general public and law enforcement; and 4) To effectively utilize media to raise awareness of critical issues.

While our work began in direct response to 9-11, it is clear that we fill a need that existed well before then, a need that has taken on a new urgency. We believe it is critical to give voice to immigrant communities that are too often not represented in our political and social conversations. We operate under the fundamental premise that we speak more loudly as a coordinated coalition, and we strive to bring together our immigrant communities with more mainstream communities, recognizing that the erosion of fundamental rights of one community often leads to the erosion of rights of all of our communities.

We find that the tragedy of 9-11 and its aftermath has also provided a tremendous opportunity to mobilize and build leadership within immigrant communities of color that are being targeted, to educate them about their rights, to encourage them to speak out and become engaged with other communities in partnership; and to become active in political decision-making processes, and taking on the responsibilities of participatory democracy.

HFZ Campaign works closely with a number of partner agencies to accomplish its mission and goals. These include: The Arab American Community Coalition, Japanese American Citizens League, Asian Counseling and Referral Service, Chaya (an agency serving South Asian Women), The

Hate Free Zone Campaign of Washington

The amount of money requested appears in the first sentence; the reader doesn't have to search for it.

Narrative

The momentum of the Hate Free Zone Campaign (HFZ) is evident right from the start. In just one paragraph, the authors establish the organization in terms of the following:

- The timeliness of the work.

- The remarkable growth of their group; they have seven full-time staff members, seventy-five volunteers, and twenty partner groups after just fifteen months in business.

- Their niche: what makes them unique. (Notice the word "only.")

- The credibility of their organization, as evidenced by an award from the city of Seattle.

For me, the most compelling factor is the timing. Faced with a crisis, HFZ was founded in just a week. Their initial strategy—combining service with advocacy—has proven effective, which is not always the case when groups are created in a moment of crisis. The success of their approach is a testament to their clear vision and community organizing wisdom.

The statement of mission and goals is clear and uncompromising, including the inspiring language, "where acts of hatred and discrimination will not be tolerated."

To highlight their goals visually—they get lost in the middle of this paragraph—the authors could indent and stack the list, and perhaps use bold type for key phrases:

1. To advocate politically . . .

2. To provide direct support . . .

3. To provide anti-bias education and training . . .

4. To effectively utilize media . . .

This would add visual variety and create more blank space on the page.

This paragraph includes strong language linking issues and constituencies. This is really a problem statement—immigrant communities are targeted, in part, because they are uneducated and politically inactive—but it reads like a call to action. By defining the problem this way, the authors are planting the seeds of the solution they develop later in the proposal.

This is an amazing and diverse mix of partners. Note the use of names; rather than saying, "We work with a broad cross section of the immigrant community," the authors list their partner groups. This makes the coalition specific and tangible. The power is in the names.

Sikh Temple of Renton, Somali Women and Children Skills for Change, Somali Social Development Resource Center, The American Civil Liberties Union, Northwest Immigrant Rights Project, Asian Pacific Islanders' Coalition, and the Organization of Chinese Americans.

Hate Free Zone's constituency and community. According to 2000 US Census figures, 10% of Washington State's 5.75 million residents is foreign born and nearly half of these citizens arrived in the past decade. In King County alone, there are over 73,000 refugees. Immigrants hail from countries including Vietnam, Laos, Cambodia, Eritrea, Ethiopia, Somalia, the former Soviet Union and the Near and Middle East. It is estimated that there are 40-60,000 South Asians, 20-25,000 Somalis and 15,000 Arab Americans in Washington State. Many of these immigrants are struggling to meet their families' basic needs and learn the customs, practices and language of a new country. These challenges are compounded by harassment and hate crimes and the threat of them due to backlash and fear of those who appear to be "other" exacerbated by the September 11 events. In addition, we work in solidarity with many progressive Caucasian groups, as well as other communities of color. The actions of the Federal government continue to erode constitutional and civil rights for all individuals, and we believe our only course of action to challenge these actions is to bring communities together to speak to policy makers.

Strategy and Plan of Action. We work on four different platform areas to effect long-term systemic change in the arena of immigrant civil rights. Our platforms and plans for 2003 are described below:

1. **Political Advocacy**
   - Drafting and responding to legislation that affects the communities we serve, responding to anti-terrorism legislation, or promoting anti-hate legislation.
   - Mobilizing and educating targeted communities to become involved in the political process around critical legislation that affects civil and workers' rights.
   - Raising awareness of city and state legislators around immigrant issues, facilitating communication between legislators and targeted communities.
   - Facilitating efforts to form hate free zones in other parts of the country.

2. **Safety and Support Services**
   - Staffing statewide hotline for hate incident and discrimination reporting.
   - Providing training to targeted community individuals and leaders on civil rights, immigrant rights, discrimination reporting options, and other resources.
   - Establishing a central resource list of legal and other pertinent referral sources.
   - Assisting communities in developing appropriate responses and training people within their own communities to act as resources.

3. **Education and Training**
   - Developing, in conjunction with a number of different communities, a multicultural, anti-bias K-12 curriculum for introduction into state schools.
   - Developing culturally responsible training material for law enforcement and other appropriate agencies
   - Conducting outreach and education into individual schools.
   - Utilizing existing efforts of Japanese American groups in schools and communities to publicly talk about the parallels between their experiences and the possible consequences of post-

2

When I look at this list of partners, I wonder: Has anyone, anywhere tried this before? On one hand, this underscores the difficulty of their work; on the other, it sets the Hate Free Zone apart as a unusual group.

Constituency and community. Statistics are effectively used to define their constituency.

What are the data on hate crimes since September 11, 2001—nationally and in Washington State? The problem undoubtedly exists; here's an opportunity to quantify it. This would also be a terrific place for a quote or anecdote about an immigrant affected by hate crime. Can the authors take one family's experience (anonymity or changing names is acceptable) and use it to represent the scope of the backlash?

Strategy and plan of action. This section expands on the four goals outlined on the first page of the proposal, using the same sequence. The bulleted layout is clean and easy to read.

The question about replication is answered here, with a specific objective about starting and serving groups in other regions.

This proposal doesn't include a formal "objectives" section (it doesn't really need one), but a few numerical goals here would help to define the scope of service. For example, how many hotline calls are anticipated in the next year? How many people will receive training on civil and immigration rights? This kind of thinking could be applied to several of the methods listed in this section.

Here's a strong point on peer education and improving the capacity of the affected communities.

A terrific strategy with great emotional resonance. A large majority of Americans, regardless of their politics, now accept that Japanese Americans got a raw deal during World War II. Highlighting their experience provides a sobering antidote to the present anti-immigrant hysteria.

September 11 events and legislation

4. Media and Public Awareness
- Implementing public awareness campaigns to raise awareness and understanding around targeted cultures and religions, and to support hate free communities.

Social Values: HFZ Campaign revolves around a fundamental assumption that immigrant communities of color need to be given the opportunity and resources to have a voice on issues that affect them. By doing this, communities will begin to understand the political process and how to make a difference. Our holistic program addresses both immediate needs and systemic change through coalition–building of communities that have often never spoken to each other or known about each other. We believe power comes in standing together. We are wholly committed to seeing the full democratic participation of all individuals in America, to ensuring that justice is truly for ALL, and to organizational diversity, including being led by individuals from the communities we serve.

Benchmarks of Success: We evaluate our efforts in five ways: 1) Assess success in reaching and working with communities we serve (have we built trust? Do communities want to keep working with us? Do individuals come to us when they are in need? Do community members agree or proactively ask to take leadership on critical issues?); 2) Compare target outcomes with actual activities, and progress towards our mission and goals; 3) Assess effect in media (Are we relied upon by the media as a credible authority on immigrant issues? Do people learn about our efforts through media coverage?) 4) Evaluate constant feedback from and collaborations with the organizations, partners and communities with whom we work; 5) Utilize evaluation forms on specific forums and panels we conduct; 6) Obtain feedback from political representatives with whom we work. In addition to the targets we've set for ourselves with measurable outcomes (such as number of forums conducted, number of clients served, etc.), we are using built-in measures of effectiveness such as success with the legislative process, high attendance at community forums and meetings, increasing activist engagement both in numbers and depth of involvement, and continued media coverage.

Partial List of Accomplishments: In the 15 months since HFZ Campaign began, we have been able accomplish a tremendous amount. Some highlights of our work include:

- Operationalized (February 2002) a statewide hotline for hate crimes/incidents reporting and referral. Assisted over 125 clients from the Sikh, South Asian, Arab American and Somali communities with issues involving harassment, bullying, racial profiling, and targeted by Federal agencies.
- On September 21, 2002, HFZ Campaign led over 30 partner organizations and almost 100 local and national co-sponsoring agencies to organize a public hearing, "Justice for ALL: The Aftermath of September 11." Over 1,100 people heard 22 people tell their personal stories to a panel of eight high-level Commissioners from Congress, City and County Council, INS, FBI, and DOJ. This event, modeled after the Japanese American redress hearings following the WWII-era Japanese Internment, provided a groundbreaking opportunity to present how hate based violence, discrimination and unjust government action is affecting immigrants.
- Post 9-11, Sikhs suffered brutal hate crimes nationally because their visibly ethnic clothing was associated with Osama bin Laden. The local Sikh community was initially extremely hesitant to speak out. However, HFZ was able to impress upon the President of the Gurudwara (Sikh

The Media and Public Awareness strategy sounds useful; a bit more detail on the publicity campaigns would be helpful.

Social values. This paragraph defines the ways that constituent service and political organizing are integrated.

Once again, the authors use simple, declarative language: "We believe power comes in standing together." If you want to write with emotional impact, this is the way to do it.

Benchmarks of success. The evaluation process described here is sophisticated in the way that it seeks out feedback from a wide range of constituents: community members, collaborating organizations, elected officials and their staff, even the news media. Visually, this could be seen as a series of concentric circles radiating outward from the center of the organization. This section could be improved with the following changes:

- Reordering the list from the inside out.

- Indenting and stacking the list to create more space instead of jamming everything into a long paragraph, which makes it harder to read and digest. (These kinds of layout tricks tend to take up more space; at this stage, I'm wondering if the authors were faced with a five-page limit and opted to squeeze in as much information as possible—a risky approach.)

- Adding measurables: How many forums will they conduct? How many clients will they serve?

Partial list of accomplishments. Here are the numbers relating to past accomplishments, and they are impressive. Quantifying your impact by collecting the data is another way to establish credibility. Many groups use these numbers to create benchmarks for the future.

Here's a great place for a brief excerpt from testimony provided at the event. As a reader, I want to hear directly from the affected communities in their own voices.

Here's another specific story with emotional impact.

Temple) the importance that Sikh community concerns be heard. Invited to testify before legislators, he was so visibly moved by the opportunity to speak and be heard that he and others have since become actively involved. 70 Sikhs went to Asian Pacific American Legislative Day in Olympia, and local Sikhs have since begun actively bringing forward issues and proposing solutions for problems such as bullying in schools.

- When Somali community members' money transmittal businesses were closed down by the Federal government, HFZ arranged for them to speak directly with the Chair of the State Legislative Financial Services Committee that drafts legislation to monitor money transmitters. This was doubly remarkable: First, the proposed legislation failed to pass. Second, Somalis from different factions, who had never earlier been able to put ethnic and political differences aside, experienced the power of speaking with one voice.

- Provided eight Know Your Right forums in the Sikh, Somali, Oromo, Latino and Arab communities, in conjunction with Northwest Immigrant Rights Project

- Helped three Somali grocery store owners win back USDA Food Stamp privileges with pro bono legal defense from Perkins Coie; raised emergency food funds for affected families, apprised key legislators and media of the issues

- Gathered panels of community members from varied communities to testify regarding proposed state anti-terrorism legislation and its effects on those communities; successfully defeated legislation

- Established relationships with key members of the Arab American, Somali, Oromo, and Sikh communities, as well as with currently non-targeted communities of color including Japanese American, Chinese American, and other Asian Pacific Islander communities.

- Responded to calls from New Jersey, Ann Arbor and Detroit, MI groups who are interested in a similar campaign; worked on putting together a toolkit for other cities and counties who want to establish hate free zones.

- Spoke at over 25 junior high and high school classrooms and over 70 public forums and panels, often bringing together members of targeted communities to speak about their experiences.

- Established a basic organizational infrastructure, attained a fiscal sponsor, acquired office space, computers and equipment and hired staff.

Leadership and Diversity: We are committed to diversity of staff, board and volunteers, as this is a cornerstone of our mission. Our organization and board are both led by individuals from affected communities. **Pramila Jayapal,** Executive Director, is an activist and writer born in India who has worked across Africa, Latin America and Asia. She has been involved in international and domestic social justice issues for over twelve years. She has an MBA and BA in English Literature. **Kush Bambrah,** Associate Director, is a Sikh American who previously worked for National Asian Pacific American Legal Consortium on issues of hate crimes and discrimination. He has a JD and a BA. **Asha Mohamed,** Community Outreach Coordinator, is from Somalia and has grown up in Kenya and Europe. She speaks five languages and hails from Dante Alighieri Universita in Nairobi. **Liza Wilcox,** Community Services Manager, has held roles in nonprofits including Tibetan Government in Exile and National Citizen Action. **Amelia Derr,** Education Coordinator, focuses on multicultural, anti-bias curriculum and has an MSW from the University of Washington. **Nancy Johnson,** Grants and Office Administrator, holds a PhD in English from University of Louisiana, and a BS, Geology and MS, Mineralogy from University of Michigan. **Advisory Board** includes **Aaliyah Gupta,** Executive Director, Chaya; **Diane Narasaki,** Executive Director, Asian Counseling and Referral Services, **Ibrahim al-Husseini,** co-founder of Arab American Community Coalition; **Dorry Elias,**

An interesting pattern emerges in this proposal: HFZ reaches out to communities that have been politically inactive. Propelled by threats to their safety and their livelihoods, they come together, develop solutions, and begin to implement them. The cumulative effect is uplifting: through strength in numbers, potential victims create change and in this way, can no longer be victimized. The reader feels, "Yes, something can be done because it is being done."

Funders want to feel good about giving, and one way to feel good is to see results. HFZ's results are well documented throughout this section.

It's useful to learn that the work of the Hate Free Zone is known beyond Washington State and that they are working to share their expertise with other communities. Do they have the potential to earn income by selling their toolkits or providing consulting and training services?

Leadership and diversity. This list of leaders is notable in its diversity, relevant expertise, and representation from the affected communities.

Printing the names in bold type is a nice touch—they stand out—but the paragraph feels very dense. This would be a good opportunity for a table: names on the left, credentials on the right.

If you knew that Nairobi, Kenya hosts a university named after Dante Alighieri, raise your hand. (He's the Italian author of *The Inferno,* the great Renaissance poem about sin, politics, and hell.) The world is filled with surprises, isn't it? Since grant reviewers are besieged with hundreds of documents that often read and look the same, sometimes the quirky details will make a proposal stand out.

Executive Director, Minority Executive Directors Coalition; **Susan Foster**, Partner, Perkins Coie LLP; **Karol Brown**, Attorney, Perkins Coie, LLP; **Ann Benson**, Directing Attorney, Washington Defenders Association Immigration Project; and **Sharon Tomiko Santos**, Washington State Representative.

Fundraising Information. To date, we have raised $303,000, with an additional $165,000 in funding committed for 2003. Our major supporters are the Paul G. Allen Foundation ($100,000 over two years), Bill and Melinda Gates Foundation ($75,000), Virginia Wellington Cabot Foundation ($70,000 over two years), Seattle Foundation ($63,500), Seattle Office of Civil Rights ($30,000), United Way Venture Fund ($20,000), Greenville Foundation ($15,000), Seattle Peoples Fund ($12,000), Massena Foundation ($10,000) and Allstate Foundation ($9,500). We have requested three-year funding from Gates Foundation ($150,000), and have submitted proposals to NCCJ, Universalist Veatch Foundation, and Stern Family Fund. A grant from The Neighborhood Assistance Center for strategic planning will assist us in streamlining our work and preparing for the future. A direct appeal campaign has raised almost $20,000 to date. We have applied for a grant to plan the development and implementation of an overall fundraising strategy. We plan to provide our trainings to organizations and companies for a fee, and will be developing fee schedules for this work. Finally, we are considering a fee-based membership as another long-term revenue source.

Summary. We are proud to say that in the post 9-11 backlash area, we have emerged as one of the leading models around the nation for community capacity building within the broad spectrum of communities that have suffered. National organizations conducting research around the country applaud our proactive, replicable model: Human Rights Watch, Applied Research Coalition and the National Asian Pacific American Legal Consortium report that HFZ Campaign is unique in its approach and ability to serve not just one but many different ethnic communities. A leading local newspaper, Northwest Asian Weekly, has awarded our Executive Director, Pramila Jayapal, with a 2002 Leadership Award. In addition, Pramila will deliver the keynote speech for the 2003 Seattle Chapter of Japanese American Citizens League Installation, an honor generally reserved only for Japanese American leaders, in recognition of HFZ Campaign's exceptional efforts to highlight similarities between the current situation in immigrant communities and the post-WWII Japanese Internment. Perhaps the biggest tribute to our work comes from the communities we serve:

> *The HFZ Campaign has been working with the Sikh community to educate community members about legislation that affects our basic rights, to mobilize community members to become involved and to assist Sikhs who have been victims of hate crimes...We believe that Hate Free Zone is doing something no one else is doing. —Sharanjit Singh Sarang, President, Gurudwara Singh Sabha of Washington*

> *Hate Free Zone has become a part of the Somali community. Even though it was created after September 11, its services to Somali community exceeds to all other organizations that had existed before Hate Free Zone. Your help and continuous support is recognized and admired by the grocery store owners and the community at large. –Abdurahman Jama, Somali spokesman*

We believe we are truly a perfect fit for the Coexistence and Community Committee. Support from Threshold Foundation will help us to continue our efforts to build better shared communities in Washington State.

Fundraising information. This is a striking list of funders, especially for a new group. The grants are relatively large; both mainstream and progressive foundations are included.

Much of this information appears in the budget on the next page. To save space, the authors could simply refer the reader to the budget.

For a new organization, $20,000 in donor income looks encouraging. How many individuals contribute? HFZ is smart to look for diversified income so early in the life of the organization, including from fees for service (answering the question raised earlier in the proposal) and membership development. Given the volatility of their issue, it's crucial that they diversify their funding as soon as possible. Grantmakers understand this, too, which is why a proposal for fundraising planning is a sensible idea.

Summary. Even more credibility: attention from respected national organizations.

Another compelling story, again highlighting the parallels between the Japanese American experience in World War II and the current climate for immigrants, especially those from the Muslim world.

Great quotes! They really illuminate the case for this work. Indeed, they almost get lost at the end of the proposal. At least one could be moved to the first page, or perhaps they could be used as transitions between the sections of the proposal. An additional two or three testimonials would go even further. Let's fill this proposal with a chorus of voices.

It's appropriate to refer to how your work meets the funder's priorities, but the specifics are missing. What's the nature of the "fit"? Nothing complicated required; one more sentence would do the job.

HATE FREE ZONE CAMPAIGN OF WASHINGTON
2002-2003 Budget

	2002	2003
Salaries	163,430	264,000
Payroll Taxes	13,387	18,876
Benefits	7,683	11,400
Employee Support	1,220	1,201
Consultants	14,408	10,000
Rent	12,200	21,600
Utilities	1,942	2,000
Telephone/Telecomm.	4,933	7,200
Postage	800	1,200
Office Supplies	3,346	3,600
Equipment	3,812	5,000
Computers	4,614	5,500
Program Supplies	4,610	5,000
Printing/Copying	2,603	10,000
Reference Materials	16	
Memberships	45	600
Insurance	125	501
Travel	979	3,600
Conferences	0	1,000
Tides Service Fees	8,051	6,602
Other Expenses	3,976	1,000
Special Projects		10,000
TOTAL	**252,180**	**389,880**

Funding Received 2001-2002		Additional Funding Committed/Received	
FOUNDATION FUNDING			
Bill & Melinda Gates Foundation	$75,000	Paul Allen Foundation (2003-2004)	$50,000
Seattle Foundation (11/01)	45,000	Massena Foundation	$10,000
Seattle Foundation Leadership Init.10/02	18,500	Greenville Foundation	15,000
Virginia Wellington Cabot Foundation	30,000	A Territory Resource	5,000
Paul Allen Foundation (2002-2003)	50,000	Unitarian Universalist Veatch Foundation	30,000
Dancing Hill Fund	10,000	Virginia Wellington Cabot Foundation	40,000
MEDC	835		
Neighbor to Neighbor (11/01)	5,000	Individual Donors	20,000
Neighbor to Neighbor (11/02)	5,000		
British Petroleum	5,000	Contract Revenue –School Training	2,000
Funding Exchange	3,000	SOCR-Dept of Justice Contract	30,000
Chaya/9-11 Pooled Funds	4,000	**Total Committed + Carryover for 2003**	**253,270**
Seattle Peoples Fund	12,000	**Proposals Submitted /Prospective Funding**	
A Territory Resource	3,500	Joyce Mertz Gilmore Foundation	50,000
		Arca Foundation	50,000
United Way Venture Fund	20,000	NCCJ	60,000
		Ford Fdn- Leadership for a Changing World	100,000
Individual Donors	6,680	Public Welfare Foundation	50,000
		Threshold Foundation	20,000
Contract Revenue	9,835	Ms. Foundation Democracy Funding Circle	20,000
TOTAL RECEIVED	**303,450**	**TOTAL PROSPECTIVE**	**350,000**

6

Budget

The budget is cleanly organized and provides the right level of detail. One additional point: how many FTEs (full-time equivalents) are included under "salaries"? We know from the proposal that HFZ employs seven people, but it would be useful to restate that in the budget.

HFZ's quick growth—a $250,000 budget in its second year, nearly $400,000 in the third—raises a host of questions. Do they have the infrastructure in place to handle the complexity of planning, staffing, financial management, fundraising, and governance? Can they build a sustainable organization with this kind of rapid growth? Is sustainability even an issue? (Perhaps they plan to build capacity rapidly in their partner organizations and work themselves out of a job.) These concerns are not really addressed in the proposal. Any diligent grantmaker would ask a lot of follow-up questions relating to the growth of the group.

As mentioned earlier, this is a very diverse income mix. It demonstrates that their work is valued by a wide cross section of the community. (I can't recall hearing about a group that received funding from both British Petroleum and the Funding Exchange, not to mention the United Way.)

Jargon note: it's helpful to spell out acronyms—MEDC, SOCR, NCCJ—whenever possible.

Supportive Parents Information Network, Inc. (SPIN)
Proposal Narrative
"Through the Eyes of Children:
An Experiential Exhibit of the Lives of Children in Poverty"

Organization

History

SPIN began in August 1998, when 12 parents came together with a volunteer lawyer to understand how they could receive education, training, counseling and supportive services necessary to prepare for self-sufficiency. At that time, the local welfare department was refusing counseling, many supportive services and education, forcing parents to take hotel cleaning jobs or other low-wage, part-time temporary work that offered no chance at self-sufficiency. SPIN provided accurate, reliable information about what opportunities existed under welfare reform and how parents could advocate for them. Since that time, SPIN's credibility, accomplishments and presence have grown dramatically. SPIN now has nearly 1,500 members and is growing at the rate of about 20 new members per month. Our all-volunteer staff helps any one who needs us, but only parents who agree to participate in SPIN's efforts to help parents on welfare is allowed to become a member. **Our mission** is to help parents on welfare achieve self-sufficiency by providing: (1) a safe space to acquire the information and courage they need to make informed choices, (2) member-generated activities that develop leadership, peer support and family strength, and (3) a sense of importance in contributing one's knowledge, talents and experience to the community as a whole, and (4) public awareness of the effects of public policy and institutional practices on poor families.

Constituency, Target Population, and the Community We Serve

SPIN offers information, advocacy training, peer support, leadership development, and community involvement activities for parents and children on welfare. Almost all of our members are women. About 70% of our membership is Hispanic, 22% Caucasian, 6% African or African-American, and the remainder Asian and a mixture of racial or ethnic identities. SPIN serves any parent on welfare in San Diego County. There is no membership fee except the willingness to help other parents on welfare. SPIN also offers free training in welfare regulations and other advocacy issues for community-based organization staff members and other agencies, in order to strengthen the quality and capacity of community-wide advocacy efforts.

How Is Our Constituency Involved in Our Work?

SPIN does not simply encourage the participation of our members; we require it. SPIN's motto is: "In good times or in bad, life is never just about you. It is about trying to make the world a better place for everyone." Because we are an all-volunteer organization, we rely on parents to help us reach our many families. We call on members for operational leadership and service on our Board of Directors. Our activities and events, from conception to planning and participation, arise entirely from our members. We are committed to finishing what we start, keeping our promises to members and their children and furthering a view of community that

Supportive Parents Information Network (SPIN)

SPIN's proposal is structured as an extended narrative; in other words, a rather detailed story. This strategy offers both strengths and weaknesses, as you will see. Given the content and the nature of the organization, it works quite well here.

History

The document begins with a founding story. Their primary goal—self-sufficiency for low-income parents—is made clear in the first sentence. Note the language: simple declarative sentences and a complete absence of social work or welfare-to-work jargon.

The authors quickly establish momentum—as a reader, you can sense that change is in the air. Their group is expanding rapidly, even with the requirement that all members participate actively. The proposal builds a compelling argument, sentence by sentence: welfare recipients may not have much money, but they have skills, energy, and commitment.

The mission statement is important and deserves more weight. It's currently buried in the middle of a long paragraph—even when highlighted with bold text, it tends to get lost. To give it further emphasis, the numbered points could be indented and stacked:

1. A safe space . . .

2. Member-generated activities . . .

. . . and so on.

Constituency

Who's involved? The use of data helps to delineate the membership.

SPIN includes in its constituency other agencies that serve welfare recipients and engages those agencies through education and service. This outreach helps to expand and strengthen the movement.

How Is Our Constituency Involved?

I'm impressed by the fearlessness of the opening sentence—"SPIN does not simply encourage the participation of our members; we require it"—and the clear sense of purpose behind it. Again, the language here is straightforward, empowering, and free of jargon. This is more than a grant proposal: it's a policy statement, or even a call to battle.

It's interesting that SPIN members feel so strong about government funding. In a sophisticated way, they have taken their own experience with the government and applied it to their group. This indicates a depth of ownership over the organization and its mission.

embraces persons from all socio-economic, racial, ethnic and religious circumstances. We do all of this without accepting a single penny of government funds. At the insistence of our members, SPIN refuses to apply for government funding. Members view such funding as a perpetuation of their economic dependency and as a potential source of unwanted influence over their determination to comment upon practices and policies which affect their ability to achieve self-sufficiency.

Our Work With Local Groups

SPIN is a sought-after collaborator by other groups and individuals in our community. We believe this is for three reasons: (1) we complete every project we start, (2) **we are the only grassroots organization for parents on welfare in San Diego County**, and (3) we are devoted to maintaining an atmosphere of respect, dignity and kindness towards every person we encounter. We have worked successfully with innumerable organizations, agencies and schools.[1]

We have worked with such groups in the following ways: (1) provided parent testimony about poverty policies, practices and circumstances in community and public forums; (2) staged many workshops for parents on welfare and CBO staff on welfare-to-work planning, special education laws, leadership and communications, kinship and guardianship, and other matters that require fundamental knowledge in order to advocate for positive outcomes. Our workshops are free; we provide small meals. Our desire is to strengthen the capacity of parents on welfare and the agencies that serve them and other low-income people.

How Does the Project We Now Propose Fit Into the Larger Work of SPIN?

Poor people are not without tools to improve their lives. But they are trying to close a socio-economic gap that gets bigger all the time. Their most valiant efforts to achieve self-sufficiency can be made futile by unthinking or unrepresentative public policy, or by administrative practices employed by government for the sole purpose of regulating eligibility of poor people for public benefits. In every aspect of SPIN's activities, we have been unwavering in our insistence on educating the public and policy makers about the effects their assumptions and actions have on real lives of parents and children who are poor. We insist that parents be allowed to speak for themselves in the places where public policy originates and becomes law. We teach parents that when they speak in such forums, they are not just there to tell their own story, but to remind mainstream society that everyone is part of our community, and that there are thousands with similar stories who have no way to be heard.

---

[1] Among our collaborators are: The Caring Council, Los Angeles Coalition to End Hunger & Homelessness, National Campaign for Jobs & Income Support, Coalition for Family Economic Self-Sufficiency, First United Methodist Church Mentor Program, Empl oyee Rights Center, SEIU Local 535, SEIU Local 2028, Team Advocates for Special Kids, California State University San Marcos sociology department, San Diego State University Women's Studies classes, Mid-City Nazarene refugee congregations, Southwestern College, Grossmont College, City College CARE Program, San Diego State University EOP, Montgomery Adult Education, Mid-City Community Advocacy Network, and San Diego County Health & Human Services Agency.

Our Work with Local Groups

For the second time, we are told that the organization finishes what it starts. This is clearly an important issue for the authors. As a reader, I wonder, "Why?"

These paragraphs offer additional opportunities to "break up the page" by indenting and stacking the numbered items.

Here's a specific description of how SPIN works with other groups. To get a sense of the scale, numbers would be helpful: How many parents testified? How many workshops were organized? How many people attended? These questions lead to a larger question: Is it fair to expect an all-volunteer, understaffed group to collect data? If so, how much? For me, the answers are "yes" and "at least a little." Perhaps the data collection piece can be framed in terms of self-reliance or even the development of job-related skills. It might say, for example, "We know our approach is effective because *we* collect the numbers to prove it, and our members are trained to do it."

How Does the Project We Now Propose Fit into the Larger Work of SPIN?

Another strongly written section. Their clear and uncompromising vision is reflected in their language.

What a diverse mix of collaborators! Unions, social service agencies, universities, government agencies, policy groups, and community organizations at both the local and national level. As in the Hate Free Zone proposal on the preceding pages, the breadth of the coalition is evident in the names. This list makes a compelling case for collaboration, since, at least at a cursory level, so many organizations have an interest in seeing the poor empower themselves.

Over the past few years, we have learned that America's heart may be hardened to the poor, that many people in this great nation have been encouraged to, and have adopted, such cruel assumptions about the poor, that there is no longer a national desire to improve the lives of the women, children, disabled, elderly and forgotten residents of our country. This is not rhetoric. The shredding of the national safety net is virtually accomplished, with little else to do but demolish Head Start and privatize Social Security. California's own budgetary nightmare looks as if it will go on for 10 years at least, with the bulk of remedies composed of severe cuts to health, nutrition, education, and subsistence of the poor.

In an environment where social justice is relegated to the status of a luxury, rather than a necessity, it becomes paramount that grassroots organizations develop intensely effective ways to change the public consciousness to embrace at least a rudimentary understanding of the humanity of the poor. Only then will the public dialogue that precedes public policy be changed.

With that in mind, SPIN has embarked on an effort to mobilize all of SPIN's assets to accomplish this goal. We have not abandoned any of our other efforts. We have simply taken on a more comprehensive view of involvement. For the past 14 months, we have been developing the volunteer leadership of our children, ages 3 through 16, to help convey to the public and policy makers the impact of governmental actions and decisions on the quality of low-income children's lives.

We began this work in November 2001, when the San Diego City Council's Land Use Committee was considering an inclusionary housing ordinance. This ordinance was by no means a panacea to cure the severe lack of affordable housing in San Diego, because ultimately it produces no residential units for persons at the low levels of income of welfare families, but rather for persons at 50-80% of the median income. But the ordinance was widely regarded as a beginning, a test of the City Council's will to address the affordable housing problem by making a political choice the building industry had fought successfully for 10 years.

SPIN fielded the first and only delegation of children who testified before the Land Use Committee one afternoon, bringing the committee staff and members of the audience to tears. Children spoke of their experience in shelters and overcrowded apartments, in cars, and on the streets. They spoke of their hopes and their pain with simple clarity. They asked that their futures be considered in the decision-making process. The next time the Land Use Committee met, the public comment period was mysteriously moved from the end to the beginning of the meeting, a time when the children, whom the committee had been informed would once again testify, were still in school. No matter. It was very near Martin Luther King, Jr., Day, and the children decided to march through downtown with the drawings of their "dream homes" which they had planned to hold aloft during the committee meeting and testimony.

From that point, SPIN developed a leadership and communications workshop that took place over a period of six weeks in the summer of 2002. The culmination of those workshops was a compelling Power Point presentation composed of the children's pictures, drawings, words and musical accompaniment. It focused on the issues of homelessness and how it affects children's lives and feelings. It took the building industry to task for efforts to arm-twist the

Again, the authors rely on straightforward, declarative language: " . . . there is no longer a national desire to improve the lives of the women, children, disabled, elderly, and forgotten residents of our country. This is not rhetoric. The shredding of the national safety net is virtually accomplished. . . . " The simplicity of these words gives them emotional power.

This paragraph sets up the need for the project: if the public is callous because people don't understand the lives of the poor, then let's educate them. The remainder of the proposal describes SPIN's outreach strategy to the public and decision makers.

The phrasing is a bit awkward here: "SPIN has embarked on an effort to mobilize all of SPIN's assets. . . . " Shifting to the first-person voice would solve this problem: "We have embarked on an effort to mobilize our assets. . . . " If the "we" is unclear, then perhaps, "At SPIN, we have embarked" and so forth. Always refer to your organization and your work in the first-person voice.

This paragraph sets up the local context for their programs.

A powerful story—lots of emotion without sentimentality.

This would be a great place for a few quotes from the kids. Describing their testimony works well, but allowing us to hear their voices would work even better.

SPIN's response to the Land Use Committee's schedule change shows a lot of creativity and flexibility. The result: a great visual image that places organizing for affordable housing and against poverty within the context of the civil rights movement. If the authors were inclined to insert a photo (as in the Native Seeds/SEARCH example in Chapter Seven), this would be the place to do it.

As a substitute for photos (or perhaps in addition to photos), a sampling of the children's PowerPoint slides could easily be inserted here, making this proposal a visual feast and really setting it apart from so many other wordy grant applications.

realty association into revoking support for the inclusionary housing ordinance. On August 6, 2002, 18 SPIN children from ages 5 through 15, presented the Power Point to the City Council's massive housing meeting attended by more than 1,000 persons. The children anchored the presentation with speeches they wrote themselves, and they waited nearly six hours to give their presentation. They were animated, involved, and intent on being heard.

The project we describe in this proposal is the next step in the evolution of our children's voices. We have fashioned this step, "Through the Eyes of Children," into a series of events that will include the support, assistance, and consultation of SPIN parents, community organizations, and student interns to help the children prepare and construct a moveable exhibit that will allow the public and other visitors a window into the lives of children in poverty — into the physical spaces and emotional landscapes these children call "home."

In order to accomplish this, we will enlist the assistance of artists, photographers, videographers, and others to teach the children the arts they wish to use in depicting their hopes, dreams, joys, frustrations and suffering. In the process, the children will learn strategies for individual expression and they will combine these into a larger voice. We plan to stage this exhibit in schools, colleges, public buildings and spaces, museums and other venues throughout San Diego County. We plan to have the children on hand to explain the works and to witness the impact of their efforts. We also plan to offer exhibit visitors the opportunity to record in written, audio or video form, their impression, and we will provide visitors with post cards and a list of addresses of public officials and policy makers.

We are requesting $5,000 for this project, although we estimate it will cost just over three times that much. We will seek the remainder from other foundations and individual donors. We will use the $5,000 to acquire the supplies necessary to develop the children's expressive techniques and subject matter, including the purchase of art supplies, film, development and enlargement costs. We expect a minimum of 30 children to participate; their parents will accompany them to assist with every activity. To a small extent, we must help with mileage expenses, since the children live throughout the County. We know we can accomplish this project, because we already have achieved this level of commitment by parents and children for previous efforts in affordable housing, and parents and children have promised it for this project as well.

Because socialization is an important part of children's achievements as a team, we will use a small portion of the funding to pay for simple foods we cannot get donated in large enough amounts to feed the participating children, parents and other helpers. SPIN has a tradition of silently acknowledging that hunger is a fact of life among these children and parents. We provide simple, nutritious meals or snacks as part of a warm hospitality offered to our members and their families whenever we meet. It may seem like a luxury, but to our members, it is gift they accept with humility and restraint.

The San Diego Foundation for Change was the first funder of SPIN with a grant of $4,000 in 1999. Two years later, we applied again to SDFC and were granted $3,000. We have been funded by a number of foundations and some individual donors since we began, but it is the San Diego Foundation that made our organization possible. For almost five years, we have

A great organizing moment is described here in the children's experience at the meeting; as a reader, you can feel the energy.

This would be a good spot for another subheading: *Organizing Plan* or maybe *The Next Step*. Because this page looks exactly like the previous one, readers are likely to get lost. Subheadings serve as place markers to guide the reader through the proposal. They are particularly useful for people who review hundreds of grant applications and need to skim them from time to time.

Any venues secured so far? Exhibition dates?

By including a bit more detail than we need—for example, why the group pays mileage expenses—the proposal begins to lose focus and bog down. As an alternative, a work plan with tasks, deliverables, and deadlines would provide a nice change of tone and demonstrate the steps for completing the project. A work plan could also cover the same ground with about half the words.

Touching language here: Providing food "may seem like a luxury, but to our members, it is a gift they accept with humility and restraint."

By outlining their history together—the San Diego Foundation for Change (SDFC) provided start-up funding for SPIN—the writers express their gratitude and encourage the funder to feel a sense of ownership, pride, and partnership.

grown, developed and remained true to our mission. We have waited for the voices of our members to indicate our next steps, and now our children have spoken. We seek partial funding for this project from the San Diego Foundation for Change for two reasons: (1) because support by the Foundation is an endorsement from a community leader in social justice that signifies the legitimacy of our purpose, and (2) because what we are trying to accomplish — changing the public mind, essentially — is difficult, and when one begins a difficult journey, one must choose one's partners well. Their endurance, commitment, and understanding make the road seem safer and the destination shorter. SDFC is such a partner.

We have already brought together the team of student interns and the group of parents and children who will participate in this project. We are gathering the expertise of artists, photographers and display experts. Our second planning meeting will take place March 16, and our third, which will center on the discussion with the children, will take place March 19. We are engaged in consultations with three artists and one photographer. We will recruit film and audio expertise from our student interns.

Our goal will be to elicit strategies and the components of the exhibit's message from the children. We have done this successfully before when we elicited their participation in the affordable housing issue. We require parent involvement in SPIN's children's projects to develop the bonds between parent and child, to provide a place where parents can observe successful parenting techniques among other parents and community volunteers, to allow children to experience a setting in which their parents are treated with respect and dignity instead of the way institutions tend to treat low-income parents, and to ensure that parents and children are committed to the project and do not feel exploited by it.

Evaluation

We will evaluate this project according to three goals: (1) skills and opportunities acquired by the children; (2) completion of the project and display in numerous venues throughout San Diego County, and (3) impact of the exhibit on visitors.

Skills and Opportunities Acquired by the Children

Children will be exposed to all media employed in the exhibit. They will be allowed to choose those media in which they feel they are best able to express their message. They will also spend time in discussions and team activities to determine what their message will be. What aspects of the lives of low-income children do they think are important for others in the community to know about? (SPIN children have already shown themselves responsive to that question by writing and illustrating two annual issues of *SPIN Kids' World*, for which they selected the topics.) Children will be asked to share their work with peers and parents, and final selection of exhibition works will be made by the children themselves. Children will be asked to accompany the exhibit to venues to greet visitors and participate in pre- or post-exhibition events sponsored by SPIN or the hosts. SPIN will record the children's evaluation of their experiences at various intervals in the preparation and execution of this project. Finally, SPIN will honor the

The sentence that begins, "We seek partial funding. . . " is a direct pitch to the reader; for emphasis, it should start a new paragraph.

The paragraph ends with a lovely appeal: "When one begins a difficult journey, one must choose one's partners well. Their endurance, commitment, and understanding make the road seem safer and the destination shorter. SDFC is such a partner."

Much of this information is covered earlier in the document. Good proposals are stories, and stories are often created through the repetition of themes and images. For better or worse, storytellers tend to cover the same ground to make a point, even when it's unwarranted. Many grantwriters fall into this trap. The solution is easy: Ask one or two people outside your organization to review your proposal and point out places where the writing is unclear or the content redundant.

Here's a great opportunity to use bullets for highlighting and visual variety:

- To develop the bonds . . .
- To provide a place . . .
- To allow children . . .
- To ensure that parents and children . . .

Evaluation

This is an interesting strategy: name the evaluation points first, then detail them below.

Skills and Opportunities Acquired by the Children

What are the youth interested in? What topics have they chosen for their publication? One additional sentence would make this more tangible.

children whose efforts make this exhibition possible, providing press releases and other statements of their contributions to media, school officials and others in the community.

Completion of the Project and Display in Numerous Venues

SPIN has already reached out to its community and agency collaborators concerning our desire to stage this exhibit in as many venues as possible in San Diego County. Proper venues include public and private facilities such as schools, civic buildings, museums, churches and other places accessible to the community. SPIN expects this exhibit to endure for a minimum of three months to six months in San Diego County, with a minimum of six exhibition sites at locations in North County, East County, South Bay, Mid-City, La Jolla and Downtown San Diego. Thereafter, SPIN will seek exhibition sites in Southern California, with funding for transportation and other expenses by sponsors from those venues.

Impact on Visitors

SPIN will seek the attendance of every legislator from local, state and federal government representing San Diego County constituents. We will also seek to record legislators' comments after they view the exhibit. We will record the reactions of members of the public who visit the exhibit. We will ask visitors to complete a post card to public officials concerning their reaction to the exhibit. We will compile the reactions we have recorded and provide a broad sampling of these responses to individuals and organizations funding this project.

Organizational Structure / Administration

SPIN policy is set by a Board of Directors composed of nine members, five of whom are parents on welfare or parents have reached self-sufficiency after being on welfare. Board members often help plan and participate in SPIN activities. They are also responsible for developing non-grant funding sources and individual donors. This task is fairly new to our board, but they have formed a development committee and are hard at work identifying resources. For example, our treasurer prepared our application for inclusion in the Combined Federal Campaign, and we were accepted. Another board member has begun the preparation of a press packet and mailing list for individual donors. Still another has kept a network of organizations informed about SPIN's accomplishments. SPIN's board consists of the following: Cecelia Blanks, an African-American woman, former welfare mother, now a college counselor with a master's in social work; Maria Luz Lopez, Hispanic, a CalWORKs parent, married with three girls, recently named Student of the Year in the social work department at SDSU; Hilda Rivera, Hispanic, CalWORKs parent, mother of two daughters, survivor of domestic violence, soon to graduate from Southwestern College with an associate's degree in child development; Carl Steward, African-American, former CalWORKs parent who reached self-sufficiency after graduating from Grossmont College with a computer science degree and obtaining a job in his field; Tami Thompson, Caucasian, former Medi-Cal employee, with a master's in applied sociology, owner of a small business; Dr. Linda Shaw, Caucasian, associate professor of sociology at Cal State San Marcos, expert in qualitative evaluation of social service programs, author of peer-reviewed papers and a soon-to-be published book on welfare reform; Sharon

Completion of the Project and Display in Numerous Venues

The authors begin to define the scope of the project, with at least six exhibition sites around San Diego County. If two or three venues could be lined up and named before the proposal is submitted, that would inspire confidence.

Impact on Visitors

This paragraph outlines a simple but effective strategy for using the exhibit to change public opinion and public policy. It also describes how funders will be notified.

What's lacking is a publicity plan. How will they promote the event to ensure maximum turnout?

Organizational Structure/Administration

Paragraphs of this length are tough on the reader—when the eyes wander, the mind is close behind. If you're using a narrative format with lots of text, keep your paragraphs to a reasonable length.

This discussion about board members and fundraising works because it outlines specific tasks.

SPIN has a diverse board with a variety of relevant life experiences and professional expertise. This formatting is a problem, however. At the very least, the authors could highlight the names by using bold text. Even better, they might create a table with names on the left and credentials on the right.

Cullity, Caucasian, adjunct professor of sociology at Cal State San Marcos, master's in sociology, former small business owner; Brenda Popma, Caucasian, IRS attorney and SPIN board treasurer, and Irene Macias, Hispanic, CalWORKs parent, soon to obtain her teaching credential in elementary bilingual education.

Day-to-day leadership is provided by a core of parent leaders who have decided against formal leadership roles. From the beginning, SPIN parents have rejected formal leadership positions, because they would place too much responsibility on persons in those positions and would deprive others of leadership roles. Consequently, SPIN operates by consensus among parent leaders. Leadership group sizes vary according to the event or activity being planned and executed. SPIN takes pride in the diversity of races, nationalities, creeds and sexual orientation of its members, volunteers and community participants in our events and activities.

SPIN's daily fiscal and operational responsibilities are met by a full-time volunteer director, the attorney who started SPIN with 12 original members. She is assisted by a full-time volunteer bilingual community outreach coordinator and a host of parent and children volunteers. The director and community outreach coordinator oversee all planning and execution of activities and events, relationships with collaborators, production of training materials, carrying out of training and other workshop activities, coordination of parent volunteers, and maintenance of organizational responsibilities, including the development of grant funding.

Supplemental Information

A.   SPIN accepts no funding whatsoever from government. We have not received any funding from church foundations or the United Way.

B.   We received a start-up grant of $4,000 in 1999 from the San Diego Foundation for Change, as well as a $3,000 grant from SDFC in 2001. The second grant was for parent advocacy training.

C.   Our organization obtained 501(c)(3) status in July 2001.

This is an interesting take on leadership. I wouldn't mind a bit more detail on the trade-offs created by this type of structure. For example, does additional work fall to the "all-volunteer staff" because of the lack of formal leadership? Is it ever difficult to reach consensus? If so, how does the group deal with it? This would be a good place for a quote from one of the board members about why they chose this model and how it works for SPIN.

I suspect that most funders would be curious about a long-term staffing plan. SPIN's day-to-day operations rely on the work of two apparently very dedicated volunteers. Do the leaders have plans to hire paid staff? What will happen if one of the key volunteers moves on to other work?

Supplemental Information

The authors are responding to questions posed by the foundation in the application materials.

PROJECTED EXPENSES
Children's Project

DIRECT COSTS

Personnel
Director	0
Community Outreach Coordinator	0

Operating Expenses
Equipment and Site Rental	4,500
Events (six venues, prep events, honors Ceremony, etc.)	4,000
Insurance	2,000
Postage and delivery	200
Printing and Reproduction	2,500
Supplies	2,500

Other operating expenses:
Mileage (for low-income parent drivers)	200
Consumable supplies	1,000
Total	**$16.900**

PROJECTED INCOME

San Diego Foundation for Change (projected)	5,000
Ben & Jerry's Foundation (projected)	10,000
Individual Donors (confirmed)	2,000
Total	**$17,000**

Budget

This budget offers the right level of detail for an organization of this size, but it's missing one very large number: the cash value of donated time. (There's a discussion of in-kind services in Chapter Nine.) To capture this information, the organization might consider a two-column budget: one for cash expenses and income, the other for in-kind expenses and income. When the value of volunteer time is factored in, SPIN looks more like a $100,000-per-year organization.

It would take additional record keeping to log volunteer hours and tally their value, but these totals would be helpful for a number of reasons:

- They would demonstrate the breadth and depth of community commitment.

- They would provide a way to quantify the leverage that funders get for their investment. A little bit of money is matched by a lot of free labor.

- Seeing the numbers would make the volunteers feel good and reinforce their commitment to the organization. ("Look at how much our donated time is worth!")

A proposal to The New-Land Foundation, Inc.
The Spine of the Continent Implementation Program
Amount requested: $10,000

Needs Statement

Biodiversity loss is one of the world's most pressing problems and there is growing global concern about the status of the biological resources on which all life depends. Many species are declining to critical population levels as important habitats are being destroyed, fragmented, and degraded, and ecosystems are being destabilized by climate change, invasive species, and direct human impacts. Leading scientists now agree that the current species extinction rate is between 1,000 and 10,000 times higher than historical averages.

Existing protected areas, while absolutely necessary, are often too small, too fragmented, and represent too few types of ecosystems to protect biodiversity at all levels. Moreover, immediate threats to biodiversity in the United States are likely to increase in the coming years as anti-conservation forces assume key leadership posts in important government agencies, the federal courts, and Congress. At the same time, the ongoing decline in foundation assets and the continued slow pace of economic recovery has left the conservation community with considerably fewer resources with which to defend wild nature than in the past.

In this new environment in which both political and economic capital is limited, conservationists must seek out new ways of protecting biodiversity that provide the greatest ecological benefit at the lowest possible cost. Much of this work will necessarily be opportunistic, taking advantage of short-term strategic alliances and the like to protect certain areas. In order to be most effective, however, this work must be based on the best available science, careful long-term planning, and, most importantly, an overarching vision of wildlands protection that addresses key conservation problems at local, regional, and continental scales.

Goals

With these needs in mind, the Wildlands Project has set the following three major goals for our work across North America:

1. Identify, document, publicize, and defend the continent's most ecologically significant wild places, with priority on core wildlands and wildlife linkage areas.
2. Use the science of conservation biology to defend ecologically important lands and derail anti-conservation initiatives at the local, state, and federal levels.
3. Give conservationists and the general public hope and a plan for the future by providing a positive, long-term vision of ecological restoration and recovery.

Wildlands Project

The first thing that jumps out at you here is the logo, which includes three elements:

- A simple, evocative name

- A stylized paw print, suggesting wild places and fierce creatures

- A slogan that encapsulates the mission with three active verbs: *reconnect* wild lands by linking them together, *restore* wilderness by reducing human impacts, and *rewild* these places by ensuring that they have a full range of native species

The page is balanced and inviting, with lots of white space. It looks like an easy read.

Needs Statement

This discussion will work for people who have a basic understanding of environmental science, but phrases such as "critical population levels" and "ecosystems are being destabilized" may scare off the less-educated reader. This detail raises a crucial question about audience: Can you assume that reviewers share your language and values? This proposal seeks a renewal grant, so the likely answer in this case is yes. Under most circumstances, however, don't assume anything.

Here's a staggering statistic: We are losing species to extinction at least one thousand times faster than the average rate during the history of the Earth. This can't be a good thing, right?

This paragraph addresses the need in several dimensions:

- *Environmental.* There aren't enough protected areas.

- *Political.* There is no commitment to conservation among elected leaders.

- *Financial.* Less money is available from traditional environmental funders.

It's amazingly concise. Given three sentences to define a complex problem, it would be hard to do a better job.

This is an interesting, counterintuitive argument: Faced with a hostile situation that limits our options, we have no choice but to think big. The boldness of the idea is compelling, and sets up the next portion of the proposal.

Goals

No explicit organizational history is included in the proposal, though some of this information is worked into the narrative throughout. As before, this approach assumes a certain level of familiarity on the part of the readers.

The action verbs in the first goal—identify, document, publicize, and defend—really summarize the work.

Goals two and three nicely balance each other; one is defensive, the other proactive. Successful conservation work requires both types of strategies.

The Spine of the Continent Implementation Program

The New-Land Foundation has been an important partner in our ongoing efforts to advance these three goals over the past decade. Thanks in part to your support,

- our vision for a big, wild, and connected North America continues to be refined and disseminated to a growing audience;

- our conservation planning program is widely recognized as being on the cutting edge of conservation science and ecological reserve design; and

- our conservation action program in the Sky Islands of the Southwest has taught us much about how to take the vision of landscape-scale conservation and translate it into effective, on-the-ground strategies to protect wild nature.

We invite the New-Land Foundation to join us again this year as we enter an exciting new phase in our history and development as an organization. In the coming year, the Wildlands Project moves from vision to action on an even larger scale with our "Spine of the Continent"

Wildlands Conservation Planning Efforts along the Spine of the Continent

implementation program. Running from Canada's Yukon Territory to Mexico's Sierra Madre Occidental, the Spine of the Continent is one of four proposed "MegaLinkages"—giant systems of conservation lands that will tie North American ecosystems together for wide-ranging species and ecological processes (see the map at left). Each MegaLinkage is comprised of several "Wildlands Network Designs" or WNDs. WNDs are science-based conservation plans that use cutting-edge research to establish conservation priorities for very large regions. A typical WND covers several million acres, ecologically reconnecting habitat

The Spine of the Continent Implementation Program

This section thanks the donor for past support, and strives to link that support to tangible success. The bulleted items echo the three goals from the previous page—a clever approach—but they feel a bit generic. More specific results might work better.

In the second bullet, the phrase "widely recognized" begs the question of widely recognized by whom? This would be a good spot for a quote from a prominent scientist, environmentalist, or even an elected official, praising the efforts of the Wildlands Project.

Nice phrase: "moves from vision to action."

The map on this page defines the scale of their vision and their work better than any written description ever could. Indeed, the Wildlands Project could not exist without maps. If you can use maps to tell your story (see Chapter Seven), do so.

A lot of proper names and jargon are introduced in one paragraph, including "Spine of the Continent," "MegaLinkages," and "Wildlands Network Designs or WNDs." Some of this is unavoidable, but if you must introduce new terms, don't add too many at once.

Choose your acronyms with care. WND is reminiscent of WMD, or weapons of mass destruction. You may provoke an unintended subliminal response in your reader.

across county, state, and international borders.

To advance this continental vision, the Wildlands Project and its regional partners will publish three WNDs along the Spine of the Continent in 2003: the "Heart of the West," which follows the Rockies south from the southern end of the Yellowstone to Yukon planning area to northern Colorado; the "Southern Rockies Wildlands Network," which covers most of central and western Colorado and parts of northern New Mexico; and the "New Mexico Highlands Wildlands Network," (formerly New Mexico Link) which connects the Sky Islands Wildlands Network to the southern Rockies. These landscape-scale conservation plans will be similar in scale and scope to our Sky Islands Wildlands Network conservation plan, a first-of-its-kind proposal for connecting wilderness areas via landscape linkages in southeastern Arizona, southwestern New Mexico, and northern Mexico.

The Wildlands Project is the primary author of the New Mexico Highlands Wildlands Network, and we are working in partnership with the Southern Rockies Ecosystem Project (SREP) and the Denver Zoo as a major sponsor of the Southern Rockies plan. The Heart of the West conservation plan is being directed by Wild Utah, with the Wildlands Project serving as a consultant and scientific adviser. All three plans will be published as professional quality reports and will be distributed to conservationists, agency staff, public officials, and other opinion leaders from across the Mountain West later this year.

In coordination with the release of these three plans, the Wildlands Project will publish a "Spine of the Continent" brochure, which will serve as a general outreach piece for our work in all of the Rocky Mountain states. This brochure will include brief descriptions of the Sky Islands, New Mexico Highlands, Southern Rockies, and Heart of the West WNDs, and may include a brief description of ongoing science-based conservation planning efforts in the Yellowstone to Yukon region as well. By including all of these programs in a single brochure, we remind readers of the Wildlands Project's broader mission—to develop a *continental* system of protected areas and interconnected wildlife linkage areas capable of protecting the full diversity of life in North America.

As we prepare for the plans' release, our field staff will continue ongoing efforts to secure endorsements for our plans from key constituencies and increase public awareness of our methods and goals through workshops, one-on-one meetings, and public presentations. For example, this past fall we held a two-day workshop in Albuquerque to review core elements of the New Mexico Highlands plan and solicit feedback from regional experts. Attendees included staff from New Mexico Department of Game and Fish, the U.S. Forest Service, the New Mexico Wilderness Alliance, the New Mexico Fish & Wildlife Research Unit, The Nature Conservancy, Defenders of Wildlife, Forest Guardians, the Taos Land Trust, and many others. By enlisting the support of key stakeholders early on in the process, many of whom hold key positions of power locally, we hope to develop a coalition of supporters who will then speak on our behalf on important land protection initiatives across the Rocky Mountain region.

For all the layout skill that went into this proposal, this page is very weak. There's nothing here to guide the reader or break up the page.

For example, this section could have been handled with bullets and bold text:

- **The Heart of the West,** which follows . . .
- **The Southern Rockies Wildlands Network,** which covers . . .
- **The New Mexico Highlands Wildlands Network,** which connects . . .

On a positive note, these plans are built on a successful model ("first-of-its-kind") pioneered by the Wildlands Project.

Naming partners is always a good strategy. In terms of formatting, the information is handled more skillfully in the chart that appears on page five of the proposal, so this paragraph is unnecessary.

Notice the deadline: "later this year." Deadlines help to promote productivity within the organization and ensure accountability for the funder.

This would be a good spot for another subheading; perhaps Outreach Strategy.

Their brochure sounds like a useful tool; how many will they print? How will they be distributed?

This section establishes the credibility of the Wildlands Project in two ways: by listing the names of participants, including several government land management agencies, and by including the decision makers in the planning process, which gives them a much better chance of having their plans implemented once they are published. In the long run, these plans won't count for much unless the land managers use them to guide purchase and protection strategies.

Attract national attention to the region through an "Endangered Linkage" campaign

We will increase public awareness of the importance of landscape connectivity in the Rocky Mountains through a "Most Threatened Linkage" campaign. Drawing from the expertise of a leading media consultant, this campaign will attract public attention to critical habitat areas in imminent danger along the Spine of the Continent. This campaign will be modeled after several other highly successful "most threatened" programs, such as Conservation International's "25 Biodiversity Hotspots" program and the National Parks Conservation Association's "Ten Most Endangered Parks" campaign.

This program will highlight one critical linkage area located within the boundaries of each Wildlands Network Design along the Spine of the Continent. Each linkage was selected based on three criteria. First, they had to be located in a wildlife linkage area of high biological importance. Second, they had to be linked to some larger threat explicitly related to government policy at the federal, state, or local level. Third, each linkage had to be associated with an existing, locally directed campaign. Our intention with this program is not to create new projects that compete with other campaigns, but rather to add value to important local efforts already taking place on the ground.

Running from north to south, the Most Endangered Linkages are:

1. The Crowsnest Pass. In the Y2Y planning region, the Crowsnest Pass in southwest Alberta and southeast British Columbia provides important wildlife habitat and connectivity for a number of species, including the grizzly bear. The future doubling of traffic lanes on Highway 3, which runs through Crowsnest Pass at one of the lowest elevations in the Rocky Mountains, threatens to forever sever important habitat areas to the north and south. Dr. Chris Servheen, director of the U.S. Interagency Grizzly Bear Recovery Team, has stated flatly that if the Crowsnest Pass is lost to conservation, grizzly bears will be lost to the United States.

2. The Powder Rim. Located within the boundaries of the Heart of the West Wildlands Network, this important wildlife linkage in southern Wyoming is under increasing pressure as a site for oil and gas exploration. Such development would threaten several rare species and habitats, including important mating grounds for the sage grouse and the only known population of the beard tongue penstemon, a rare member of the snapdragon family. As part of this campaign, we will work with Biodiversity Conservation Associates and others to ask that the Bureau of Land Management designate the region as an "Area of Critical Environmental Concern."

3. The Vail Pass. Interstate 70 at the Vail Pass has been called the "Berlin Wall" for wildlife in Colorado because so many wildlife deaths, including a reintroduced lynx, have been documented there. This campaign will focus on I-70 around the Vail Pass in Colorado to draw attention to both lynx reintroduction and the impact of roads on habitat connectivity. We will highlight how ongoing expansion of the Vail ski resort has resulted in the loss of important lynx habitat. We will also look at how the tremendous growth in highway traffic—a direct result of increased development at Vail and other nearby ski

4

Attract National Attention to the Region . . .

Any seasoned publicist would study previous publicity campaigns to learn what works. This proposal outlines a similar approach for designing the "Most Threatened Linkages" campaign.

Here's another opportunity for bullets to highlight campaign selection criteria.

Funders are wary of duplication. Rather than duplicate the work of other conservation groups, this project is meant to build on local work already under way. This would be a good opportunity for a partner quote testifying to the "value added" by the involvement of the Wildlands Project.

For me, this is the most interesting portion of the proposal for a number of reasons:

- The place names are evocative; every one hints at a story.
- Each location faces a different combination of threats, from highways and snowmobiles or oil and gas drilling to suburban development or "national security." Taken together, they serve as a diverse laboratory for testing the Wildlands Project approach to conservation.
- Each area has its own unique habitat and wildlife.

Chris Servheen's statement really underlines the threat and legitimizes the choice of Crowsnest Pass as a priority area for protection. Don't just take it from us, say the authors, here's a respected expert who agrees with our analysis. (When our "constituents" are other species, we are forced to rely on the opinions of humans who know them well.)

Sage grouse, beard tongue penstemon, snapdragon . . . the diversity of place is encoded in the names. When these species are gone, argues the proposal, the place itself is diminished.

"The Berlin Wall for wildlife": what a shattering image! Data would strengthen the case: How many casualties? How many species?

Each profile suggests opportunities for additional graphics, such as a conceptual map showing how wildlife move through these threatened areas, or a before-and-after map showing the impacts of development.

areas—has impacted wildlife. Finally, we will highlight the impact of snowmobile use on the lynx. The trails that snowmobilers create allow other species (such as coyotes) access to remote lynx habitat, thus causing additional competition for prey.

4. <u>Tijeras Canyon</u>. In the New Mexico Highlands, Interstate 40 east of Albuquerque cuts through the heart of Tijeras Canyon, severely limiting movement of black bears, mountain lions, and other species between the canyon and the Sandía Mountains. This campaign will focus on the impact of both urban sprawl and roads on wildlife habitat. The Wildlands Project and our partners will use this opportunity to educate government agencies on overpass and underpass alternatives to the status quo on state and federal highways. We also will work with municipal officials to educate them on the impact of suburban sprawl on wildlife habitat.

5. <u>The U.S.-Mexico Border</u>. Lastly, current proposals for greatly expanded border security infrastructure at the U.S.-Mexico border, including fencing, roads, and lighting will seriously disrupt wildlife migration patterns in the region, effectively reducing the native range of several species, including the jaguar.

Most Endangered Linkages – Program Summary				
WND	**Linkage**	**Major threat**	**Celebrity Species**	**Partners**
Yellowstone to Yukon	Crowsnest Pass	highway expansion	grizzly bear	Y2Y Conservation Initiative
Heart of the West	Powder Rim	oil & gas exploration	sage grouse	Biodiversity Conservation Associates
Southern Rockies	Vail Pass	roads, development	lynx	Southern Rockies Ecosystem Project
New Mexico Highlands	Tijeras Canyon	roads, sprawl	black bear	New Mexico Wilderness Alliance
Sky Islands	U.S.-Mexico Border	fencing	jaguar	Defenders of Wildlife

To announce the list's release, we plan on distributing printed and electronic media kits and fact sheets for use by news agencies, the conservation community, policymakers, and the general public. We will use a variety of means to distribute these materials, including hosting a reception at the Society of Environmental Journalists annual meeting in New Orleans this September. We also intend to work with LightHawk, a volunteer-based aviation organization with more than 100 volunteer pilots, to provide over flights with media and decision makers for each wildlife linkage.

Anticipated Outcomes

The Spine of the Continent Implementation Program represents the first time ever that a series of complementary landscape-scale conservation plans have been linked together to span the entire

The idea of overpasses and underpasses is intriguing. Have they been tried before? Do animals actually use them? What do they look like? This is a story waiting to be told.

This table is an elegant way to summarize the proposal. The basics are all here: where, why, what's at stake, who's involved. I love the term "celebrity species"; it conjures up great images without resorting to ecological jargon (focal species, keystone species). In fact, the phrase is clever enough to stand a little repetition, and could be used once or twice in the narrative.

Here's a brief but comprehensive plan for promoting the campaign. The earlier discussion of publicity centered on the "most endangered" concept; this one deals with nuts and bolts of getting news coverage and reaching opinion leaders. As ever, a few measurables—how many media kits, news stories, overflights—would strengthen this section.

Anticipated Outcomes

Here is the case for uniqueness: conservation has never been attempted on this scale. The sheer chutzpah of the Wildlands Project might scare off some funders, but others will be attracted to its ambitious, comprehensive approach.

continent from north to south. It is a bold, positive vision comprised of a clear and compelling long-term goal (continental connectivity); a set of rigorous, science-based roadmaps for how to accomplish that goal (WNDs); and an action plan for achieving tangible results in a political environment that requires immediate, on-the-ground action (Endangered Linkage campaign).

In sum, by framing current ecological threats within a larger framework of ecological restoration and recovery, we have created a method for implementing large-scale conservation action that

1) is easy to understand;
2) creates opportunities for media exposure and increases public awareness of the Wildlands Project and other partner organizations;
3) responds in an effective way to immediate ecological threats;
4) educates both conservationists and the general public on the importance of landscape-scale habitat connectivity;
5) increases the impact and effectiveness of several ongoing wildlands protection campaigns; and most importantly,
6) begins to build an on-the-ground network of interconnected protected areas that spans the entire North American continent.

We thank you for past support and encourage you to join us again this year as we turn our vision of healthy, connected landscapes along the Spine of the Continent into reality.

6

This paragraph restates the campaign in terms of vision, strategy, and methods; each one links logically to the others.

Here's a clean, jargon-free, easy-to-understand list of what they hope to accomplish through this project. It's a stretch to label these "outcomes," as the authors have done, since outcomes are generally measurable. Rather than saying their actions will "create opportunities for media exposure," I would encourage benchmarks stating how many times the Wildlands Project expects this campaign to be covered in the major news media during the next year. Some of these items are almost impossible to measure. How will we know when "conservationists and the general public" have been successfully educated?

Perhaps I am guilty of nitpicking. The broad goals of the Wildlands Project will likely take a century to accomplish. Given that kind of timeline, it's tough to create one-year measurable outcomes. Funders who support the work are likely to do so based on the vision, accepting that the details will be worked out along the way.

Finally, the authors remind the foundation of its previous grant support and request a renewal.

Wildlands Project 2003 Budget - Selected Programs*
Prepared for New-Land Foundation

Expense	Sky Islands	Rewild the Rockies	New Mexico Highlands	S. Rockies & Heart of West	Education & Advocacy
Accounting	-	-	100.00	100.00	450.00
Advertising	-	-	-	-	100.00
Bank Service Charges	-	35.00	187.00	187.00	750.00
Business Insurance	425.00	383.00	300.00	300.00	1,800.00
Contract Labor	-	-	1,000.00	-	-
Equipment Purchases	-	1651.63	-	-	2,000.00
Miscellaneous Expense	500.00	-	-	-	-
Office Expense	500.00	156.23	-	-	4,000.00
Office Rent/Maintenance	4000.00	2797.20	150.00	150.00	1,700.00
Personnel Expenses*	55613.00	38093.25	42,317.00	29082.73	251,209.96
Postage	650.00	153.68	1,000.00	350.00	16,500.00
Production (Printing etc.)	3500.00	82.41	5,500.00	500.00	57,074.00
Professional Services	0.00	400.00	525.00	525.00	5,200.00
Telephone	2800.00	1627.29	750.00	750.00	4,200.00
Travel\Conf	4000.00	12327.07	2,000.00	2000.00	9,000.00
Utilities	-	-	175.00	175.00	500.00
WE Research Fund	-	-	-	-	3,000.00
Website	-	-	-	-	5,000.00
Total Direct Expense	71,988.00	57,706.76	54,004.00	34,119.73	362,483.96
Indirect Costs @10%	7,198.80	5,770.68	5,400.40	3,411.97	36,248.40
Total Expense	79,186.80	63,477.44	59,404.40	37,531.70	398,732.36

* **NOTE:** The Spine of the Continent Endangered Linkage Campaign draws from several program budgets, listed above. If awarded, New-Land Foundation funds would be applied to the Rewild the Rockies program, which is responsible for coordinating the campaign.

1

Budget

This is a more complex budget than we have seen in this book, which bespeaks a larger and more sophisticated organization. The formatting makes it easy to understand, despite the complexity of the project.

The New-Land Foundation is being asked for $10,000 toward a $63,000 goal for the Rewild the Rockies program. That program is a component of the Spine of the Continent Endangered Linkage Campaign, whose budget totals more than $600,000. (The annual budget for the organization is just over $1 million.)

Why would a foundation invest $10,000 toward a $600,000 price tag? A few possible answers:

- They want to be part of something ambitious, substantial and successful, and $10,000 is all they have to give. (Millions of individual donors send $25 checks to large national nonprofits for the same reason.)

- They were satisfied with the work funded by their last grant.

- They have the option of steering their money to a subset of the larger project. (For another take on how to structure a complex budget with restricted grants, see the Canadian Parks and Wilderness Society budget in Exhibit 7.5.)

- Perhaps they like the people involved and want to see them succeed.

Don't be shy about asking for partial funding. Many project budgets have been successfully pieced together from smaller grants.

"Indirect costs" is another term for overhead. These are the basic costs of staying in business: bookkeeping, utilities, office supplies, and so on. Many funders refuse to pay indirect costs, in part because there is little accountability for how that money will be spent. The alternative is to itemize each overhead expense, showing the percentage that falls within the program for which you seek funding. This creates more work for you but provides a higher level of accountability for the grantmaker.

In this budget, the Wildlands Project appears to have done both. For the reader, it's unclear which indirect costs are not covered in the itemized list. An additional budget note at the bottom of the page would resolve the mystery and spare the funder a follow-up phone call.

chapter
9

Creative Ways to Leverage Your Grants

For every dollar we give, the Southern Partners Fund must raise an additional dollar from another source: a dollar-for-dollar match. That idea came from one of the founding grantee leaders—not the funder—which was extremely gratifying.

—BARBARA MEYER, Bert and Mary Meyer Foundation

Most fundraising books and magazines are filled with jargon, such as database-driven telemarketing, resource stewardship, human capital, and charitable remainder trusts. I try to avoid this kind of fundraiser-speak, since I don't know what most of these phrases mean, but there's one word I can't get around: leverage. *Leverage* refers to creative ways to use money on hand or already pledged to raise additional money. This chapter will teach you how it works.

Matching and Challenge Grants

Some foundations and many government agencies give grants on a matching basis. For every dollar they provide, you are required to raise another dollar from a different source, such as your membership or another foundation. In a two-for-one match, you must raise two dollars for every one they pledge. Sometimes these are called "challenge grants" because you use the promise of funding to challenge other donors to give.

Matching grants add a level of complexity and so can add extra work, but they serve as a kind of insurance policy for the funder and can actually help you raise more money. Let's say you need $15,000 for a project, and Foundation A pledges $5,000 on a two-for-one matching basis. First, they're protected. They write the check only if you solicit enough money to complete the project, so their grant won't be wasted on a partially funded, less-than-effective program. Second, you can use their pledge as a lever to pry loose donations from other sources. You go to Foundation B and Major Donor C and say, "Listen, we have $5,000 already committed. If you'll each contribute $5,000, we can collect the $5,000 waiting in the bank and the project will be fully funded." With the first commitment in hand, your request carries a lot of credibility.

Challenge grants are also a great way to motivate your regular donors to make additional gifts. When I worked at Native Seeds/SEARCH, a regional conservation group in Tucson, we used challenge grants to begin and end a capital campaign for a new seed bank, library, and grow-out garden. One of our foundation supporters pledged $10,000 on the condition that we raise an equal amount from our members. We promoted this challenge in our newsletter and sent a special mailing to the entire membership requesting gifts for the match. We also phoned selected donors. The result: nearly $30,000 in member contributions!

This strategy worked so well, we tried it again two years later when we neared the end of our campaign. We approached the same funder with a similar request: you helped us initiate the campaign, now help us finish it. They obliged with another $10,000 grant and once again we prepared a mailing and announced the new challenge on the front page of our newsletter. Our members came through with an additional $22,000 in gifts. Overall, nearly one thousand members—one-quarter of the membership—made donations to the capital campaign, which eventually raised more than $250,000.

If you do receive a challenge grant, it's often possible to "draw" some of the money before the match is completed. With both grants described above, we requested half the total—$5,000—once we were able to demonstrate $5,000 in matching contributions. We photocopied all appropriate checks as they came in, then sent the folder of photocopies to the foundation when we reached the threshold.

For most projects, the first grant is the hardest to secure. You might improve your odds by suggesting a challenge grant in your proposal, especially if you are confident you can raise the match from your members or the people you serve. Grassroots support sends a powerful signal that your work is valued by the community.

An ambitious example is under way in Atlanta, where the Bert and Mary Meyer Foundation has pledged to transfer all of its assets to a new community-based grantmaker, the Southern Partners Fund. The fund is planning a capital campaign to raise the millions of dollars needed to complete the match. For more on this story, see Chapter One.

In-Kind Donations

In-kind donations are any goods or services you receive for free. For many groups, this area is an unexplored gold mine. Just to get you thinking about how you might improve your work life at little or no cost, here's a short list of possible in-kind goods and services:

- *Goods:* artwork, audiovisual equipment, books and magazines, buildings, cars and trucks, computer equipment, construction materials, food and drink (for events or volunteers), furniture, house plants, land, landscaping plants, mailing lists, meeting rooms, office supplies, photocopy machines, software, tools, telephones.

- *Services:* accounting, advertising, banking and investment, building maintenance, catering, computer support and networking, construction and remodeling, entertainment (for events), event planning, graphic design, housing (for interns, consultants, or staff), landscaping, legal, mailing, marketing and publicity, office space, payroll, photography, printing, storage, travel, training and consulting, videos.

Notice that most of these goods and services are best provided by businesses. In-kind gifts are a great way to involve your local small-business community, since it's always easier to solicit goods or services than cash donations. Even if you're turned down, you might be able to negotiate a substantial discount, which will reduce your expenses. You won't get anything for free, or at a discount, unless you ask.

Many organizations request free items—airplane tickets, bicycles, hotel rooms, restaurant meals, and the like—to use in their fundraising raffles and auctions. Businesses want their generosity to be publicized, so be sure to acknowledge their gifts in your newsletter and annual report, at your benefit events, in your news releases, and any other way you can.

Like challenge grants, in-kind contributions are an opportunity to show community support for your work. Many funding agencies will allow you to use in-kind donations to fulfill a percentage of your matching grant requirements. Appropriate noncash contributions can include outside gifts, such as free consulting services, or donations from within your organization, such as supervisory staff time not funded by the grant you seek but paid for through other means, such as membership dues.

Most groups do a poor job keeping track of their noncash gifts. If you take the time to itemize and tally the value of all in-kind donations, your group will benefit in several ways:

- By putting a cash value on these contributions, you will impress your members, donors, and foundation prospects. This, in turn, will help you secure additional in-kind gifts, cash donations, and grants. Oregon's farm worker union, Pineros y Campesinos Unidos del Noroeste, receives $150,000 worth of in-kind services per year—and includes the data in their grant proposals. Given their relatively modest annual budget of $400,000, free goods and volunteer labor greatly increase the number of people they are able to organize and serve.

- By quantifying the value of volunteer time, you can give volunteers the respect they deserve and avoid taking them for granted. Most of us immediately understand the importance of donated legal fees or accounting support, but the people who stuff envelopes are worth a lot, too. Convert hours into dollars and it's harder to overlook their contributions. For example, Native Seeds/SEARCH receives about six thousand hours of volunteer time each year for planting crops, weeding, cleaning seeds, packaging products for sale, and so on. The monetary value of this work is at least $42,000.

- As mentioned above, these gifts can be used to meet the matching requirements on some grants. Remember to include a brief explanation of how you calculate the cash value of in-kind gifts.

Program-Related Investments and Loans

Foundations have traditionally earned money from stocks, bonds, real estate, and other investments, then used the earnings to fund their grant programs. A handful of funders also support nonprofits through program-related investments (also known as PRIs), sometimes called "recoverable grants." In plain English, the funders loan money directly to their grantees. Charitable investing of this sort has been used to underwrite low-income housing, historic preservation, small-business development, community revitalization, and other program areas. In addition to their typical portfolios, funders use program-related investments as a way to invest directly in social change and earn a small return. According to the Foundation Center, foundations provided $266 million in program-related investments in 1999, nearly double the 1998 total.

Other "social lenders" sometimes assist nonprofits in the following ways:

- *Community loan funds* support small businesses—and in some cases, nonprofits—in underserved areas: inner-city neighborhoods, rural communities, Native American reservations, and so forth.

- *Revolving loan funds* are loan pools set up to help nonprofits diversify income. Repayments replenish the funds, providing capital for other organizations. Examples include the Independent Press Association (www.indypress.org), which loans money to members for subscription development, and the Environmental Support Center (www.envsc.org), whose loan fund helps environmental groups build their membership or launch earned-income ventures.

- *Credit unions* are membership-owned financial institutions, in the same way that cooperatives are owned by their members. Some credit unions have progressive lending and investing policies. VanCity, for example, offers both grants and loans to entrepreneurial nonprofits in its home base of Vancouver, British Columbia.

Involving investors in your programs—even when those investors are foundations—is a tricky strategy. A program-related investment is not, technically speaking, a loan, but from the perspective of the grantee organization it functions like a loan, because the principal must be repaid with interest. If you are unable to repay the funder, you will have a hard time getting grants in the future. Make sure you have sufficient collateral to cover the debt, or another guaranteed source of income lined up for the near future. Many worthy organizations have failed due to unwise borrowing. If you can't pay for it, don't do it. Even better, find another way to do it that requires less cash.

On the other hand, there are times when a well-established, broadly funded organization can successfully manage a program-related investment or even a traditional bank loan. If your group is creating a venture to earn money from your programs, you might need money to get started. Income from the business would then be used to retire the debt. Capital campaigns offer another good example, because land and buildings purchased with investment or loan money can serve as collateral. If you were unable to raise the necessary funds to cover the loan, you could sell the property—as a last resort—and repay the lender.

To illustrate how this works, let's review the capital campaign at Native Seeds/SEARCH described earlier in this chapter. The group received two challenge grants to help buy and restore two old adobe buildings and the adjacent land for a new seed bank and grow-out garden. The foundation that provided the matching grants also invested $40,000 through a program-related investment at 3.5 percent interest, a much lower rate than we would have received from a commercial lender. We combined this investment with money from a bequest and bought the property outright for $90,000.

While we were obligated to repay the investor within fifteen years, we did so within three years. Although we used most of the money raised from members and other grantmakers for renovation costs, a portion was set aside for payments to the foundation. Whenever our capital campaign account had a big enough cushion, we made another $5,000 payment on the principal.

This brief description makes the process look simple. In fact, it took tremendous time and energy. To put things in perspective, consider this: the $40,000 investment was only 16 percent of the total project budget. We raised the rest as we went along. After receiving this initial investment, we spent only what we had available and incurred no additional debt.

When fully repaid, the cost of the loan was only $1,400, which qualifies as "cheap money." Furthermore, the foundation was duly impressed with our ability to manage debt and fulfill our commitments. They continued to support the organization with traditional grants for several years.

If you're blessed with a diverse funding base and can manage your money this prudently, your group might be ready for a program-related investment or a loan. The more prudent option for most groups is to raise the money you need before you spend it.

If you've read this far, and you diligently use the tools and tips in this book, you're going to raise money. How will you handle success? I'm reminded of the old line, "Be careful what you wish for—you might get it." The hardest part of the grantseeking process comes after you get the grant: you have to be accountable for spending it wisely and fulfilling your obligations. Chapter Ten focuses on the best ways to manage your grant money and keep the grantmaker happy.

Successful Grants Administration

Don't apply for a foundation grant unless you're truly ready for the scrutiny of outsiders regarding everything from your office's appearance to the documentation of your organization's impact and the accuracy of your accounting.

—JEFF ANDERSON, Oregon Community Foundation

Many grant proposals—indeed, some of the best grant proposals—are nothing more than dreams committed to paper. Even the most practical, well-planned projects always include a big dose of uncertainty. Dreaming dreams is easy, but designing a project—diagramming the dream—is hard work. Writing the proposal is even harder. Convincing someone to pay for it is harder still. Each stage of the process is progressively more difficult.

This chapter focuses on the really hard part: what to do after you've won the grant. The money is in the bank, but now you must test your dream against reality. To pass the test, you need to run the program effectively, handle the money scrupulously, and keep the donor informed.

The goal of this entire process—creating a project, writing a proposal, securing a grant, implementing your plan—is to make a tangible, measurable difference in the world. It's tempting to fixate on the money, but remember, you apply for grants to fund your work, not to build up your bank account. Money in the bank does not guarantee success in the community.

If you manage the project well and get the work done, you will find it easier to raise money in the future. Do a sloppy job, and you may not be considered for future funding. Even worse, word will get around that your organization is disorganized and irresponsible. This brings us back to one of the first questions to ask when designing a new program: Do we have the capacity to both implement and manage it properly? Be realistic in your assessment.

Record Keeping and Reporting

If you receive grants, you will write reports. This is one of the great truths of nonprofit life. A few small family foundations want nothing more than a newsletter, but everyone else insists on a formal accounting of your work. Many foundations request an interim report—say, six months into a one-year grant—and virtually all require a final report at the end of the project.

Grant reports fill several functions:

Accountability. The people who pay for your work have a right to know what you accomplished (and didn't accomplish) with their money. Foundation staff are accountable to their boards and grantmaking committees, and the foundations themselves must report to the Internal Revenue Service. Your report is part of a very long paper trail designed to ensure that the community is being served through the grantmaking process. The fancy phrase for this work is "due diligence."

Management oversight. Most people behave more cautiously when someone important is looking over their shoulder. By requiring grant reports, funders help their grantees stay on schedule, honor the work plan, and avoid impulsive behavior.

Publicity. Foundations use reporting information in their Web sites, annual reports, press releases, and other publications, which helps your group gain added exposure and recognition.

Fundraising. Some grantmakers—especially community-based foundations—solicit donations from the community to pass through to their grantees. If these funders can demonstrate effective grantmaking, their credibility improves and they raise more money. This, in turn, helps local organizations by increasing the pool of funds available for grants.

Adaptive learning. Grantmakers rely on their grantees to bring them news from the front lines—what's working, what isn't—so they can adapt their programs accordingly. "Grantees help us with our planning," says Tia Oros Peters of the Seventh Generation Fund. "They see emerging issues and help to link us up with other funders."

Feedback also helps grantmakers serve their grantees more effectively. "We have constantly sought comment on our application forms, processes, and grant limitations and have made and will continue to make changes in response to those comments," says Jim Abernathy of the Environmental Support Center.

The key to grants administration is common sense. Invest a little thought and effort along the way and everything will work to your advantage. The following ideas will help you stay on track:

Review progress periodically. Project organizers should meet on a regular basis to evaluate their work. For some projects, quarterly meetings are adequate; for others, you'll need to get together every week. Ask tough questions. How does the actual program compare with your proposal? Are you sticking with the timeline? Do you need to make changes? Are you spending money at an appropriate rate?

Minor adjustments are normal, since grant proposals always contain an element of improvisation. If you find that you require a major change of program, however, notify the grantmaker and negotiate these changes. A grant proposal is a contract, so any significant alterations must be approved by both parties—grantor and grantee. Better to adapt and achieve a good result than stick with the original program and accomplish less. Foundation officers understand this and want you to succeed.

Take lots of notes. You can't write an accurate final report unless you keep track of what you do all year. Without documentation, you will also find it difficult to analyze your work. How many people are you reaching? What's working and what isn't? What are you learning? If your proposal includes numerical objectives or evaluation points (and it should), how are you doing with the numbers? Collect lots of data. Document everything.

Save all articles, reviews, brochures, and other materials. If your project is written up in the local newspaper, clip and save the article. If the grant pays for production of publications, save copies. These items should be enclosed with the relevant reports.

Follow instructions. Foundations always tell you what to include in your final report. Give them what they want.

Honor the deadlines (or negotiate better ones). When asked what annoys her, Marjorie Fine of the Unitarian Universalist Veatch Program at Shelter Rock says, "People who miss deadlines and don't call to warn us. Deadlines are tools that I need to do my job." Irene Vlach of the Lazar Foundation concurs: "I can't count how many reminders I have to send to get reports. I actually like it when people ask for more time on their own initiative and don't need to be reminded."

Keep it simple. Grant officers don't have time to wade through piles of paper. Be selective about what you write and attach. For most grant reports, two pages of narrative, a budget detailing actual spending, and one or two attachments is plenty of information.

Don't expect a reaction from the foundation. You probably won't hear from them unless you do something wrong or leave something out. In most cases, a staff member will flip through the grant report, extract whatever information he or she needs, and file it. Your report will sit in the file cabinet until the editor starts gathering material for the foundation's annual summary. When you submit your next proposal, someone will pull the file to see if you fulfilled the reporting requirements. That's about it.

In his essay, "Foundation Leadership," which appears in the book *Environmental Leadership* (1993, p. 259), Jon Jensen of the George Gund Foundation tells a cautionary tale:

> Most foundations are primarily in the business of making grants, as opposed to following up on grants and evaluating how they worked. . . . Following up on the progress and impact of funded projects takes on lower priority in the day-to-day activities of the staff person. . . .
>
> For example, I once asked a colleague in another foundation what grants were on the agenda that had been voted on by his board a few weeks ago. I received, in reply, a blank stare. . . . He was already so focused on the next set of grants, he had forgotten those he had just finished.
>
> The pressure to keep moving forward is so great that looking back becomes a luxury. As might be expected, grantees may feel neglected because they receive few if any follow-up calls from the foundation and get little or no comment in response to the lengthy and carefully crafted progress reports they submit.

The moral of this story is, no news is good news. Do a careful, competent job with your grant reports, but don't expect much in the way of praise or criticism. Follow the lead of foundation staff—write it, submit it, and don't worry about it.

Exhibit 10.1 shows a grant report prepared for the Albuquerque Community Foundation, which provided funds for the Native Seeds/SEARCH project outlined in Chapter Four. It's brief, detailed, and specific, giving foundation staff a clear, measurable idea of how their money was spent.

In just two pages, this report accomplishes a lot:

- It restates the goals and objectives of the project. (This format is required by the foundation, but it's a good idea for all grant reports.)

- It identifies fourteen community groups that participated in outreach programs.

- It lists fifteen traditional crops grown in the demonstration garden.

EXHIBIT 10.1

Example of a Final Grant Report

TO: Laura Hueter Bass, Albuquerque Community Foundation
FR: Angelo Joaquin, Jr., Executive Director, Native Seeds/SEARCH
RE: Final Grant Report

Last September, the Foundation granted $1,500 to Native Seeds/SEARCH to support our community education and outreach programs in Albuquerque and northern New Mexico. An interim report was submitted in April; this report should complete our requirements for the grant. Financial documentation is enclosed.

Goals and objectives (as outlined in proposal): Brett Bakker, our New Mexico staff, will assist Native American farmers by distributing seeds, providing technical support for local and tribal seed-saving, and networking growers through the Traditional Native American Farmers Association. Through outreach programs, seed sales, gardening workshops, and contacts with the local news media, he will educate the public about the need to preserve genetic diversity and support indigenous culture and agriculture. He will also manage a small demonstration and grow-out garden in Albuquerque, while keeping the office open one day each week for walk-ins.

Results: Brett continues as a half-time employee for Native Seeds/SEARCH (he makes his real living maintaining the grounds at the University of New Mexico). In the past year, he provided educational programs and consultation to a variety of community groups across the region:

o Albuquerque Organic Gardening Association
o Santo Domingo Pueblo Senior Citizen Project
o Flowering Tree Permaculture Institute, Santa Clara Pueblo
o Huichol Center for Cultural Survival and Traditional Arts
o Ramah Navajo Weavers Association

o Indian Pueblo Cultural Center
o Albuquerque Master Gardeners
o Jefferson Middle School
o High Desert Research Farm
o Uptown Garden Club
o Albuquerque Public Library
o Cornstalk Institute
o La Montanita Food Co-op
o UNM Anthropology Department

We had another successful year in our grow-out garden, with land and water donated by Shepherd of the Valley Presbyterian Church at Rio Grande and Montano. Among the winners:

o Alvarón temporal peas
o Hopi white lima beans
o Punta Banda tomatoes

o Wenk's yellow hot pepper
o Cuartelas fava beans
o New Mexico melons

EXHIBIT 10.1 *(continued)*

Example of a Final Grant Report

o   Mostaza roja
o   Acoma mixed gourds
o   Hopi black sunflowers
o   Jemez mission grapes

o   Taos brown beans
o   Orach
o   San Juan squash, chiles, and
     watermelons

Seeds from the harvest will be sold to interested gardeners through our catalog, distributed for free to indigenous farmers, and preserved in our seed bank. While Brett was unable to organize any formal gardening workshops at the site, several volunteers helped out informally throughout the growing season with planting, weeding, and harvesting.

Brett collected seeds and cuttings from heirloom fruit trees at San Felipe, Isleta, Santo Domingo, Zia, Jemez, and San Juan Pueblos, and the Spanish community of El Guique. Thanks to a grant from the Educational Foundation of America, Brett will be able to focus more of his time on collecting endangered crops. He is preparing for a series of trips throughout northern New Mexico, southern Colorado and southern Utah. His goal: bring in at least 50 uncollected varieties over the next eighteen months. The first trip, a collaboration with the High Desert Research Farm at Ghost Ranch, will take place next month.

Brett continues as our local liaison to the Traditional Native American Farmers Association (TNAFA), an all-indigenous group convened by Native Seeds/SEARCH to support traditional agriculture in New Mexico and Arizona. Brett met with TNAFA staff about ten times during the past year, attended their last annual conference at Camp Verde, Arizona, and will participate in their 1994 conference next month in Santa Fe.

The news media was once again supportive and interested in our conservation efforts. Brett was interviewed on KUNM Radio and showed off our crops on *The New Garden*, a program syndicated nationally on PBS. (TNAFA director Calvin Aragon, of Acoma, was also profiled on the show.) Our work was mentioned in *The New Mexican* and *Arellano,* a quarterly publication from Embudo, New Mexico. Brett also writes a regular column for La Montanita's *Co-op Connection* newsletter; here's a recent excerpt:

> *"There's a sense of wholeness journeying the backroads. Piles of corn wait to be shucked; there's a new way to learn of tying red chile into ristras. The cattle will soon be brought down from the hills to clear the cornstalks. Even with the harvest tasks, no one's too busy not to offer a cup of coffee around the kitchen table and talk of the year's crops, recipes for chile caribe, and how's Tio Florencio feeling lately?"*

In this season of plenty, we thank you – again! – for your enthusiastic support.

Expense Report

Salary, payroll tax (.5 FTE)	$11,359	Travel	440
Rent and office supplies	1,583	Professional fees	606
Garden supplies and seeds	849	Miscellaneous	74
Printing and postage	210		
Telephone	428	**Total**	**$15,549**

- It names seven indigenous communities where staff collected seeds and cuttings from heirloom fruit trees.
- It describes the group's upcoming projects and next steps.
- It includes an excerpt from an article by the New Mexico field manager.
- It itemizes how the money was spent.

By naming names and providing details, this work is made real for the reader. We could have written, "We offered educational programs to fourteen organizations and grew fifteen traditional crop varieties," but the lists of crops and cooperating groups paint a much more vivid picture. The work of Native Seeds is embodied in these names because they reflect the diversity of the group's constituency and the crops they grow. That sense of connection with the community and the land is reinforced at the end of the narrative, in the words of the man who did the work.

Managing Grant Money

Financial management is the weak link in many grassroots groups. Planning and budgeting combine all the money taboos with that common ailment, "math phobia." Put a spreadsheet in front of most activists and they will run screaming from the room. As financial management trainer Terry Miller writes in his book, *Managing for Change* (1992, pp. i-ii), "For people driven to work in the nonprofit sector . . . there is often the sense that managing money is tantamount to making a deal with the devil."

Your bookkeeping skills will have a big impact on your ability to raise money and do your program work. Many otherwise successful groups have folded because they didn't take the necessary steps to put their books in order. "If you try to avoid financial management," Miller says, "the ironic thing is that you may spend more of your time on it than you would have otherwise—like any good discipline, good financial management systems make life more systematic, easier to get the work done."

For detailed information on accounting systems and evaluating what level of complexity is appropriate for your organization, I refer you to Miller's book. "There is no magic or secret to financial management," he writes. "You know more about it than you think you do." To start you thinking about the subject, and to reinforce your better instincts, here are a few broad suggestions:

If you need help, hire a professional. For many grassroots groups, it makes sense to hire a bookkeeping service. Contract bookkeepers don't cost that much because you pay only for the hours you use each month and in return you get a breadth of experience. If you can find someone who supports your mission, she or he might donate the service or offer a discount. Select a bookkeeper with non-profit experience. Ask other groups in your community for recommendations.

Set up your books to track income and expenses by department or program. Don't try to track expenses by individual grant. You will create unnecessary work for yourself, since most funders don't want or need that level of detail. For the same reason, don't open a separate bank account for each grant unless required by the funder to do so.

When you track your expenses by program (and not by individual grant), you are more likely to seek grant support for your own priorities and initiatives instead of responding to the grantmaker's priorities. This is one of the subtle ways that financial management systems influence your program work. All successful fundraising strategies address the interests of both funder and recipient to some degree, but if you want your group to be successful over the long run, stick to your mission and don't get sidetracked in pursuit of money.

Spend grant money on relevant program expenses only. Most grants are restricted to the activities outlined in your proposal, according to the financial plan reflected in your project budget. Unless you receive money for general support, don't treat your grant as an emergency slush fund or rewrite the budget as you go. Minor changes are fine, but if your project budget needs significant adjustments, notify the funder and negotiate the alterations. If you have the foresight to anticipate these changes and the diligence and honesty to initiate the contact, the grantmaker is bound to be impressed. This makes for an easy, straightforward negotiation.

Review project expenses each month. Track your cash flow. Be careful you don't spend all your grant funds long before the project is supposed to end (unless you finish the work early).

If you receive multiple grants for a project, you may be able to exhaust the first grant before the work is complete and still have money in the bank from the second or third grant. In this situation—depending upon your relationship with the funder—you could submit an early final report and perhaps even apply for a follow-up grant while the project continues. If you're not clear about how to proceed, check with foundation staff. In many cases, they will ask you to stick with the original reporting schedule.

Keep receipts for all expenses. You won't need to submit them with your grant report, but it's useful to have receipts on hand in case you run into questions from foundation staff. More important, receipts and appropriate documentation help to maintain an "audit trail" and demonstrate your stewardship of community funds. Good internal control has a big impact on your effectiveness and credibility; saving documentation for all expenditures is the most important part of good control.

Once again, keep it simple. When it comes to reporting grant-funded expenses, keep it simple. For most grants, six to ten line items are sufficient for a grant report budget.

The Value of Honesty, Revisited

Many years ago I was involved with "the little project that couldn't." Every problem spawned three new problems, delay led to delay, and after a year of doing nothing it was time to submit our final report. We wrote to the foundation, detailing our troubles, and described our plan to revive the project. After explaining the financial situation—we had spent only $3,000 of their $15,000 grant—we requested a nine-month extension.

Their response arrived in the mail a few weeks later. One of my coworkers was expecting a letter addressed, "You stupid jerks," but the tone was respectful and supportive. "Thank you," the foundation officer wrote, "for being so careful with our money. Your extension is approved. Good luck."

It's easy to think of foundation staff as "them," especially if they work in another city. It's easy to withhold information, especially if it makes you look bad. It's easy to rearrange the truth. But remember, funders are your partners and peers. If you lie, you put that partnership at risk.

There is no such thing as a flawless project. Grantmakers understand this, which is why they value honesty. As Marjorie Fine says, "Be honest, even when things go bad. Be sensitive to different outcomes than the ones you expected. In social justice work, outcomes are more nuanced."

Every problem has a solution; describe yours. Don't run around like Chicken Little shouting, "The sky is falling!" Tell them about your strategy: you've hired an engineer and you're building a scaffold and you plan to prop it up while you figure out what to do next. Show your ingenuity. You might even be rewarded for your candor. "If we know about the challenges you're facing," says Denise Joines of the Wilburforce Foundation, "we can sometimes provide additional resources to address them."

Your Mother Was Right: The Value of Good Manners

Once, at a conference, I heard a grants officer lecturing a room full of grant recipients. He was angry because so few of them had bothered to add his name to their mailing lists. "If I gave you $20," he said, "you would send me a newsletter. I give you $1,000 and never hear from you again. What's wrong with this picture?"

Once you receive the grant, your relationship with the grantmaker enters a new phase. Up to that point, all your communications—phone calls, proposal, site visit—are a form of courtship. When that check is written, the relationship gets serious. Unfortunately, many groups deposit the check and become deadbeat partners—they're silent and invisible until it's time to ask for more money.

"When you receive the grant, don't disappear," says Irene Vlach. "When you have a victory or a change in program staff, let us know. Pick up the phone. By being educated, we become better grantmakers."

It takes very little work to "stay on the radar screen" and maintain healthy foundation relations. As Jon Jensen indicated, you probably won't get a reaction, since foundation staff are so busy, but they'll notice your effort. Down the road, when you apply for another grant, you will see the results. Keep these suggestions in mind:

Send a thank-you letter and pick up the phone. As soon as you are notified of the grant, get in touch with the grantmaker. The phone call is a courtesy; the letter will be added to your file at the foundation office, along with whatever paperwork you are required to fill out to receive the check.

Put all funders on your mailing list. Make sure they receive your newsletter, annual report (if you produce one), and other publications.

Acknowledge the grantmakers. Mention foundation supporters on your Web site and in your publications and relevant news releases, unless they wish to remain anonymous.

Ask before adding them to your listserv or e-news list. This is a courtesy you should extend to everyone, not just people who give you money.

If something exciting happens, mail a postcard or a brief handwritten note. "I thought you might like to hear about . . . " E-mail is also effective, but if you send paper it is more likely to end up in your grant file, which is still a paper process in nearly all foundation offices. Your good manners will be remembered when the file is pulled for the next proposal review.

Share your press coverage. When an organization I worked for was featured in *Time* magazine, we photocopied the article and sent it to all major donors and foundation supporters. The key here is to be selective—do not distribute a three-sentence calendar announcement of your next event or a fifteen-second video clip from the local evening news.

Send photographs where relevant. A good photo packs a lot of emotional appeal and provides a nice break from all the words. Plus, a busy program officer can absorb a photo in about five seconds, think about your group, feel good about your work, and move on to other things.

Invite funders to everything. Make sure they know about your upcoming annual meeting, nature hike, youth program, protest, performance, candidate accountability session, press conference, volunteer recognition event, member picnic, paint-the-office party—whatever. They might actually show up, which will give you the opportunity to showcase your group in action.

Offer to meet with them. If you're traveling and plan to be in their neighborhood, offer to meet with foundation staff and give them a progress report. You might be turned down, but the offer will be appreciated.

Don't overdo it. Three or four extra contacts per year—press clips, postcards, and the like—are plenty. If, however, you have questions about your current project or need assistance with your upcoming proposal, don't be shy about calling for help.

When I reviewed this list with one of my classes, a student raised her hand and said, "So, we're supposed to do all the things our mothers taught us to do." That sums it up pretty well, at least in the case of my mother. Treat funders like respected peers and generous friends. Say thank you. Stay in touch. Invite them to participate. Share the spotlight; don't claim all the attention. Use your manners. Be a credit to your mother and your organization, too.

By now you've learned how to think like a program officer and design your work to make the most of grant opportunities, identify prospective funders and get to know them, prepare a terrific proposal, manage all the money that's about to come rolling in (well, trickling in), and keep in touch with the grantmaker.

Here's the final test: do you have the smarts and the staying power to carry on for the next decade or two or three? Money makes it easier to keep going, but in the end it's not about the funding—it's about your heart and your passion for change. How will you keep yourself energized? You'll find tips for the long haul in Chapter Eleven.

The Grantseeker's Guide to Surviving and Thriving

We're seeing larger, democratically run groups with more sophisticated strategies. They're willing to take on big targets and win. Thousands of these organizations are doing pretty well; they run on people's energy, which is higher than ever before. From my perspective, the administration in Washington is a blip on the screen. We're getting closer to creating a democratic society from the bottom up.

—RON WHITE, formerly of the Tides Foundation

Fundraising is organizing. Resources go where change happens.

—BILL DEMPSEY, formerly of the Unitarian Universalist
Veatch Program at Shelter Rock

In 1980, a few weeks after Ronald Reagan was first elected president, I answered a classified advertisement in the Portland *Oregonian*. The first word was ACTIVIST. I can't remember the rest of the ad, but the main idea was that I would get paid to work for social justice. I was adrift and anxious about the future, and this seemed to me a small, tangible miracle.

The next day I was sitting on a cracked vinyl sofa, waiting for my interview. The linoleum was streaked with dirt and a pile of dead office machines (remember mimeographs?) rusted quietly in the corner, but the atmosphere was electric. Phones rang, people ran in and out with picket signs, a typewriter (remember typewriters?) chattered in the back room, and I overheard an argument in which the word "tactics" played a big role. I didn't know what was going on, but I wanted *in*.

That night I started knocking on doors, asking strangers for money to fight the utility company. I was—surprise!—a fundraiser. By the time I left Oregon Fair Share in 1983, I had received lots of training in community organizing and tactical research, but my door-to-door experience—talking with people about a better world and asking them to help pay for it—was the most compelling, frustrating, and empowering part of the job. My fundraising skills, coupled with an abiding desire for justice, have kept me in the movement for social change ever since.

Few of us set out to be fundraisers, but we see the need and we go to it with courage and persistence. We lead with our hearts, which is how it should be. Unfortunately, this leads to a lot of broken hearts. I was a terrific door-knocker, but at the end of my canvassing career, after ten thousand pitches on ten thousand doorsteps, I found myself sitting on the curb, crying in the rain. At that moment—I remember it vividly—I was convinced that I had nothing left to give. The twenty years since have proven me wrong.

Nearly every day I feel profoundly grateful for my work. That doesn't mean I'm not tired or angry or discouraged, because I am. Still, I persevere. I've learned that real social change takes generations, and unless we're in it for the long run, we just skim the surface and nothing really changes.

As Gandhi said, "We must *be* the change we wish to see." Here are a few humble suggestions to help you redesign your heart and your mind for the long haul.

Dealing with Rejection

As a door-to-door canvasser, I was expected to talk with forty people per shift and recruit five members. For every enthusiastic person who said, "Great, let me write you a check," seven others said, "Get lost." Some nights were much easier, others were brutal. I spent very little time arguing or convincing; my job was to find the right people and leave everyone else alone. In some ways, rejection was helpful. The quicker the refusal, the sooner I could move on to the next house. The law of averages eventually bailed me out.

The odds of having your grant proposals approved are about the same. At some point in your grantseeking life—probably very early—you will face rejection. Perhaps you just received a rejection letter, which is why you're reading this book.

You've heard this before, but if you're like me, you need to hear it again: Don't take it personally. As Lois DeBacker of the Charles Stewart Mott Foundation says,

"I understand that people pour their lives into this. I feel terrible about turning down really, really compelling work, but we turn down good ideas all the time for lack of funds. It's not a judgment on the validity of the work."

For many activists, however, it's hard to separate the personal from the professional. As a first step, you need to sort out the things you can, and can't, control. Most proposals are rejected because of lack of money, which has nothing to do with you, your organization, your project, or your writing skills. The vast majority of funders can't (or won't) allocate sufficient funds for every proposal they receive. "The hard news," says Hubert Sapp of the Hartford Foundation, "is that we get more good ideas than we can fund." If you send out grant applications, you will accumulate your share of rejection letters. That's the way it works.

You should also understand that the "Sorry, we can't help you" letter can move you to the next stage in the relationship, not the end. As Jon Jensen of the George Gund Foundation says, "I write a bland rejection letter that says, 'Call me.' Then I tune my comments to how they are reacting. I've told applicants, 'You get points for persistence.' The proposal is an educational process—we're educating each other—and people don't always get it the first time."

Jason Halbert of the Oak Hill Fund takes the same point even further: "As a former coordinator of a grassroots program with an annual budget of roughly $100,000, I often felt rejected by foundations and never really thought of trying again. Often people turn initial rejection into bitterness or spite and that only hurts the organization and the individual in the long run. Cultivate the relationship and deepen the knowledge of those you seek funding from and you'll have a better chance. Don't burn any bridges; fundraising is not war."

Of course, the best antidote for rejection is success. By targeting your proposals and building solid relationships, you can greatly improve your odds. Before knocking on a door with your proposal, know who lives inside, what they care about, and how they want to be approached. If you know in advance that they won't be interested in your work—because you don't fit the guidelines—don't knock.

If you take one message from this book, let it be this: do your homework. You will raise more money, waste less time, and feel better about your efforts. For more information on grant research, see Chapter Five.

There's another, more subtle reason for doing a thorough job on the research. During five years as development director at Native Seeds/SEARCH, a regional conservation group in Tucson, I built a prospect base of 250 foundations, corporations, and other funding sources. Over time, we applied to perhaps half the list. Several others we tracked for our long-term capital project, a conservation farm. The remaining prospects were fairly marginal, but that file cabinet, stuffed to the limit with foundation guidelines and annual reports, was a great comfort to me. As I filed away each rejection letter, I would think, "If you don't want to work with us, we'll find someone else who does." In many cases, "someone else" was right at my fingertips. Rejection doesn't feel so bad when you have other options.

Diversifying Your Funding

In collaboration with my colleagues at the Institute for Conservation Leadership, I've helped to create a new program called "The Complete Fundraiser." We work intensively with fifteen to twenty organizations over the course of twelve months, providing them with training, consulting, mentoring, and a whole lot of moral support.

When we recently met with participants at the opening workshop, a disturbing pattern emerged: several groups were on the brink of insolvency. Their financial problems went far beyond the usual year-end scrambling endemic to grassroots organizations. Many of these folks faced genuine crises. They had enough money to cover payroll for a month, maybe two, and little or nothing in the pipeline.

What do you think they had in common, besides being broke? You guessed it—a deep reliance on foundation grants.

If your organization survives on grant money, it will die without it. Who, then, controls the fate of your group? No funder can underwrite your work forever. Very few will fund you for more than two or three years in a row. You can improve your financial health by developing relationships with several grantmakers, but that won't protect you if their priorities shift. Issues rise and fall on the public agenda, and a lot of grant money moves with the trends. Some funders simply close up shop. "In our state," says David Karoff of the Rhode Island Foundation, "the philanthropic community is shrinking due to moves and corporate mergers. Demand is up, while the number of givers is down. This drives the need for creating a donor base of individuals."

"At this point," says Roxanne Turnage of the CS Fund, "no one should put all their eggs in the foundation basket."

If you're serious about creating real change in your community, you must develop grassroots financial support. Change takes time and requires a steady stream of money. A diverse funding base of individual gifts, major donors, benefit events, and earned income is the best way to ensure the long-term survival and success of your organization.

Unlike most foundations, individuals have been known to support specific groups for decades. When I went to work at the Tucson Planned Parenthood affiliate in 1988, we began transferring donor information from file cards to a computer database. Some of those cards had been marked on for twenty years! Many $10 and $20 contributors had, over the years, become major donors, giving annual gifts of $500 or more. Their commitment increased as their financial situation improved and they became more involved with the group and saw how their money was being used. In some cases, their children (and even grandchildren) were also donors. This happens when an organization lives to be sixty years old and maintains its relevance and vitality.

If you'd like a quick refresher on the whys and hows of diversifying your funding, take another look at Chapter Two. "Get training to do this well," says David Karoff. "People should seek mentoring and coaching through the Association of Fundraising Professionals and take advantage of other training opportunities." (You can find the association at www.afpnet.org.)

Using Your Time and Energy Effectively

I once wrote on a job application, "I've learned to keep my sense of balance and my sense of humor under the usual constraints of not enough time and never enough money." It's a clever sentence, but in one sense it's a lie. When I wrote it, I felt overwhelmed by the problems we face, and I still do.

Take an honest look at the world—it's easy to be overwhelmed. Your goal, as activist-for-life, is to put that feeling in perspective and enjoy the victories you earn along the way. You need both balance and humor to survive, but mostly you need faith—faith in the power of change and your ability to create change. The following ideas will help you keep the faith and get the work done.

Honor your priorities. When I first met my wife, I told her the two things I couldn't tolerate were gross injustice and moldy dishes. In the intervening years, nothing has really changed. I've washed a lot of dishes and devoted most of my waking hours to community organizing and raising money. Work is the biggest part of my life, because it gives me a sense of community and purpose. I am sustained by what I do all day.

Your priorities may be different. Learn what they are and honor them. If you spend time in meetings thinking about your children, go to fewer meetings and enjoy your kids more. If you feel the need to make things grow, put your hands in the dirt. If your faith is wavering, find quiet time and space to strengthen yourself spiritually. If you're exhausted, take a nap.

The main point is, figure out what moves you most and then do it. Burnout is caused by people doing what they *should* instead of what they *want*.

Give your favorite organization whatever time you can afford—give it whole-heartedly and passionately—then draw the line. In the long run, you will have more time and energy to share.

Pick your fights. It pains me to say this, but you must develop an aversion to lost causes. If you can't see your way to victory—even if that victory won't occur for years or decades—pick another fight. To maintain your sanity and stamina, focus your energy where it will have the greatest impact.

Go easy on the ideological purity. Don't get sucked into petty arguments with coworkers and allies. The history of the social change movement is filled with campaigns that failed because allies could only agree—only!—on 90 percent of the program. If you're spending a lot of time arguing about turf, or the wording of your news release, or how to divide up the credit, something is wrong. Check your ego at the door and focus on areas of agreement, not disagreement.

Learn how to juggle. Sort through the pile on your desk daily and put the most pressing items on top; deal with them first. Buy a calendar—paper or electronic, it doesn't matter—and use it. Don't go to meetings just for the sake of being there. Spend some time each day raising money. Keep track of the bank balance, but don't be obsessed. Say "thank you" whenever possible, for any reason. When you make a mistake, accept responsibility and solve the problem. Most of all, keep your wits about you. When in doubt, think.

Create something good, then use it again and again. After you and your coworkers have laid out your organization's priorities for the year, sit down and write the "master proposal" for each project. Don't think about the funders yet; keep wrestling with the words until you've found the language that best describes why the project is needed, how you'll organize it, and why you're the best group to undertake the work. After you've got the basic language down for each program, you can adapt the length and format to meet the requirements of various funders.

Recycling your work in this way will save you vast amounts of time. In fact, you can take this strategy even further by pulling paragraphs or phrases from your proposals and using them in your mail solicitations, news releases, brochures, newsletters, and any other written materials. During my time at Native Seeds/SEARCH, the membership renewal letters (six per year) were built from language first created for grant proposals.

Don't be a drudge. Last and best, give yourself lots of credit, then take a long break. Hike, swim, sleep, dance, ride a bike, go see a movie, make love with your sweetheart, cook an extravagant meal, stay up all night and read a good book. Forget about the sorry state of the world for a few hours, and revel in the wondrous state of the world. To quote the late author and troublemaker

Edward Abbey, "Be as I am—a reluctant enthusiast, a part-time crusader, a half-hearted fanatic. Save the other half of yourselves and your lives for pleasure and adventure. It is not enough to fight for the land; it is even more important to enjoy it."

I am the worst person to offer this advice, since I'm usually the last one to heed it. When this book is finished, however, I plan to take a long hike into woods, swim in my favorite pond, and lay on a big rock in the sun. You should do the same.

The Perfect Organization

People rarely call a doctor when they're healthy, and nobody looks for a consultant when their nonprofit is running smoothly. I spend a lot of time talking with folks who feel that their organizations are sick, and that makes them feel sick.

The first thing I ask is, "When you walked into the office this morning and flipped the switch, did the lights go on?"

"Sure."

"Aha! That's a victory. You found enough money to pay the electric bill. How about the phone?"

"We're talking, aren't we?"

"Terrific. Another victory."

This is a useful strategy for a therapist—my unofficial job title—but it's probably cost me some consulting work. People don't want to spend money to learn what they're doing right; they want me to fix what's wrong. Most of us tend to ignore the things we accomplish just by showing up each day, plowing through the e-mail, answering the phone, digging through the pile on the desk, pushing the work forward, and flying the flag of hope for everyone to see and admire.

Corporate gurus have a name for this strategy. They call it "muddle-through management," and as far as I'm concerned, it's a legitimate way to run a small business or even a nonprofit. It's especially effective for small, over-worked, underfunded social change organizations with big ideas. Muddle-through management might be the best way to save the world, which is a very muddled place.

In the perfect world, every group would have a comprehensive strategic plan, an ample budget, a hard-working board, and lots of staff. Everyone would be paid a living wage. All problems would have obvious solutions.

Alas, there is no perfect world, except the one we carry inside our hearts. The perfect organization doesn't exist, except in our fantasies. Every nonprofit—even the most pragmatic, diverse, visionary, well-funded group—has a truckload of troubles. So don't assume that your group is the only one that's broke and disorganized. You're in excellent company, and you're doing good work in spite of everything.

It's okay to strive for perfection, but don't let your fantasies or frustrations interfere with that pile on your desk. Keep digging.

resource

A

Useful
Publications

This resource list includes publications I have reviewed and, in many cases, used. Hundreds of additional books and periodicals are available to help you with fundraising, proposal development, and other organizational needs. I urge you to visit your nearest Foundation Center Cooperating Collection (look for the list at www.fdncenter.org) and spend some time browsing. The Internet also offers many terrific resources for nonprofits; see Resource B and also below.

Before ordering any of these materials, call to confirm availability and current price. Some publishers require an additional charge for shipping and handling.

Board Development and Fundraising

The Board of Directors, Kim Klein and Stephanie Roth, 2000. 40 pages. $12. Grassroots Fundraising Journal, 3781 Broadway, Oakland, CA 94611, 888/458-8588, www.grassrootsfundraising.org.

> *This booklet includes ten articles reprinted from the* Grassroots Fundraising Journal, *including several on board fundraising responsibilities and strategies. My favorite: "53 Ways Board Members Can Raise $1,000."*

Boards from Hell, Susan M. Scribner, 1998. 62 pages. $15. Scribner & Associates, 3939 Virginia Road, Suite #210, Long Beach, CA 90807, 562/426-9444, www.susanscribner.com.

> *A humorous look at everything that can go wrong with your board of directors. Includes sections on how to create a healthy, productive board and then involve board members in strategic planning.*

Canadian Resources

Canadian FundRaiser, Box 86, Station C, Toronto, Ontario M6J 3M7, 416/345-9403, www.canadianfundraiser.com. Twenty-four issues a year, $227.

> *A broad range of fundraising news and tips, designed primarily for mainstream charities. Free e-newsletter available.*

Green Source, www.ec.gc.ca/ecoaction/grnsrc/index_e.cfm.

> *This Web site is maintained by the EcoAction Community Funding Program, a project of Environment Canada that provides "financial support to community groups for projects that have measurable, positive impacts on the environment." This free database includes funding from government, foundation, corporate, and nonprofit sources.*

2004 Canadian Directory to Foundations and Grants, Jason Tanaguchi, ed., 2003. $375 ($275 for members). Canadian Centre for Philanthropy, 425 University Avenue, Suite 700, Toronto, Ontario M5G 1T6, 416/597-2293, www.ccp.ca.

> *The most comprehensive guide to Canadian foundations, with more than 2,200 funders and 24,000 grants; also available in an on-line version for $450 a year ($350 for members). The CCP publishes a variety of materials for Canadian nonprofits.*

Community-Based Fundraising

Fundraising for Social Change, 4th ed., Kim Klein, 2001. 403 pages. $35. Jossey-Bass, 989 Market Street, San Francisco, CA 94103, 800/956-7739, www.josseybass.com.

> *One of the most accessible books on fundraising, and one of the few that addresses the needs and concerns of progressive groups.*

The Fundraising Houseparty, Morrie Warshawski, 2002. 58 pages. $14.95 plus $4 shipping. Available from the author, 1408 W. Washington Street, Ann Arbor, MI 48103, 734/332-9768, www.warshawski.com.

> *This thin but thorough book covers everything you need to know to raise money at cocktail parties, brunches, and the like. Includes sample invitations, scripts, and checklists.*

Fundraising in Times of Crisis, Kim Klein, 2003. 192 pages. $24.95. Jossey-Bass, 989 Market Street, San Francisco, CA 94103, 800/956-7739, www.josseybass.com.

> *A practical, hands-on guide for dealing with crises—financial and otherwise—and working your way back to fiscal and organizational health.*

Getting Major Gifts, Kim Klein and Stephanie Roth, 2000. 40 pages. $12. Grassroots Fundraising Journal, 3781 Broadway, Oakland, CA 94611, 888/458-8588, www.grassrootsfundraising.org.

This booklet includes twelve articles reprinted from the Grassroots Fundraising Journal. *It contains enough information to allow the reader to design and initiate a major donor program.*

The Nonprofit Membership Toolkit, Ellis M. M. Robinson, 2003. 291 pages. $35. Jossey-Bass, 989 Market Street, San Francisco, CA 94103, 800/956-7739, www.josseybass.com.

A step-by-step approach for building a strong membership program to increase your income and improve the effectiveness and clout of your organization.

Raise More Money: The Best of the Grassroots Fundraising Journal, Kim Klein and Stephanie Roth, eds., 2001. 200 pages. $29. Jossey-Bass, 989 Market Street, San Francisco, CA 94103, 800/956-7739, www.josseybass.com.

This "greatest hits" collection spans two decades, fifty-five articles, and nineteen authors. It covers everything from organizational and board development to nuts-and-bolts fundraising strategies.

Successful Fundraising, 2nd ed., Joan Flanagan, 1999. 324 pages. $18.95. McGraw Hill/Contemporary, One Prudential Plaza, 1300 Randolph Street #400, Chicago, IL 60601, 800/621-1918, books.mcgraw-hill.com.

A witty, thorough approach to fundraising (including foundation and corporate grants) from one of the pioneers of grassroots fundraising.

Computer Products and Services for Grant Research

See Resource B for product evaluations and contact information.

Earned Income

Selling Social Change (Without Selling Out): Earned Income Strategies for Nonprofits, Andy Robinson, 2002. 229 pages. $25.95. Jossey-Bass, 989 Market Street, San Francisco, CA 94103, 800/956-7739, www.josseybass.com.

In addition to raising money through grants and donations from individuals, nonprofits can earn income by selling products and services. This book uses case studies from two dozen grassroots organizations and a variety of worksheets to illustrate the process.

Venture Forth! The Essential Guide to Starting a Moneymaking Business in Your Nonprofit Organization, Rolfe Larson, 2002. 272 pages. $30. Amherst W. Wilder Foundation, 919 Lafond Avenue, St. Paul, MN 55104, 651/642-4000, www.wilder.org.

A thorough, step-by-step guide to creating nonprofit business ventures, with an especially good section on nonprofit business planning.

Grant Directories

Most grant directories are large, expensive books that grassroots organizations should consider using (for free) at the library. The most significant publishers are the Foundation Center (www. fdncenter.org) and Taft Group, an imprint of Gale (www.galegroup.com/taft.htm).

The following specialized directories are more affordable and more likely to address the needs of grassroots groups. A state or regional directory may also be available for your area; check the Foundation Center's Web site at fdncenter.org/learn/topical.sl_dir.html.

Environmental Grantmaking Foundations 2003, Corinne S. Thiele, ed., 2003. 1,008 pages. $110. Resources for Global Sustainability, P.O. Box 3665, Cary, NC 27619, 800/724-1857, www.environmentalgrants.com.

The most comprehensive resource for environmental grantseekers, with profiles of 892 funders, including 55 Canadian grantmakers. A CD version of this directory is available from the publisher for $120.

Grantmakers Directory 2000–2001, Nicole Trombley, ed., 2001. 336 pages. $25. National Network of Grantmakers, 138 Court Street #427, Brooklyn, NY 11201, 718/643-8814, www.nng.org.

The National Network of Grantmakers is a consortium of funders that support social and economic justice, human rights, cultural diversity, and grassroots democracy. This directory profiles two hundred grantmaking institutions, including more than sixty that accept a common application form.

2000 Religious Funding Resource Guide, Eileen Paul, ed., 2000. 517 pages. $92.50. ResourceWomen, 4527 South Dakota Avenue, N.W., Washington, DC 20017, 202/832-8071.

A compendium of guidelines and application forms for thirty-nine grant and loan programs, plus a handy table explaining the hierarchy of each major denomination and suggestions for how to approach and address clergy.

Grant Research

The Foundation Center Guide to Grantseeking on the Web, 2003 Edition, Kief Schladmeiler, ed., 2003. 852 pages. $29.95. The Foundation Center, 79 Fifth Avenue, New York, NY 10003, 212/620-4230, www.fdncenter.org.

A comprehensive, inexpensive guide to research on foundations, corporations, government agencies, public charities that give grants, and even individual donor prospecting. Also available in CD-ROM format at the same price.

Foundation Fundamentals: A Guide for Grantseekers, 6th ed., Pattie J. Johnson, ed., 1999. 257 pages. $24.95. The Foundation Center, 79 Fifth Avenue, New York, NY 10003, 212/620-4230, www.fdncenter.org.

One of the first and best guides to grants research. Includes sample entries from various foundation directories, which you can use to orient yourself before beginning your research.

Nonprofit Advocacy

The Alliance for Justice (11 Dupont Circle, N.W., 2nd Floor, Washington, DC 20036, 202/822-6070, www.afj.org) publishes a series of booklets to help non-profits understand the rules regarding advocacy, lobbying, and elections. Here are some of their titles:

- *Being a Player: A Guide to the IRS Lobbying Regulations for Advocacy Charities,* 1995. 57 pages. $15. A plain-language roadmap of lobbying reg-ulations.

- *The Connection: Strategies for Creating and Operating 501(c)(3)s, 501(c)(4)s, and PACs,* 1998. 62 pages. $25. This booklet explains the advan-tages and issues to be considered in establishing each of these types of nonprofit organization.

- *The Rules of the Game: An Election Year Legal Guide for Nonprofit Orga-nizations,* 1996. 52 pages. $20. Explains the right (and wrong) ways to organize specific voter education activities.

- *Seize the Initiative,* 1996. 56 pages. $20. This guide answers questions that are frequently asked by nonprofits about working on ballot initiatives.

Periodicals

Several of these publishers also offer free on-line newsletters.

The Chronicle of Philanthropy, 1255 23rd Street, N.W., Suite 700, Washington, DC 20037, 202/466-1234, www.philanthropy.com. Twenty-four issues per year, $69.50.

The most thorough coverage of the nonprofit sector, including fundraising issues and strategies. Regular "New Grants" feature describes recent founda-tion and corporate grants; "Deadlines" lists current grant opportunities.

Foundation News and Commentary, Council on Foundations, 1828 L Street, N.W., Washington, DC 20090-6043, 800/771-8187, www.cof.org. Six issues per year, $60.

This magazine is written primarily for foundation officers. Most articles focus on philanthropic trends and the profession of grantmaking.

The Grantsmanship Center Magazine, P.O. Box 17220, Los Angeles, CA 90017, 213/482-9860, www.tgci.com. Four issues per year, free to nonprofits at their business addresses.

Part newsletter, part promotional brochure for Grantsmanship Center trainings and publications.

Grassroots Fundraising Journal, 3781 Broadway, Oakland, CA 94611, 888/458-8588, www.grassrootsfundraising.org. Six issues per year, $32.

Brief, easy-to-read articles designed for social change activists and small non-profits. Lots of useful nuts-and-bolts information on community-based fundraising.

NonProfit Times, 120 Littleton Road Suite #120, Parsippany, NJ 07054, 973/394-1800, www.nptimes.org. Twenty-four issues per year; free to "full-time nonprofit executives." All others, $65.

Covers a wide range of nonprofit fundraising and management issues, with a focus on "direct response"—direct mail, telemarketing, and Internet fundraising—and financial management.

Responsive Philanthropy, National Committee for Responsive Philanthropy, 2001 S Street, N.W. Suite #620, Washington, DC 20009, 202/387-9177, www.ncrp.org. Four issues per year, $25.

The National Committee for Responsive Philanthropy works to promote progressive philanthropy, including grantmaking for social change. Their newsletter analyzes federal legislation as it relates to philanthropy and includes occasional features on fundraising for social justice.

Program-Related Investments

The PRI Directory: Charitable Loans and Other Program-Related Investments by Foundations, 2nd ed., 2003. 155 pages. $75. The Foundation Center, 79 Fifth Avenue, New York, NY 10003, 212/620-4230, www.fdncenter.org.

A list of funders that provide program-related investments, with tips on how to approach them and manage charitable loans if your application is successful.

Proposal Writing

Demystifying Grant Seeking: What You REALLY Need to Know to Get Grants, Larissa Golden Brown and Martin John Brown, 2001. 241 pages. $26.95. Jossey-Bass, 989 Market Street, San Francisco, CA 94103, 800/956-7739, www.josseybass.com.

A systematic approach that begins with identifying your internal needs and moves through the process of research, proposal development, and outreach to funders. Myths are addressed along the way; for example, grants are not "something for nothing," but rather "rational deals between colleagues."

The Foundation Center's Guide to Proposal Writing, 3rd ed., Jane C. Geever, 2001. 226 pages. $29.95. Foundation Center, 79 Fifth Avenue, New York, NY 10003, 212/620-4230, www.fdncenter.org.

While this book is designed for mainstream nonprofits, it contains lots of helpful information for grassroots groups, including a lengthy appendix with suggestions from foundation officers.

Program Planning & Proposal Writing, Norton J. Kiritz, 1980. 48 pages. $4. The Grantsmanship Center, P.O. Box 17220, Los Angeles, CA 90017, 213/482-9860, www.tgci.com.

A brief, inexpensive, and thorough guide with many helpful examples.

Winning Grants Step by Step, 2nd ed., Mim Carlson, 2002. 128 pages. $29. Jossey-Bass, 989 Market Street, San Francisco, CA 94103, 800/956-7739, www.josseybass.com/nonprofit.

This workbook walks you through the process of developing and writing a grant proposal, asking provocative questions at every stage. CD-ROM included.

Writing for a Good Cause, Joseph Barbato and Danielle Furlich, 2000. 336 pages. $15. Fireside Books, 1230 Avenue of the Americas, New York, NY 10020, www.simonsays.com.

Practical, hands-on advice leavened with humor and attitude. The final section—how to get your proposal out the door in a hurry—is a great resource for all the procrastinators among us.

Strategic Planning and Financial Management

Benchmarking Your Organization's Development, 2002. 59 pages. $10.50. Institute for Conservation Leadership, 6930 Carroll Avenue, Suite #420, Takoma Park, MD 20912, 301/270-2900, www.icl.org.

An easy-to-use workbook designed to help you evaluate your organization using "best practices" for the nonprofit community—how you organize your programs, raise and manage money, recruit volunteers and leaders, supervise staff, and so on.

Managing for Change: A Common Sense Guide to Evaluating Financial Management Health for Grassroots Organizations, Terry Miller, 1992. 137 pages. $22.50. Available from the author, 250 Parnassus #204, San Francisco, CA 94117, 415/664-1576, e-mail: 70611.165@compuserve.com.

This book, originally developed for the Partnership for Democracy, is a plain-English guide to planning, budgeting, record keeping, reporting, and other non-profit management issues. It is designed specifically for social change organizations.

Strategic Planning Workbook for Nonprofit Organizations, Bryan W. Barry, 1997. 144 pages. $28. Amherst A. Wilder Foundation, 919 Lafond Avenue, St. Paul, MN 55104, 651/642-4000, www.wilder.org.

This easy-to-use guide contains a sample strategic plan, plus several exercises and worksheets you can photocopy and share with your board or planning committee.

Grant Database Tools

Jean Lewis, Tucson Pima Public Library

In recent years, grant databases have emerged as important tools for identifying potential funders for nonprofit organizations and projects. When used properly, these databases can help you identify a wide range of sources while reducing research time. With prices ranging from $500 to $2,000 a year, purchasing these products and services makes the most sense for staffed organizations with budgets of at least $200,000 per year.

Smaller groups will want to look for free access at the public library. You will find 230 locations with free access to one of the Foundation Center databases at fdncenter.org/collections/index.html. When you go to the library, ask about training opportunities or seek out the librarian who has the most experience using the database.

If you're considering a purchase, ask for a free trial; if a trial is not available, consider subscribing for one month and then make your decision. Invest time to learn how to master the relevant features of each database. Use the phone or on-line tutorials, read the print instruction manual, or print out and study the help screens. With practice, your searches will yield better results.

As you'll see in the product evaluations that follow, these databases emphasize different strategies and philosophies. Some providers focus on the largest and most active grantmakers, since they provide a majority of private grant dollars. Other databases include most or all grantmakers, which allows identification of small local foundations that are more inclined to support small local projects. Some include government funding opportunities; others do not.

Unfortunately, the most comprehensive databases tend to be the most expensive. If the price exceeds your budget, use the library and free on-line resources. State and local grant directories, also available at the library in both print and on-line formats, will help you identify supporters of projects that have immediate and direct benefit to your own community.

A note on government funding: If you're looking for information on government funds, investigate the free on-line Catalog of Federal Domestic Assistance, www.cfda.gov; Federal Register, www.gpoaccess.gov/fr/index.html; and the Web sites of state and local government agencies.

Canadian grantseekers should look into the Canadian Directory to Foundations & Grants and the Online Directory; both are prepared by the Canadian Centre for Philanthropy, www.ccp.ca.

In Exhibit B.1, you'll find profiles of eight national database products and services that were available in August 2003.

Exhibits B.2 and B.3 offer comparisons of these databases. Exhibit B.2 compares search fields available for each database. Exhibit B.3 shows a sampling of search results by recipient. Recipient searches are useful because you can learn which funders support peer organizations with programs or constituencies that overlap yours. A range of conservation and social justice organizations were selected for this search, including a few groups featured in this book.

EXHIBIT B.1

Database Products and Services (evaluated August 2003)

CHRONICLE OF PHILANTHROPY'S GUIDE TO GRANTS

Format	Internet http://philanthropy.com/grants/
Coverage	Foundation and corporate grants of $10,000 or more that have been reported to the Chronicle of Philanthropy over previous three years. Approximately 1,250 funders.
Updates	Biweekly
Price	Annual subscription ranges from $199 for Chronicle subscribers to $295 for non-Chronicle subscribers. Monthly subscription ranges from $65 to $95.
Target audience	Researchers; research and higher education; school systems; large organizations. Does not target small to mid-sized organizations.
Strengths	Currency; includes grants awarded in current year and the previous two years. Detailed listing of grants awarded by large funders. Easy to use. Search fields: keyword, grantmaker, recipient, subject, and year. Helpful sort options promote relevance. Search for other funded projects by same subject. Links to news stories in the Chronicle relevant to search criteria.
Weaknesses	Limited to largest funders. Insufficient descriptive information about funders. Cannot limit search by some important criteria. Web link to some funders not always included. Grants are categorized under multiple topics and appear more than once on a list.
Help	On-line Search Tips E-mail: help@philanthropy.com with search questions No phone number provided for database assistance
Contact information	Chronicle of Philanthropy 1255 23rd St. N.W., Suite 700 Washington, D.C. 20037 http://philanthropy.com/grants/ 202/466-1200
Notes	Intent is to provide access to the grant award announcements as listed in the biweekly Chronicle of Philanthropy.

FC SEARCH: THE FOUNDATION CENTER'S DATABASE ON CD-ROM

Format	CD-ROM
Coverage	72,000 U.S. foundations, corporate givers, and grantmaking public charities
	313,000 past grants of $10,000 or more awarded by largest funders
	324,000 trustees, officers, and donors
Updates	Semi-annually in spring and fall
Price	$1,195 single user; $1,895 single location, up to eight users
Target audience	All levels of grantseekers
Strengths	Broad scope; contains all grantmaking private foundations including small and mid-sized funders excluded from other databases.
	Includes major corporate foundations.
	Twenty-one search fields to refine search.
	In-depth program descriptions and application guidelines for larger funders provides excellent depth of information.
	Links to 5,000 grantmaker and corporate Web sites and to foundations' most recent 990-PF.
	Search results can be marked and printed or saved as a group.
	Results easier to view than some other databases.
Weaknesses	Smaller funders lack detail.
	Most effective use requires completing the guided tour or study of manual or help screens.
Help	800/478-4661
	E-mail: fcsearch@fdncenter.org
	Guided tour at http://fdncenter.org/marketplace/fcsearch_tour/index.html
	Help screens; print user manual
	FC Search electronic newsletter with tips and news
Contact information	The Foundation Center
	79 Fifth Avenue
	New York, NY 10003
	www.fdncenter.org/marketplace
	800/478-4661
Notes	Available for searching free-of-charge at many libraries. Find these at http://fdncenter.org/collections/

FOUNDATION DIRECTORY ONLINE

Format	Internet
	www.fconline.fdncenter.org
Coverage	Four on-line subscription plans range from 10,000 to 74,000 funders. Up to 250,000 past grants, 300,000 trustees, officers and donors, and 4,000 Web sites of funders.
	Platinum Plan is the most comprehensive.
Updates	Bimonthly
Price	Ranges from $195 to $995 annually, or from $20 to $150 per month.
Target audience	All levels of grantseekers.
	Small organizations need Platinum Plan to access smaller funders.
Strengths	Broad scope; contains all grantmaking private foundations including small and mid-sized funders excluded from other databases.
	Includes major corporate foundations.
	In-depth program descriptions and application guidelines for larger funders provide excellent depth of information.
	Eleven to fifteen search fields, depending on which plan used.
	Easy navigation; very flexible.
	Direct link to funders' Web site and 990 PF.
Weaknesses	Smaller funders lack detail.
	Cannot save records to disk; can view or print individual records but cannot save or print group of records.
Help	800/478-4661
	FDONLINE@fdncenter.org
	Tutorial at http://fconline.fdncenter.org/help_fdoplatinum_tutorial.html
	On-line help screens; troubleshooting guide
	Message board, FAQs, Foundation Directory Online News
Contact information	The Foundation Center
	79 Fifth Avenue
	New York, NY 10003
	www.fconline.fdncenter.org
	800/478-4661
Notes	Similar to FC Search but easier to use and less expensive.
	Of the four levels, Platinum Plan is recommended.

GRANTSELECT

Format	Internet
	http://www.grantselect.com
Coverage	10,000 funding programs provided by

- 4,000 government agencies, corporations, foundations, associations, research institutes, universities.
- 300 grants provided by Canadian private sources and 175 by Canadian government sources.

Updates	Daily to quarterly
Price	Ranges from $750 to $1,500 per year.
Target audience	Universities, researchers, larger arts, health, and educational institutions; fellowships.
Strengths	Searchable by nine search fields including keyword, funder's geographic location and focus, field of interest, type of support, region.
	Easy to use.
	Good for sponsored research opportunities.
	Detailed list of subject headings.
	Link to funder's Web site.
	Includes some government funding and some Canadian sources.
	Links to federal government grant sites.
Weaknesses	Relatively small number of funding sources.
	Cannot search by recipient name or by phrase in keyword, such as "racial justice."
	No link to 990 PFs.
	Less suitable for small nonprofits.
Help	800/225-5800
	On-line help screens
	grantsadmin@greenwood.com
Contact information	Greenwood Electronic Media/Oryx Press
	A division of Greenwood Publishing Group
	88 Post Road West, Westport, CT 06881
	http://www.grantselect.com/
	800/225-5800
	grantsadmin@greenwood.com
Notes	E-mail alert service for extra fee.
	Can select from seven customized segments for $300 to $600 each: Arts and Humanities; Biomedical and Health Care; Children and Youth; Community Development; K-12 and Adult Basic Education; International Programs; Operating Grants.

GRANTSTATION

Format	Internet
	http://www.grantstation.com/
Coverage	5,000 grantmakers
Updates	Annually
Price	$599 per year
Target audience	Most grantseekers
Strengths	Differs significantly from the other databases by emphasis on grantmaker's current interests rather than past giving.
	Searchable by geographic focus, areas of interest and types of support.
	Results are moderately good matches.
	Detailed information on funder's areas of interest.
	Links to funders' Web site.
	Upcoming federal government deadlines and links to state programs.
Weaknesses	Because of limited number of foundations, may not be suitable for some smaller organizations seeking local funding.
	No keyword searching.
	Cannot search by grant recipient or examples of grants awarded.
	No direct link to funder's 990 PF but link to GuideStar.
Help	877/784-7268
	clientsupport@grantstation.com
	Detailed tutorial provided by phone
	On-line help page
Contact information	GrantStation.com, Inc.
	3677 College Road, Suite 11B
	Fairbanks, AK 99709
	http://www.grantstation.com/
	877/784-7268
	E-mail: info@grantstation.com
Notes	Weekly bulletin of grantseeking opportunities.
	Funding strategy and assessment tools.
	Tutorials on different approaches to corporations, foundations, and government; conducting a grants search.
	Proposal writing tools and resources.
	Questions to ask the funder to determine the "fit."

GUIDESTAR GRANT EXPLORER

Format	Internet www.guidestar.org
Coverage	42,000 foundations 1,200,000 past grants of $5,000 or more
Updates	Weekly
Price	$499 per year for single user $49 per month
Target audience	All levels of grantseekers.
Strengths	The most comprehensive list of grants awarded of $5,000 or more in previous two years by each funder in database. Searchable by funder, grantee, and people (trustees, and so on). Limit by funder asset size, grant size. Direct link to funder's Web site and 990 PF. Can track almost all recipients of a given funder.
Weaknesses	No description of funders' field of interest; must surmise from grant recipients or inadequately detailed "program breakdown." No details on grants awarded, only link to recipients. In the absence of funder's "field of interest" search field, the importance of the search field "Grantee NTEE" for type of recipient is not self-evident to novice.
Help	800/784-9378 On-line tutorials, search tips, and help screens customerservice@guidestar.org
Contact information	Philanthropic Research, Inc. GuideStar Customer Service 427 Scotland Street Williamsburg, VA 23185 www.guidestar.org 800/784-9378 customerservice@guidestar.org
Notes	Database growing rapidly. Free monthly electronic newsletter. Other fee-based products available, especially for grantmakers and donors.

PROSPECT RESEARCH ONLINE

Format	Internet
	www.iwave.com
Coverage	8,000 U.S. foundations; 1,000 Canadian foundations
	4,500 U.S. corporations; 550 Canadian corporations
	3 million individuals, U.S. and Canada combined
Updates	Daily updates; each record updated at least annually
Price	$1,995 per year for single user, one location
	Twelve free special search requests with annual subscription
Target audience	Most nonprofits
Strengths	Detailed information on each funder and corporation in the database.
	Detailed biographical and philanthropic data on donors, board members, and so on.
	Although some important search fields are not available, these missing categories can be searched using "keyword."
	Sorts by relevance; best matches appear first.
	Very strong on prospect research for individuals.
	Valuable supplementary information such as special events, news articles, trends and ideas, grantwriting tips.
	Good Canadian coverage.
	Can save search strategy and create list of prospects.
Weaknesses	May not be suitable for some smaller organizations seeking local funding.
	Hard to read; cannot enlarge small font.
	Requires training for effective use.
Help	800/655-7729
	help@iwave.com
	Detailed tutorial provided by phone.
	On-line help screens.
	Live "chat" assistance during business hours.
	Convenient mechanism for sending request for assistance at other times.
Contact information	iWave
	P.O. Box 143
	Charlottetown, PEI C1A 7K2 Canada
	http://www.iwave.com/
	800/655-7729
	info@iwave.com
Notes	Offers other databases:

- Foundation Finder links to 990 PFs, fee-based.
- PRO Who's Who provides biographical data from Marquis Who's Who series free with PRO 2.0 subscription.

PROSPECTOR'S CHOICE

Format	CD-ROM
Coverage	10,000 corporate and private foundations, and direct corporate giving programs.
Updates	Annually
Price	$849 per year for up to eight users, single location
Target audience	All grantseekers
Strengths	Keyword searching.
	Searchable by name of funder, officer, officer's alma mater, location of funder and recipient, type of grant and recipient.
	Can combine search fields.
	Biographical information on some officers.
	Can exclude funders that give to preselected recipients.
	Save and recall feature easy to use.
Weaknesses	Cannot search by field of interest or giving priorities although the detailed recipient type helps.
	Some results lack relevance.
	Phrase (text string) searching does not work as promised.
	No live links to funder's Web site or to 990 PFs.
	Difficult to find search terms in record.
	Results more dated than other databases.
Help	800/877-4253
	http://www.gale.com/customer_service/technical_information/index.htm
	Print User's Guide and Help Screens on CD-ROM
Contact information	Thomson Gale
	27500 Drake Road
	Farmington Hills, MI 48331
	http://www.gale.com/
	800/877-4253
	E-mail: gale.salesassistance@thomson.com
Notes	Permits saving to a comma-delimited file that allows importing the saved data into a spreadsheet or database.

| | Database | | | | | | | |
Search Fields	Chronicle of Philanthropy	FC Search	Foundation Directory Online	GrantSelect	GrantStation	GuideStar Grant Explorer	Prospect Research Online	Prospector's Choice
Grantmaker								
Name	Yes	Yes	Yes	Yes	Yes	Yes	Yes	Yes
Field of interest	No	Yes	Yes	Yes	Yes	No	Yes	No
Geographic location of funder: state	Yes	Yes	Yes	Yes	No	Yes	Yes	Yes
Geographic location of funder: city	Yes	Yes	Yes	No	No	Yes	No, but can retrieve using keyword	Yes
Geographic focus for grants: national	No	Yes	Yes	Yes	Yes	Yes	No	No
Geographic focus for grants: state	No	Yes	Yes	Yes	Yes	Yes	No	No
Board members, officers, donors	No	Yes	Yes	No	No	Yes	Yes	Yes
Asset size	No	Yes	Yes	No	No	Yes	Yes	No
Grant size/range	No	Yes	No	No	No	Yes	No	No
Direct/live link to funder's Web site	No	Yes	Yes	Yes	Yes	Yes	Yes	No
Direct/live link to funder's 990 PF	No	Yes	Yes	No	No, but link to GuideStar to retrieve 990 PF	Yes	No, but link to GuideStar to retrieve 990 PF	No

Grants

Recipient name	Yes	Yes	No	No	Yes	No, but can retrieve using keyword	No
Recipient type or grant subject	Yes	Yes	No	No	Yes	No, but can retrieve using keyword	Yes
Recipient geographic location: state and city	Yes	Yes	No	No	Yes	No	Yes

Other Features

Keyword or text searching	Yes	Yes	Yes	No	Yes	Yes	Yes
Phrase searching	Yes	Yes	No	No	Yes	Yes	Yes, but results sometimes lack relevance
Save and recall searches	Yes	No	No	No	No	Yes	Yes
Some government funding	No	No	Yes	Yes	No	No	No
Some Canadian funding	No	No	Yes	No	No	Yes	No

EXHIBIT B.3

Database Results of Searching by Grant Recipient (August 2003)

	Database							
Search Fields	Chronicle of Philanthropy	FC Search	Foundation Directory Online	GrantSelect	GrantStation	GuideStar Grant Explorer	Prospect Research Online	Prospector's Choice
Typical years covered as tested in August 2003	2001–2003	1999–2001	2000–2002			1999–2002	2000–2001	
Canadian Parks & Wilderness Society	2 grants/ 1 funder	10 grants/ 4 funders	8 grants/ 5 funders	Cannot search by grant recipient name	Cannot search by grant recipient name	0	1 grant/ 1 funder	Cannot search by grant recipient name
Global Exchange (CA)	0	16 grants/ 12 funders	8 grants/ 7 funders			34 grants/ 25 funders	13 grants/ 13 funders	
Grassroots Leadership (NC)	2 grants/ 2 funders	20 grants/ 12 funders	10 grants/ 6 funders			26 grants/ 17 funders	3 grants/ 3 funders	
Los Angeles Alliance for a New Economy (CA)	4 grants/ 4 funders	21 grants/ 10 funders	19 grants/ 8 funders			32 grants/ 18 funders	7 grants/ 7 funders	
Native Seeds/SEARCH (AZ)	1 grant/ 1 funder	3 grants/ 3 funders	1 grant/ 1 funder			0	5 grants/ 5 funders	
New England Grassroots Environment Fund (VT)	0	7 grants/ 6 funders	9 grants/ 5 funders			16 grants/ 11 funders	6 grants/ 6 funders	

Raising Money from Faith-Based Grant Programs

For us, the relational aspect is more important than the money. The Hunger Fund is a tool that allows us to fulfill the Biblical call to be of service and to be in relationship.

—LORETTA HORTON, Domestic Hunger Program,
Evangelical Lutheran Church in America

We're interested in proposals that reflect the values of our congregation and show a plan for putting those values into action.

—BILL DEMPSEY, formerly of the Unitarian Universalist
Veatch Program at Shelter Rock

Within the nonprofit community, faith organizations—churches, synagogues, mosques, and the like—have always been the largest recipient of charitable dollars. In 2002, faith organizations received more than $84 billion, or 35 percent of all donated funds (American Association of Fundraising Counsel, 2003).

Faith groups are great at raising money—all fundraisers should study their methods—but they also excel at giving it away. Annual tallies of faith-based philanthropy vary, depending on who and what is counted. According to the National Council of the Churches of Christ in the USA, which publishes the annual *Yearbook of American and Canadian Churches,* faith organizations gave away $4.5 billion in benevolences—funds spent beyond the needs of the local congregation—in 2001 (Lindner, 2003, p. 387). The *Grassroots Fundraising Journal* (Roth, 2003, p. 3) estimates that faith-based philanthropy could total

$10 billion each year. Regardless of the exact amount, we're talking about a big pot of money. This resource is designed to help you figure out whether faith-based funders provide good opportunities for your group.

A lot of faith-based philanthropy goes to evangelizing and conservative social causes, but religious grantmakers have also been a good source of funding for progressive action. For example, significant early support for the United Farm Workers came from the Roman Catholic Church. The tradition of funding community organizing and social change continues in several denominations.

While a few faith-based funders resemble foundations in their operations and proposal review processes, the vast majority do not. Marjorie Fine of the Unitarian Universalist Veatch Program at Shelter Rock defines the difference in terms of "culture plus ethics. Faith funders are interested in the transformation of both individuals and society."

Jeannie Appleman of Interfaith Funders points out another important distinction: "Most faith funders are denominational arms—for example, religious orders. Funding is one of the things they're about, but it may not be the only thing they do. They don't necessarily think of themselves as 'funders.'"

As Eileen Paul, editor of the *2000 Religious Funding Resource Guide* puts it, "Their giving capacity is often part of a larger social justice component in their structure, and staff managing the giving program have multiple other responsibilities. . . . Religious institutions or churches will give support only if they see you and your work as part of their work" (2000, p. 1).

Faith-based grant programs draw their ideals and values from deep historical roots, so they tend to have a long-term perspective on social change. They also have a broad base in their community. Gary Delgado of the Applied Research Center addresses this issue in *The Activist's Guide to Religious Funding* (1993, p. 5). "More than 40 percent of the U.S. population attends church regularly," he writes. "The percentage of church attendees in low-income organizations is often higher. Our members are their members."

Indeed, congregational and interdenominational social justice work is on the rise. Jeannie Appleman says, "There are 170 faith-based groups doing community organizing in the United States." This number doesn't include the thousands of secular organizations working with congregation-based allies on issues of peace, reproductive rights, economic and environmental justice, immigrant rights, combating racism and homophobia, and so on. "Thanks to better outreach to the foundation community," she says, "more mainstream funding is being directed to faith-based organizing."

When the secular and faith communities share common interests, money flows in both directions between them. "We fund a lot of folks outside the denomination," says Loretta Horton. "We're interested in justice and systemic change, regardless of whether there's a faith component."

If you think religious funding might fit with your programs, do your homework. Consultant Richard Male provides some suggestions for raising money from religious organizations in Exhibit C.1. For further information and strategies for approaching faith-based funding programs, the *Religious Funding Resource Guide* is an excellent starting point (see Resource A). On the local front, most community churches are listed in the Yellow Pages. You should also contact your local council of churches and ask for a directory of congregations.

EXHIBIT C.1
Tips and Strategies for Raising Money from Religious Organizations

Richard Male

The religious community in America is the most philanthropic group of people in the country. Almost every social movement in America had its roots in religious communities. They are looking for opportunities to support projects, people, and organizations that support their faith goals. If you are willing to take the time to understand their issues and develop relationships, their support can be long term and sustaining.

1. Build the relationship first, then ask for money.

2. Attend a religious service to get a feel for the congregation's interests and to meet key lay and religious leaders.

3. Read current and past editions of the religious group's bulletins and newsletters.

4. Speak about your organization and the issues it confronts at church, synagogue, or mosque meetings whenever possible and always when asked.

5. Always pass around a sign-up sheet at religious meetings to get names, addresses, and e-mail addresses for your newsletter and direct mail appeals.

6. Invite a priest, minister, rabbi, imam, or lay leader to be on your board or committee.

7. Invite members of the congregation to a meeting at your organization, or take them on a tour of your project or neighborhood.

8. Travel at least once a year to the regional and national office to meet the key funders. It is critical that they know who you are. If possible, have the congregational leader make the introduction for you.

Richard Male (www.richardmale.com) is a consultant based in Denver, Colorado. This article first appeared in the September/October 2003 issue of *Grassroots Fundraising Journal.* Used with permission.

If you choose to pursue funding from religious sources, take the following steps:

Relationships count, so reach out to the decision makers. This is true in the foundation world, but even more critical in the religious funding arena. The importance of relationships is based, in part, on the intricate pathways through which money and accountability flow: from local congregations through regional dioceses and judicatories to national denominational offices, and then back down to the local level. In many cases, decision makers rely on the opinions of colleagues who are above, below, or beside them in the hierarchy. To raise money successfully from these sources, you need a few advocates within the denomination—pastors or rabbis, administrators, lay leaders, or members of congregation social action committees. Clergy can also help you involve their peers in other denominations.

"We get handwritten applications, but that doesn't bother us," says Loretta Horton. "We know they're doing good work because we visit these programs. You can't send handwritten materials to most foundations."

Understand that faith-based fundraising is a form of community organizing. According to Eileen Paul (2000, p. 1), "Churches or temples in your local community are more than likely to be concerned about the same issues you are. They can represent powerful allies if you involve them in planning and implementing strategies for change. As a grantseeker you need to learn the social justice agenda and focus of the religious institution, and to understand that fundraising is basically an organizing task . . . because you have an additional constituency and institutional structure to relate to, to educate, and to involve in your work."

As Jeannie Appleman says, "Faith-based funders—in fact, most funders—have an interest beyond writing checks to groups. We have a granting function, but we're more than that. We see ourselves as stakeholders with interests and ideas about this field."

Study the denomination. In other words, know your customer. "Know the values of the people you're approaching," says Si Kahn of the Jewish Fund for Justice. "Know the denomination. Know something about the tradition. For example, don't ask for a meeting with the Jewish Fund for Justice on Rosh Hashanah. I notice there aren't any meetings scheduled for Christmas or Easter."

Start with local congregations. It is possible to go straight to the national religious giving programs, but many prefer an endorsement at the community level first. To qualify for grants from most denominations, you have to have a relationship with local churches. It's a more conservative climate now, and the denominations are getting more scrutiny from their congregations. Because they raise money from specific church offerings, the congregants want to know that their donations are being used for work that lines up with the denomination's values.

Si Kahn adds, "When groups approach the Jewish Fund for Justice, we ask, 'Are any of your partner organizations based in the Jewish community?' This is not as extreme as applying to a women's foundation if you don't work with women, but it's in the same ballpark."

Of course, you can also raise a lot of money directly from local churches, synagogues, and other religious institutions. Many congregations contribute to grassroots groups without going through regional or national offices. They can also help with donated office space, furniture, photocopying, volunteers, free publicity in their newsletters, public endorsements of your work, and perhaps an opportunity to give a guest sermon about your issue.

Choose quality over quantity. Unless you live in a very small town, you won't have time to develop strong relationships with all the local clergy. You're unlikely to have the stamina or patience to apply to all religious funding programs; the *2000 Religious Funding Resource Guide* includes guidelines and application materials for thirty-nine grant and loan programs. As Eileen Paul (2000) writes in that resource book, "Rather than trying to get to know all the religious bodies . . . at once, pick one or two to start with. That way, the relationships are fewer, more maintainable, and more likely to result in lasting support" (p. 6).

Follow the guidelines! Nearly all faith-based funders require forms—lots and lots of forms. Fill them out carefully and completely. Provide only the attachments requested.

Faith-based fundraising is a long-term strategy, so plan accordingly. To raise money (and make friends) among clergy, you must invest the time up front. "Once in the door, be persistent, and stay there," writes Eileen Paul (2000, p. 6). "Don't ask for money on your first visits. Remember, this is an educational process, which never happens quickly. Churches have been around for a long time, and most will likely remain."

If you build solid relationships and involve the religious community in your work, you stand a good chance of receiving financial support for several years.

Legal Issues
for Nonprofit Advocates

John Pomeranz, Alliance for Justice

> We're looking for the unexpected, a new approach, a creative
> solution that goes beyond the usual. Active, energetic engagement
> with the issue.
>
> —HUBERT SAPP, Hartford Foundation

Almost all movements for social change in the history of this country—
including movements for independence from Britain, the abolition of slavery,
protection of workers' rights, women's suffrage, civil rights, and environmental protection—had their start in nonprofit, community-based organizations. These organizations may have been churches, unions, parent-teacher
associations, advocacy groups, universities, or garden clubs. What they had
in common was the vision to see further than the political leaders of the time
and the energy to make change.

This involvement in policy issues derives from the nature of nonprofit
organizations. Nonprofits traditionally serve constituencies and issues that
have no other voice in the policy process. They frequently have the best—or
only—information on the social needs the organizations were created to
address. Their essential representative role and unique knowledge are the reasons that policymakers look to the nonprofit sector for leadership.

None of these organizations has acted alone to lead a movement. Many
strategies, some at odds with one another, have combined to accomplish great
social changes. Many organizations, each equipped for different tasks and
interested in different aspects of the underlying problem, were necessary to

shift public perception and public policy. Some sought change by convincing legislators to enact better laws, while others studied the problem and identified possible solutions. Some sought change by ensuring that elected officials who did not support change were replaced by those who did, while others educated the public and the media about the justness of their cause. Some sought change by organizing their communities and reminding their neighbors that the power to create change was (and is) theirs.

So if you're serious about making social change, you'll need different kinds of nonprofits, and that means that you'll need to know about the legal issues that those different kinds of nonprofits face—a sometimes complicated structure of laws at the federal, state, and local level, laws that govern the creation of these different types of organizations, their sources of funding, the types of advocacy they can do, and more. Each of these laws was born in response to a particular perceived problem, usually noble goals such as empowering people to create organizations to speak for them or trying to prevent scam artists from stealing by masquerading as charities, or occasionally less honorable motives, such as the desire of a powerful member of Congress to "get back" at an organization that made his life more difficult. The result is a lot of different laws that can both amaze you with the flexibility of the types of organizations you can create and frustrate you unless you're prepared to deal with it.

This chapter does not provide legal advice. Each situation needs to be analyzed by a knowledgeable professional for its specific circumstances. It does, however, provide an overview of the legal issues and briefly summarizes the strengths and weaknesses of different types of nonprofit organizations: charities and private foundations organized under Section 501(c)(3) of the federal tax law, social welfare organizations organized under Section 501(c)(4), and political organizations organized under Section 527. It tries to put these organizations into a basic structure that explains the types of advocacy for which they are best suited and introduces some of the basic rules for how these organizations can work together. This essay also touches on federal and state election laws that govern election-related activities by nonprofits (and for-profits) and various lobbyist registration and reporting laws that apply at the federal and state level.

Of course, a few pages can't cover everything you need to know about the laws governing nonprofits. You can get more information from a series of plain-language guides published by the Alliance for Justice to help nonprofits understand how to be successful advocates within the law (see Resource A). Because this is such a complex and technical set of laws and regulations, you should not rely on general summaries. You should consult a lawyer to address complicated applications of the law to your particular circumstances.

Different Types of Organizations Under Federal Law

Most nonprofit organizations are incorporated in their respective states and then seek exemption from federal tax under federal law. Organizations that meet the qualifications under one of the sections of the federal law receive various types of favorable treatment under the tax code—such as exemption from federal tax on the organization's income, the ability to offer donors a charitable tax deduction, and other advantages. However, federal tax-exempt status also comes with restrictions on the organization's activities, particularly lobbying and election-related activities. The general rule is that nonprofits receiving greater federal tax advantages are more restricted in their advocacy activities. Groups that want the tax benefits but feel too constrained by the restrictions frequently create a series of connected organizations that allow them to pursue a variety of advocacy strategies.

501(c)(3) Organizations

The most common type of tax-exempt organizations are those organized under tax code section 501(c)(3). Their activities must be almost entirely educational, charitable, or scientific, and thus these nonprofits include healthcare providers and other human service organizations, educational institutions, nonpartisan policy research organizations, churches and other religious institutions, and foundations and other grantmakers. There are two kinds of 501(c)(3) organization: public charities and private foundations.

Public Charities

In general, public charities are 501(c)(3) organizations that receive support for their activities from the general public rather than from a small number of generous benefactors. The law provides extremely favorable treatment for these nonprofits. 501(c)(3) public charities are exempt from most federal taxes, and most contributions to these organizations are tax-deductible. As the general rule suggests, these substantial federal tax advantages mean that for 501(c)(3) organizations, lobbying and other advocacy activities are limited by federal law. Nonetheless, all 501(c)(3)s are permitted to engage in advocacy activities to at least some degree.

Lobbying. 501(c)(3) public charities may lobby. The exact amount of lobbying they may do depends on the size of the organization and which of two sets of rules governing lobbying applies to the organizations.

Of the two possible tests, most public charities will be better off choosing to use the "501(h) expenditure test" (named after the section of the tax code that created it) that provides a clear definition of lobbying and limits based on how much money the organization spends on lobbying. In many cases, this test allows a 501(c)(3) to expand its advocacy, either by engaging in activities that fall outside the test's technical definitions of lobbying or by engaging in low- or no-cost lobbying (such as volunteer-based efforts) that stretch the test's expenditure-based limits further. One feature of the 501(h) test may adversely affect very large organizations: The 501(h) test, unlike its alternative, does impose an absolute cap on annual lobbying expenditures of $1 million per year.

The alternative system of limits on 501(c)(3) lobbying—the so-called "insubstantial part test"—offers only the vague guidance that a 501(c)(3) public charity may lobby if that lobbying is "no substantial part" of its activities. Under this test lobbying is left undefined and even volunteer activities that require no expenditures by the 501(c)(3) are likely to count against the limits. Many commentators have suggested that a 501(c)(3) using the insubstantial part test would be safe if it limited its lobbying to 5 percent of the organization's activities.

Unless the 501(c)(3) public charity acts to choose the 501(h) option, the generally inferior insubstantial part test will be used to measure the organization's lobbying activities. 501(c)(3) public charities can choose to have the 501(h) test apply to them by making the one-time 501(h) "election" using Internal Revenue Service Form 5768, an extremely easy-to-complete tax form. However, some types of public charities—notably churches (or similar religious institutions) and their closely connected programs—are not permitted to make the 501(h) election and must do any lobbying under the insubstantial part test.

Under the 501(h) expenditure test, public charities can spend as much as 20 percent of their budget on all lobbying, and they can spend a lesser amount—a quarter of their overall lobbying limit—on grassroots lobbying (activities designed to encourage the general public to directly lobby elected officials). For example, a 501(c)(3) public charity that spends $400,000 per year on charitable activities may spend $80,000 (20 percent) of those funds on lobbying, including as much as $20,000 (25 percent of $80,000) on grassroots lobbying. As the size of an organization's annual budget increases, the percentage of those expenditures that the organization can spend on lobbying declines.

Direct lobbying (lobbying that isn't grassroots lobbying) occurs when a representative of the organization communicates the organization's view on a specific piece of legislation to an official, such as a member of a city council or a state or federal legislator (or a staff person for such an official). It is also direct lobbying to urge the public to support or oppose an initiative, referendum, or other ballot measure (under the theory that in voting on a ballot measure the voters are acting as if they were a huge legislature). "Specific legislation" includes not merely proposed legislation that has been introduced but also any specific idea for legislation. For example, "our schools are in trouble" is not a statement about specific legislation, but "we should pay teachers more" makes a specific legislative proposal.

Grassroots lobbying occurs when the organization urges the general public to communicate the organization's position on a piece of specific legislation to these officials. Unless a communication includes a "call to action"—something to encourage the reader or listener to contact a legislator—the communication will generally not be considered lobbying. The regulations specify that a call to action occurs when the organization does one of the following:

- Explicitly urges readers to contact a legislator about the legislation

- Provides the address, telephone number or similar information for a legislator

- Provides a petition, postcard, or similar means for the reader to communicate with a legislator

- Identifies one or more legislators as being opposed or undecided about the bill, or being a member of the relevant committee or subcommittee that will vote on the bill

Fortunately, an organization's members are treated as a part of the organization, so urging them to contact public officials about legislation is considered direct, not grassroots, lobbying.

Note that both of these definitions exclude certain activities. It is *not* lobbying to bring a lawsuit. It is *not* lobbying to encourage an administrative agency (such as a state department of health or department of labor) to create or change an administrative rule. It is *not* lobbying to advocate before special-purpose bodies such as school boards and zoning boards.

In addition, there are exceptions for some activities that otherwise might appear to fit the definition of lobbying under the 501(h) rules. For example, it is *not* lobbying to prepare and distribute a "nonpartisan analysis" that provides a complete enough discussion of a legislative proposal to allow a reader to make up his or her own mind about the proposal (even if the analysis comes to a conclusion on the merits of that proposal). Nor is it lobbying to respond to a written request for assistance from a legislative committee to help the committee with a legislative proposal, such as a letter from a committee chair inviting the organization to testify before the committee.

The organization is required to track expenditures in a way sufficient to show that it hasn't exceeded its lobbying limits. Don't just count direct costs such as the expense of traveling to the state capital to lobby or the cost of printing up action alerts. Remember to include other costs, such as a portion of the salaries of any staff members or a portion of the rent on an office.

Election-related activities. 501(c)(3) public charities are more limited in their election-related activities. While 501(c)(3)s may engage in nonpartisan voter education and voter participation activities, they are absolutely prohibited from any activity that appears to support or oppose candidates for public office.

501(c)(3) public charities may not endorse, rate, contribute to, or do anything else that could seem to help or hurt a candidate. The Internal Revenue Service will examine an activity based on all the surrounding "facts and circumstances" to determine whether a 501(c)(3) organization's activities violate this rule. For example, a 501(c)(3) may criticize a legislator for failing to support an important piece of legislation during the legislative session, but if the 501(c)(3) runs a similar criticism during the legislator's campaign for reelection, the IRS might find it to be an impermissible campaign intervention.

The IRS has provided a limited amount of guidance on permissible 501(c)(3) activities during an election season. 501(c)(3)s may take the following actions:

- Publish nonpartisan voter guides that print the results of a questionnaire asking each candidate his or her position on a broad range of issues

- Sponsor nonpartisan debates or forums in which all candidates are questioned on a broad range of issues

- Encourage citizens to register to vote, and get registered voters to go to the polls on election day (but 501(c)(3)s may *not* encourage voters to support or oppose a particular candidate, even by encouraging the use of a particular policy issue as a litmus test)

- Brief all candidates who respond to the 501(c)(3)'s invitation to learn the 501(c)(3)'s stance on key policy issues

Other types of nonpartisan activities are also permitted, but, because the rules in this area are so strict, 501(c)(3)s would be wise to get more information from a knowledgeable source before launching an election-related activity.

Private Foundations

Private foundations are 501(c)(3)s that fail to meet the public support requirements that would qualify them as public charities. Typically, private foundations give grants to other organizations for charitable activities.

The rules for private foundations are substantially more strict than those for public charities. Private foundations are not allowed to lobby nor are they allowed to "earmark" grants for lobbying.

Because the rules are more strict, many foundations are under the mistaken impression that they can't fund or engage in any lobbying, but that's just plain wrong. Some even include unnecessary language in their grant agreements that forbid use of their funds for lobbying (a bad idea that needlessly puts additional burdens on their grantees). In fact, private foundations *may* give a public charity a grant for the general support of its operations, and the public charity may choose to spend that grant, in whole or in part, on lobbying. Similarly, a private foundation *may* give a public charity a grant for a specific project, even if that project includes some lobbying, as long as the amount that the foundation gives does not exceed the non-lobbying portion of the project's budget. Private foundations may even directly advocate on legislation if they are invited to do so by the legislature or if the pending legislation affects the foundation's rights, tax-exempt status, or existence.

Private foundations may support the nonpartisan election-related activities of public charities, but special rules apply when a foundation seeks to earmark a grant for a nonpartisan voter-registration or get-out-the-vote effort. Private foundations seeking to make such a grant or public charities that hope to receive such a grant should consult with a knowledgeable lawyer.

Private foundations may give grants to organizations that are not public charities, but, in general, they will have to restrict the use of these grants through a system known as "expenditure responsibility." Expenditure responsibility generally requires that the grantee not spend any of the grant funds for lobbying or partisan election-related activity and that the grantee file sufficient documentation with the private foundation to prove that the grant was spent for the intended charitable purposes. Many foundations are reluctant to make these grants to nonpublic charities, perhaps out of the mistaken belief that the rules are more burdensome than they in fact are.

501(c)(4) Organizations

A 501(c)(4) is a "social welfare organization" or "civic league" that may pursue educational, lobbying, and political activities. A 501(c)(4) organization's "primary" activities must be those to benefit the public, including any activity in which a 501(c)(3) organization may legally engage. 501(c)(4)s are exempt from most federal taxes, but contributions to a 501(c)(4) are not tax-deductible. Again following the general rule, 501(c)(4)s receive fewer benefits under the federal tax code, but face fewer restrictions on their advocacy activities.

Lobbying. 501(c)(4)s may do an unlimited amount of lobbying, including working for the passage of legislation and ballot measures.

Election-related activities. Unlike a 501(c)(3), a 501(c)(4) may carry out some partisan political activities without jeopardizing its tax-exempt status as long as such activities do not become the *primary* activity of the organization.

In addition to these requirements imposed by federal tax law, 501(c)(4)s must also comply with relevant federal or state election laws that may impose restrictions on their activities. These rules are described below. (In general, election laws have little impact on 501(c)(3)s because the federal tax rules governing their electoral activity are so strict.)

527 Organizations

Section 527 is the section of the tax code under which many different types of political organizations are organized, including political parties and campaigns and various types of non-candidate political committees. This discussion is focused on so-called "political action committees" (PACs) designed with the primary purpose of supporting or opposing candidates for office.

A PAC is generally exempt from federal taxation to the extent that it spends its funds on partisan political activities and related expenses. PACs can contribute to candidates' campaigns (up to state and federal election law limits on campaign contributions), make independent expenditures for or against candidates, and distribute materials to the general public that are skewed to support or oppose particular candidates. While tax law obligations for PACs are few, most PACs are required to report contributions and expenditures under federal or state election laws (see the discussion of election law below).

Exhibit D.1 compares the elements of 501(c)(3), 501(c)(4), and 527 organizations.

Integrated Strategies Using 501(c)(3)s, 501(c)(4)s, and PACs

As mentioned at the beginning of this chapter, meaningful social change is generally accomplished through a coordinated set of strategies. For example, the fight for civil rights in this country has been waged in the courts, the legislatures, the voting booth, and the streets. Pursuing multiple strategies to address social problems often requires the participation of several types of tax-exempt organizations with diverse skills and capacities. Frequently, 501(c)(3)s, 501(c)(4)s, and PACs will be working on the same general issue, with each engaged in activities particularly appropriate for that type of organization. In many cases, these groups are formally affiliated. For example, a 501(c)(3) may create a 501(c)(4) when an issue demands more lobbying than the amount permitted under the 501(c)(3)'s lobbying limits. Foundations are often reluctant to fund 501(c)(4)s, so a 501(c)(4) might create a 501(c)(3) to seek foundation funds to do policy research and education related to the organizations' general area of concern. Or a 501(c)(4) might create a connected PAC to encourage change at the ballot box when the 501(c)(4)'s legislative efforts fail.

The key to dealing with these relationships between organizations is to maintain appropriate separation between them. The basic idea is to keep the

EXHIBIT D.1

Different Types of Organizations Under U.S. Federal Law

	501(c)(3) (Public Charities and Private Foundations)	501(c)(4) (Social Welfare Organizations)	527 (Political Organizations)
Tax Treatment	Exempt from most federal taxes	Exempt from most federal taxes	Exempt from most federal taxes
	Contributions are tax-deductible	Contributions are not tax-deductible	Contributions are not tax-deductible
	Private foundations may give grants to charities with fewer constraints	Private foundations may only give restricted grants	Private foundations may not give grants
Lobbying Activities	Limited	Unlimited	Permitted, but may be taxed
Election-Related Activities	No intervention in candidate campaigns (activities in support of or in opposition to candidates)	Partisan activities may be a secondary activity of the organization	Partisan activities are the primary purpose of the organization
	Nonpartisan voter education, and so forth, permitted	Election laws may impose limits such as limits on campaign contributions or "express advocacy" beyond membership	Election laws may limit contributions and expenditures and may impose disclosure requirements

groups' finances and decision making independent. The different organizations that may be in the partnership—501(c)(3), 501(c)(4), 527—must maintain sufficient separation to ensure that none of the organizations pay for activities forbidden to that organization. At a minimum that requires that the nonprofits be separately incorporated and maintain separate bank accounts. In addition, each organization must cover its share of the costs for any shared staff, office space, office equipment, and the like. Because of the strict limit on partisan political activities by 501(c)(3) nonprofits, it is particularly important to maintain a clear separation between a 501(c)(3) and an affiliated 501(c)(4) engaged in political activities, either itself or through its connected 527 organization.

Election Law

In addition to federal tax law, federal and state (and sometimes even local) election laws govern the election-related activity of tax-exempt, non-profit corporations just as these laws regulate for-profit corporations. In practice, these laws rarely affect 501(c)(3) organizations, because of the strict ban on partisan activities under federal tax law. However these laws frequently affect other types of nonprofit organizations. Federal, state, and lobbyist laws are discussed here.

Federal Election Campaign Act

The Federal Election Campaign Act (FECA) governs the activities related to elections to federal offices—President, Vice President, U.S. Senator, and Member of the U.S. House of Representatives. FECA restricts the election-related activities of unions and corporations, including nonprofit corporations, but there are certain areas in which nonprofit corporations can engage in extensive electoral advocacy.

FECA has recently undergone a major change as a result of the Bipartisan Campaign Reform Act of 2002 (better known by the names of its chief sponsors, McCain-Feingold). The law was immediately attacked by its opponents as unconstitutional, and the Supreme Court has, as of this writing, yet to rule on the case. When it does, all of the laws discussed below may change, so be careful.

In general under FECA, no union or corporation, including incorporated 501(c)(4)s or other nonprofits, may directly support or oppose a federal candidate. Corporations may not take the following actions:

- Make cash or in-kind contributions to candidates

- Engage in so-called "coordinated" communications or activities at the request of or otherwise controlled by a federal candidate

- Broadcast any ad on TV or radio that features a federal candidate during certain periods just before a primary, political convention, or election

- Spend any money in support of communications that clearly identify a federal candidate and contain "express advocacy" explicitly urging voters to "elect," "vote for," "support," "defeat," "reelect," or "oppose" the candidate

In practice, these restrictions allow a huge range of electoral activity, such as "issue advocacy." Nonprofit and for-profit corporations are free to make independent expenditures for communications or activities that are *not* coordinated with a candidate and that do *not* contain the magic words of express advocacy. For example, a 501(c)(4) organization may criticize a candidate's previous support of bad legislation or run newspaper advertisements contrasting two candidates' views on an issue of importance to the organization.

In addition to this issue advocacy, corporations may also engage in partisan electoral communications that expressly support or oppose candidates by taking advantage of one of several key exceptions to the general ban on express advocacy. Corporations may say nearly anything about federal candidates to members or shareholders. They may also endorse candidates within certain limits. A few 501(c)(4) corporations that meet certain special requirements (such as refusing any funding from for-profit corporations or unions) may expressly advocate the election of federal candidates to the general public.

For activists who want even greater flexibility in electoral communications, a political committee may be the answer. Political committees can be of several different types, and the laws governing them (particularly the fundraising rules and reporting obligations) are extremely complicated. People who run PACs should get whatever help they need to learn and comply with these rules.

State Election Laws

State elections are governed not by FECA, but by state (and sometimes local) election laws. These laws vary a great deal from state to state, and a complete discussion of them would be impossible here in this short space. Some election laws mirror the FECA, prohibiting most election-related activity by corporations. Others are much more permissive—in many states corporations may make direct contributions of money or other assistance to candidates and campaigns. Check your state office of elections for more details.

One key point is that state election laws often govern advocacy for or against ballot measures. While the federal tax law treats this activity as lobbying, most states regulate it as an election-related activity. As a result, nonprofit corporations that engage in this type activity—*including 501(c)(3)s*—should check their state and local laws.

Lobbyist Registration and Reporting Laws

Every state and the federal government has some law that regulates legislative lobbying. Generally, these laws do not place any restrictions on the amount of lobbying that an organization may do, but most require lobbyists or the organizations for which they work to register as a lobbyist and report their lobbying activities.

The federal law is the Lobbying Disclosure Act, and information on its requirements is available from the Office of the Clerk of the House of Representatives. Information on most state laws is available either from the state legislature or the state ethics office.

It is important to understand that the definition of "lobbying" under these laws may vary substantially from the IRS definition of lobbying that applies to 501(c)(3) organizations under the 501(h) expenditure test. For example, the 501(h) test excludes administrative advocacy from the definition of lobbying, but many states require nonprofit (and other) lobbyists to report lobbying contacts with state agency officials that attempt to influence action on a regulatory rule or other decision.

Sharing Grants
A Strategy
for Collaborative Fundraising

Wendy Wilson, River Network

> We're seeing more collaboration among movements, not just orga-
> nizations, with new combinations of issues and constituencies.
> This is happening, in part, because groups have less money to
> work with. The attitude is, "We've got to get together or we're all
> going to die."
>
> —MARJORIE FINE, Unitarian Universalist Veatch Program at Shelter Rock

Can groups share money? Most nonprofit executive directors and development directors appear to have one of two answers regarding multi-organizational grants: No, or Hell No. Yet the biggest potential victories may be won
through collaborative efforts. In fact, many foundations are very interested in
larger-scale collaborative projects, especially environmental projects. It's a
trend that will become even more important for organizations seeking to take
their cause to a higher level and a broader public audience.

The secret is to look before you leap, according to Barbara Rusmore, who
works with organizations throughout the country for the Institute for Conservation Leadership: "We've seen three kinds of collaborative fundraising:
successful cooperation, which is a lot of work; the funder-initiated false start,
which can lead to a dead end; and the negotiated truce at the 'firing circle,'
where leaders threaten each other over their fair share."

This article first appeared in River Network's *River Fundraising Alert*, Volume 9, Number 3, Fall 2002. Used
with permission.

An important lesson learned is that money is not the reason to form a coalition. A successful coalition must have clearly shared goals, a diversity of skills and constituencies, and a strong decision-making structure. If those ingredients are there, then the prospects for program and financial success are worth exploring.

Looking for Money in Coalitions

The first step toward getting your project funded is to talk with your current funders. Ask grantmakers and major donors who already support you if they would consider a proposal for a collaborative effort. Some give larger grants to coalitions; some don't fund them at all.

Many foundations will only give to collaborative efforts through a "lead" organization that will divvy up the money according to a detailed project plan. The Environment Program at The Pew Charitable Trusts funds many collaborative efforts in that way—as many as 25 percent of their grants involve more than one organization. Jay Nelson, formerly a program officer with Pew, explains it this way: "We look at how the project objective can be achieved. Ideally one group could do it, but if they can't, then we try to figure out how many and which groups are necessary."

The General Service Foundation focuses on Western water issues and makes less than 10 percent of its grants to multi-organizational efforts. Still, notes executive director Lani Shaw, "Coalitions are definitely the trend in the funding community. Funding a collaborative proposal is more productive for a small foundation faced with twelve proposals from twelve different groups working on the same problem."

Coalitions have the potential to decrease the stack of proposals on a foundation officer's desk, but funding a coalition can be a big step. "Frankly, we got involved [on the Rio Grande] because the groups who were supposed to be allies seemed to be working at cross-purposes," says Shaw. "If the environmentalists wouldn't work together, we couldn't justify continuing to fund in New Mexico at all."

Shaw became a key supporter in a unique collaboration among funders and activist groups called the Alliance for Rio Grande Heritage, a twenty-organization, multicultural effort to restore flows and protect communities along the Rio Grande River. She gives extra time when the Alliance needs assistance. "It makes a lot of work for the funder, but we get to see how the groups really work, warts and all. And once we are involved, we can recruit others to help."

It doesn't always work so smoothly. One director involved in a difficult coalition reports, "I'm on this coalition board because I don't trust the people the foundation gave the money to, and I can't afford not to be here." This collaboration may be headed into "the firing circle." The higher the financial stakes, the worse the situation gets, until the project fails and the former partners are left to bicker over the causes of failure.

Coalition Fundraising: What Works

In the summer of 2002, River Network and the Institute for Conservation Leadership sponsored a workshop called "Living with Coalitions" to explore how successful coalitions operate. The workshop brought together activists from across the country with experience in dozens of coalitions. The group eagerly discussed their victories and their frustrations. Here's what we learned:

Shared commitment is key. Participants in a successful coalition know their specific roles and work toward a clear objective with a shared sense of commitment. Most successful environmental coalitions fund their work through a variety of sources, including foundation support, corporate support, and financial contributions from member groups. The groups' resources are pooled to allow a strong core staff to work as part of an integrated campaign plan.

The coalition's goals must come first. A large coalition grant can cause trouble when disparate groups are more interested in the money than the goals of the coalition. Our participants related horror stories of checks arriving in the mail for projects no one could explain, for work they did not understand, or with coalition partners they did not know. Participants also related problems when overeager foundation staff became too involved in sensitive coalition business. Some coalitions have gone on floundering like this for years without producing valuable results.

Funders must use their roles carefully. Nancy Dalwin, an advisor to the Tides Foundation, has seen good coalition concepts lead to dead ends. "Funder-inspired projects aren't usually as effective as activist-inspired projects. Sometimes the effort to encourage new coalitions just heightens tensions between groups over the control of money." But Brian Shields, director of Amigos Bravos and a participant in the Alliance for Rio Grande Heritage, believes that responsible funders don't have to stay at arm's length. Having the General Service Foundation and other foundations involved in the Alliance, he says, "helped avoid a feeding frenzy when money was put on the table."

The participants in the Living with Coalitions workshop agreed on a number of principles for responsible funder participation in coalitions:

- Fund the coalition process, not just action. The time dedicated to building trust is critical for success.

- Be clear with groups if a coalition project will compete with their ongoing general support request.

- Provide flexible funding to be used by a coalition for high-performing member groups to take on larger parts of the campaign.

The chart in Exhibit E.1 summarizes elements of success in working collaboratively, along with what to do and what to avoid when sharing the wealth.

The Collaborative Proposal

Jay Nelson knows what to look for in a coalition proposal: "It is clear that money alone won't hold people together, but a true convergence of interests can be encouraged by money." Even when there is a convergence of interests, some evaluators look at coalition proposals with deep concerns over the lack of accountability for funds, poor fiscal management, or just too many cooks in the kitchen.

Nelson has seen these problems emerge among coalition partners, particularly between groups that work in very different ways. "There are accountability problems and inequities between the local groups who may be doing it as a labor of love and the larger national groups who say, 'Oh well, we can always do this in the next legislative session.' But you still need them both to win."

In response to these types of concerns, the Save Our Wild Salmon Coalition has adopted a "Cooperative Agreement" between the coalition and each of its participating member groups. The agreements are tied both to specific deliverables and to the broad areas of expertise that each group will provide. These accountability mechanisms, while useful for getting potential problems out in the open, are still essentially based on good will, not actual contractual requirements. Therefore, the process of negotiating them becomes as important as what they actually say.

Bill deBuys, the former funder liaison for the Alliance for Rio Grande Heritage, discovered that the best accountability mechanism wasn't a piece of paper. "What's required is adult leadership," he says. "The anxieties over autonomy and group self-protection are inevitable. Someone needs to keep their eye on the prize and make sure that we are doing what George W. calls 'making the pie higher.'"

In the end, coalition accountability is also about communication. Participants in the Living with Coalitions workshop discussed the competing pressures on nonprofits—to meet their core mission, make budget, and service

EXHIBIT E.1

Sharing the Wealth

Elements of Success	Dos and Don'ts
Goals • Make goals clear and date-specific. • Include groups with complementary resources. • Set goals based on shared objectives, not the lure of money.	• Do meet regularly with potential partners to identify common interests. • Do communicate with funders as a group to discuss why a coalition is necessary.
Accountability • Manage coalition grants professionally. • Practice transparency between groups and with funders.	• Do write cooperative agreements tying each group's funding to expectations and deliverables. • Don't forget to talk about administrative costs and matching requirements. • Don't expect groups to devote too much of their time to a collaborative effort.
Coalition Process • Insist on mature, responsible leadership. • Make the process as complex as necessary for the size of group.	• Do build a sense of trust by working together before entering a coalition. • Do create systematic internal communications. • Don't forget to share credit for all victories. • Do try to identify economies of scale or work that can be outsourced to experts.
Funder Participation • Funders should be partners. • Include a diversity of donors and individual supporters.	• Do ask supportive foundation staff to bring other foundations into the project. • Do ask foundations if they would consider making a larger grant to a collaborative effort.
Fundraising Leadership • Appoint a lead person.	• Do support the lead group's role. • Don't be afraid to ask participating groups to help defray coalition expenses.
Honor Your Mission • Make sure that the collaborative project is compatible with your organizational goals.	• Do ask funders to continue their annual support to your group beyond their coalition grant. • Don't forget to keep your members informed of your coalition work in your newsletter and annual report.

their members—as significant reasons that they weren't able to work on collaborative projects as much as they wanted to.

Their advice to coalition staff is simple: Don't expect member groups to devote more than a fraction of their time to any collaborative effort, and understand that even the most supportive group may not be able to do much fundraising for the coalition.

As Nancy Dalwin points out, "A good collaborative project uses the capabilities of groups with complementary skills and resources. If all the groups are weak in one area, like media, a good collaborative project could provide them with the money to get outside help."

Brian Shields has seen that model in action. "The money raised by coalitions usually goes to the experts and not to local grassroots operations," he says. Amigos Bravos is also part of The New Mexico Mining Act Network, which has raised $200,000 each year primarily for legal and technical assistance. "Experts are important, but the local groups put in a lot of effort and don't get much money for general operations."

Strategic planning leading to a proposal is crucial to the proposal's success. All partner groups should be included in planning sessions well before a proposal is written.

Each group needs an official point person for the project. Some fiscal auditors recommend that the board of a group submitting a collaborative grant proposal appoint a steering committee to manage and supervise the project in their name. The steering committee helps board members understand how this new cash flow will be used, and its work provides an organizational paper trail.

The lead group submitting the proposal has extra responsibilities; if the project doesn't work out, its reputation is on the line. The lead group should anticipate and itemize administrative costs, and all partners must agree to those costs.

Once the grant proposal is submitted, follow-up is always required. The coalition must designate one person as "funder liaison" for the project, since having multiple contact people makes things muddy for the grantmakers.

In the end, your grant probably won't be as large as needed. When that happens, some groups make budget cuts across the board, while others prioritize their work. Conflicts of interests may become nearly impossible to untangle or dismiss. Partners and coalition board and staff members need to understand in advance who will make the necessary cuts.

Living with Coalitions

Mature organizations can live quite happily in coalitions by setting reasonable financial expectations and paying attention to the lessons learned by colleagues. In fact, coalitions and collaborations have become part of a diverse fundraising plan for most financially strong environmental organizations. "If you are dealing with a big campaign, a coalition is the way you have to organize," says Brian Shields.

Lani Shaw agrees: "Collaborative proposals can be better thought through than those from a single organization, so the process can create stronger ideas."

Many smaller groups feel that they have gained access to new funders for their core program work because of their work in coalitions. "We have broken bread and met each other," relates one participant. "These relationships always help."

To widen the field of funders interested in a project, you may want to consider bringing several sister organizations and constituencies into a coordinated plan or bundling smaller projects into a proposal big enough to appeal to larger foundations. For example, in some regions, members of the Waterkeepers Alliance have tied together similar approaches to clean water enforcement efforts used in different watersheds. Major regional foundations, such as William and Flora Hewlett and Charles Stewart Mott, and foundations with interest in particular states, such as McKnight and Beldon, are generally open to these proposals. Prospective applicants need to check on guidelines and make contact with the right program officer before preparing a proposal.

Other Collaborative Grantseeking Strategies

There are ways of sharing funds without creating a formal coalition. River Network Partners have worked together to secure funds, and River Network regularly solicits funds from major foundations to "pass through" to partner groups in the form of minigrants. This "regranting" could easily work at the state level as well.

River Network has also participated in projects with one or two "joint partners," or where a portion of a grant is subcontracted to another organization. Sometimes, just sharing foundation contacts with another group and exchanging mutual letters of support is the best way to work together.

Sharing More Than Money

Perhaps the most important reason to be part of a coalition is the greater potential for public outreach. Many grassroots organizations struggle to have their voice heard beyond their own membership. For those groups, collaborative projects can move their message onto a broader public stage, where people can hear it—perhaps for the first time—from messengers they relate to and trust.

Outreach comes at a cost, however, and collaborations rarely enjoy many economies of scale. Each new member creates more complexity, more communications, more time and effort to build trust and transparency. For these reasons alone, limiting the size of your group makes financial sense.

Not coincidentally, points out Bill deBuys, this level of complexity mirrors that of the environmental and social justice issues that coalitions are established to address—issues that span many different constituencies, viewpoints, and competing needs. He encourages coalitions to "get outside the comfort zone and use the ethnic and cultural diversity of the whole communityw" while recognizing that harnessing these broad energies won't save money.

River Network's vision is about building partnerships and using the diversity of communities in the art of saving rivers. We know that partnerships aren't always easy. Partners bring their own agendas, they often complain, and they always want money! So when the question of sharing grants comes up, executive directors and boards will evaluate the pros and cons—and sometimes they will discover that collaboration is the only way to win.

Advice for Handling Money in Coalitions

The following advice summarizes some useful ways to deal with money raised in coalitions.

- Identify ways your group will measure the success of the coalition and share those with your partners.

- Get clear on the amount of time required for both the work being done by the coalition and the process of being in the coalition.

- Identify how you will divide the money before you get it—insist on a strategic plan and work plan as well as a budget.

- When redistributing funds, be clear about what is expected; use a written agreement and require a written report for your records.

- Treat pass-through money received from a coalition as if the coalition were a foundation. Share any cooperative agreements or letters of agreement with your board of directors.

References

American Association of Fundraising Counsel. *Giving USA 2003*. Indianapolis, Ind.: American Association of Fundraising Counsel, 2003.

Changemakers. *Social Change Philanthropy and Community Based Philanthropy*. San Francisco: Changemakers, 2003. Also available at www.changemakers.org/pdf/Advsr-stbyst.pdf.

Delgado, Gary. "Leveraging God's Resources from Her Representatives on Earth." In Rosana Reyes and Regina Acebo (eds.), *The Activist's Guide to Religious Funding*. Oakland, Calif.: Center for Third World Organizing, 1993.

Ingram, Catherine. "Bad Magic: The Failure of Technology, An Interview with Jerry Mander." *The Sun*, Issue 192, November 1991.

Jensen, Jon M. "Foundation Leadership." In Joyce K. Berry and John C. Gordon (eds.), *Environmental Leadership: Developing Effective Skills and Styles*. Washington, D.C.: Island Press, 1993.

Klein, Kim. *Fundraising for Social Change*. (4th ed.) San Francisco: Jossey-Bass, 2001.

Lindner, Eileen W. (ed.). *Yearbook of American and Canadian Churches 2003*. New York: National Council of the Churches of Christ in the USA, 2003.

Miller, Terry. *Managing for Change: A Common Sense Guide to Evaluating Financial Management Health for Grassroots Organizations*. Portland, Oreg.: Partnership for Democracy, 1992.

National Center for Charitable Statistics. nccsdataweb.urban.org/NCCS/Public. 2003

National Center for Family Philanthropy. "Family Foundations: A Profile of Funders and Trends." www.ncfp.org/program-research-FFTrends.html. 2003.

New, Cheryl Carter, and James Aaron Quick. *The Grantseeker's Toolkit: A Comprehensive Guide to Finding Funding*. San Francisco: Jossey-Bass, 1998.

Paul, Eileen (ed.). *2000 Religious Funding Resource Guide*. Washington, D.C.: ResourceWomen, 2000.

Rosten, Leo. *The New Joys of Yiddish*. New York: Three Rivers Press, 2001.

Roth, Stephanie. "Letter from the Editor." *Grassroots Fundraising Journal*, Volume 22, Number 5, September/October 2003.

Index

Grateful acknowledgement is hereby tendered to the publishers and copyright holders for permission to use the following quotations from their works:

Quotes on planning and financial management in Chapters Four and Ten are from *Managing for Change: A Common Sense Guide to Evaluating Financial Management Health for Grassroots Organizations* by Terry Miller. Copyright © 1992 by Terry Miller. Used by permission of the author.

The case statement components outlined in Chapter Four are adapted from *Fundraising for Social Change*, 4th edition, by Kim Klein. Copyright © 2001 by Kim Klein. Used by permission of John Wiley & Sons, Inc.

The proposal evaluation form in Chapter Four, "El Paso Community Foundation: Criteria for Reviewing Proposals," was prepared by Virginia Kemendo Martinez of the El Paso Community Foundation and adapted from the work of Bill Somerville of the Philanthropic Ventures Foundation. Used by permission of the authors.

The discussion of the word *schmoozing* in Chapter Six is from *The New Joys of Yiddish* by Leo Rosten, copyright © 2001 by The Rosten Family LLC. Used by permission of Crown Publishers, a division of Random House, Inc.

The quotation on grant reporting in Chapter Ten is from "Foundation Leadership," subtitled "Life Under Water," by Jon M. Jensen, Chapter 15, page 259, in *Environmental Leadership: Developing Effective Skills and Styles*, edited by Joyce K. Berry and John C. Gordon. Copyright © 1993 Island Press, 1718 Connecticut Ave. N.W., Washington, D.C. 20009. Used by permission of the publisher and the author.

Exhibit C.1, "Tips and Strategies for Raising Money from Religious Organizations," by Richard Male first appeared in the article "Raising Money from Religious Institutions" in *Grassroots Fundraising Journal*, Volume 22, Number 5, September/October 2003. Used by permission of the publisher and the author.

Resource E, "Sharing Grants: A Strategy for Collaborative Fundraising," by Wendy Wilson first appeared in the *River Fundraising Alert*, Volume 9, Number 3, Fall 2002. Used by permission of River Network and the author.

All grant proposals and proposal excerpts reproduced in this book are used by permission of the profiled organizations.

For great advice from co-publisher Kim Klein and other experts, subscribe to the

GRASSROOTS FUNDRAISING JOURNAL

GRASSROOTS FUNDRAISING JOURNAL (6 issues/year)
KIM KLEIN AND STEPHANIE ROTH, PUBLISHERS

Do you wish fundraising would go away? It won't. Do you want to make it easier? Here's how. Learn how to increase your income and diversify your sources of funding with proven, practical strategies, including special events, direct mail, major donor programs, membership campaigns, and more. Recent articles include:
- Fundraising on the Internet • Hiring a Development Director
- Putting on a House Party • Developing a Monthly Donor Program
- Asking Current Donors: Why, How, and How Often?

"I get a year's worth of new fundraising ideas in every issue"
— KRISTEN CASHMORE, HESPERIAN FOUNDATION

$32/year — 6 issues

Don't miss these collections of favorite articles from the Grassroots Fundraising Journal:

THE BOARD OF DIRECTORS BY KIM KLEIN AND STEPHANIE ROTH

How to develop an effective — and fundraising — Board of Directors. Articles include:
- The Board and Fundraising • Building an Effective Board of Directors
- Recruiting Better Board Members • When Board Members Wriggle out of Fundraising
- Fifty-Three Ways Board Members Can Raise $500

$12 / 36 pages

GETTING MAJOR GIFTS BY KIM KLEIN

The most lucrative fundraising strategy. Twelve articles by Kim Klein, including:
- Getting Major Gifts: The Basics • The Fine Art of Asking for the Gift
- Asking for Money: The Close • Twenty-One Common Questions

$12 / 40 pages

CÓMO RECAUDAR FONDOS EN SU COMUNIDAD
(How to Raise Money in Your Community)

ARTICLES BY KIM KLEIN, STEPHANIE ROTH, MARIA GONZALES, DAVE FLEISCHER AND LUCY GRUGETT. TRANSLATED BY NORMA DEL RIO

A Spanish-language introduction to the most common and successful fundraising strategies. Small organizations can put these strategies to use immediately, even without paid staff, previous fundraising experience, technical knowledge, or expensive equipment.

$12 / 39 pages

To order call toll free at **(888) 458-8588**
or visit our website at **www.chardonpress.com**